Testaments
of
Love

Testaments
of
Love

A Study of Love in the Bible

by
LEON MORRIS

WILLIAM B. EERDMANS PUBLISHING COMPANY
GRAND RAPIDS, MICHIGAN

Library of Congress Cataloging in Publication Data

Morris, Leon, 1914–
  Testaments of love.

  Includes bibliographical references.
  1. Love (Theology)—Biblical teaching.   I. Title.
BS680.L64M67   241'.4   81-2259
ISBN 0-8028-1874-9   AACR2

Contents

CONTENTS

Preface

THERE IS a great deal written and said about love these days. It can scarcely be denied that many people think love is very important. It is also widely realized that Christianity emphasizes the practice of this virtue. Accordingly, it is curious that there are so few studies of what the Bible means when it uses the term. We usually assume that everybody knows what the word means, and that it has a generally agreed-upon meaning.

But I am not at all sure that this idea is justified, because the word *love* can be understood in any one of a multitude of ways. It seems to me that we would be better off if we did not assume quite so much and gave more thought to exactly what we understand love to be. For Christians the starting point for such an exercise must be the Bible. This book, accordingly, is meant to help Christians take this first step. It is an attempt to see what the Bible writers said about love and what they meant when they used the word. In this study I have carefully examined both the Old Testament and the New Testament, and have also discussed the Septuagint at certain points. Some parts of the discussion are rather technical, because I have examined the words used in the original languages. But the general reader may safely omit these sections without losing anything that is essential to the argument, although they are important to provide the basis for what I have written elsewhere.

This topic has interested me ever since I began to think seriously about the Christian way. How could it be otherwise for any of us? In fact, in recent years I have lectured on the topic in a number of places, notably when I delivered the Spring Lectures at Western Conservative Baptist Seminary in Portland, Oregon. I freely acknowledge my indebtedness to those who on that occasion and on others discussed aspects of the subject with me. While the opinions expressed here are, of course, my own, this book would have been much poorer without the kindly criticisms of many friends. I am grateful for their help.

I have also learned a good deal from books, and have acknowledged my indebtedness in the footnotes. But I should make special mention of C. S. Lewis, whose writings I have found especially helpful. I also owe much to Anders Nygren and to Ceslaus Spicq, whose books about love are classics. Even when one differs with these men, it must be only after careful consideration of what they have written.

I finished this book when I was visiting the United States, so I had the opportunity to discuss my subject with colleagues at Nyack College, New York, and at Trinity Evangelical Divinity School in Deerfield, Illinois. To them I owe a great debt. And I want especially to thank those people at Trinity who arranged for the typing of the final manuscript. I gratefully acknowledge the assistance of Mrs. Lois Armstrong, Mrs. Kathy Wiggins, Mrs. Karen Sich, Mrs. Bev Faugerstrom, Miss Mary Dalton, Mrs. Patty McGarvey, and Mrs. Debbie Young. Their help was invaluable.

In citing Scripture I have most often used the Revised Standard Version of the Old Testament. Unless otherwise indicated, I have used my own translation of the New Testament.

LEON MORRIS

Principal Abbreviations

AG   W.F. Arndt and F.W. Gingrich, *A Greek-English Lexicon of the New Testament,* Cambridge, 1957

ANF   *The Ante-Nicene Fathers,* 10 vols.; rpt. Grand Rapids: Eerdmans, 1951.

ASV   The American Standard Version

ATR   *Anglican Theological Review*

AV   The Authorized Version

BDB   F. Brown, S.R. Driver, and C.A. Briggs, *A Hebrew and English Lexicon of the Old Testament,* Oxford, 1952

CBQ   *Catholic Biblical Quarterly*

EB   *Encyclopaedia Biblica,* ed. T.K. Cheyne and J.S. Black, 4 vols., London, 1914

ET   *The Expository Times*

GNB   Good News Bible, The Bible in *Today's English Version*

HTR   *The Harvard Theological Review*

IB   *The Interpreter's Bible,* 12 vols., New York, 1952–57

IDB   *The Interpreter's Dictionary of the Bible,* 4 vols., New York, 1962; supplementary volume, 1976

ISBE   *The International Standard Bible Encyclopaedia,* 5 vols., Grand Rapids, 1939

JB   The Jerusalem Bible

JBL   *The Journal of Biblical Literature*

JR   *The Journal of Religion*

JTS   *The Journal of Theological Studies*

KB   L. Koehler und W. Baumgartner, *Lexicon in Veteris Testamenti Libros,* Leiden, 1953

LCC   The Library of Christian Classics

LXX   The Septuagint

NBCR   *The New Bible Commentary Revised,* ed. D. Guthrie *et al.,* London, 1970

NBD   *The New Bible Dictionary,* ed. J.D. Douglas *et al.,* London, 1962

NEB   The New English Bible

NIV   The New International Version
NPNF *A Select Library of the Nicene and Post-Nicene Fathers of the Christian Church*
NT   *Novum Testamentum*
NTS *New Testament Studies*
PTR *The Princeton Theological Review*
RSV The Revised Standard Version
RV The Revised Version
SJT *The Scottish Journal of Theology*
TDNT *Theological Dictionary of the New Testament*, a translation by G.W. Bromiley of *TWNT*, Grand Rapids, 1964–76
TDOT *Theological Dictionary of the Old Testament*, ed. G.J. Botterweck and H. Ringgren, trans. J.T. Willis, rev. ed., vols. 1– , Grand Rapids, 1977–
TEV Today's English Version
TWBB *A Theological Word Book of the Bible*, ed. A. Richardson, London, 1950
TWNT *Theologisches Wörterbuch zum Neuen Testament*, ed. G. Kittel und G. Friedrich, Stuttgart, 1933–74
VT *Vetus Testamentum*
ZAW *Zeitschrift für die Alttestamentliche Wissenschaft*

Statistics of the usage of New Testament words are usually taken from Robert Morgenthaler, *Statistik des Neutestamentlichen Wortschatzes*, Zürich, 1958.

Introduction

THERE is no need to tell our generation that love is "the greatest thing in the world." Christian and non-Christian alike, we take that for granted. We write about it, talk about it, and preach about it; we praise it and appraise it; we emblazon the word on T-shirts and on protest banners. We see ourselves as loving people, and it distresses us when others don't love as they should. Since the importance of love is so obvious, why doesn't everyone love as we do?

Because we all agree that love is so important, it is somewhat surprising that there is so little of it about. We all know that there are many unloving people. Depending on our point of view, they may be mournful moralists or licentious libertines. Some of us find intolerable those puritanical types who contend for upright living in a way that denies others the right to live promiscuously. Those of us who find this behavior upsetting see it as a denial of love, arguing that if these moralists were really loving people they would be more tolerant of the ways of others.[1] And in these days we are certainly all familiar

---

[1] Sir Arnold Lunn speaks of a sermon preached in Oxford on the subject "Why not, if we're in love?" on which a Mr. John Davies commented, "Love is supposed to be the most Christ-like of all human virtues. Because he was attacking a desire to express this feeling, the Rector's speech on Sunday was neither a very humble nor a very compassionate one." Sir Arnold goes on: "Nothing as silly as this was published in any undergraduate paper... before the First World War. Even those who described themselves as agnostics would not have risked ridicule by attacking a Christian clergyman for preaching chastity to the young. In the Oxford of my youth the hedonists suffered from no missionary urge to impose on others their own way of life. The frankly immoral were far less censorious of the moral than those prigs of the New Morality who are forever holding forth on the prurience of the pure and the inhibitions of the chaste" (Arnold Lunn and Garth Lean, *The New Morality*, London, 1964, pp. 3f.).

1

with the aggressive permissiveness that sees the conventionally moral person as somewhat less than human.

But the promiscuous do not escape, either. They usually
insist that they are truly loving, only to meet the criticism that
they are mistaking lust for love and confusing their personal
pleasure with concern for the well-being of others, which is an
integral part of real love.[2] Certainly it is not easy to avoid the
conclusion that for many of us love has become a refined selfishness, a warm affection for those of whom we approve
coupled with a hearty dislike of those of whom we disap-
prove.[3] And Christians are not guiltless in this respect. We
tend to utter the word more often than we give thought to what
it means. How do we harmonize the assurance that "God is
love" with the assertion that "our God is a consuming fire"?
Most of us never think about such problems, and in the end our
idea of love is indistinguishable from that of the world around
us.

And that idea does not reckon with the ambivalence of
love, which is something both beautiful and dangerous. C. S.
Lewis draws attention to the seeming contradiction that love
"begins to be a demon the moment he begins to be a god":

> Every human love, at its height, has a tendency to claim
> for itself a divine authority. Its voice tends to sound as if it
> were the will of God Himself. It tells us not to count the
> cost, it demands of us a total commitment, it attempts to
> over-ride all other claims and insinuates that any action
> which is sincerely done "for love's sake" is thereby lawful
> and even meritorious. That erotic love and love of one's

---

[2]Thus J. A. T. Robinson criticizes sexual relations "which are
dishonest, unchaste and immoral, because they do not express real
love, a genuine intimacy, but are casual, exploitive or merely lustful"
(*Christian Freedom in a Permissive Society*, Philadelphia, 1970, p.
49). He complains that "free love" is usually "neither 'love' nor
'free' " (p. 41): "Outside marriage sex is bound to be the expression
of less than an unreserved sharing and commitment of one person to
another" (p. 39).

[3]Douglas N. Morgan protests against "maudlin love" which he
sees as "ignorant, misdirected, and undisciplined love." He also says
forthrightly, "When sentimentality replaces sentiment, muddle-
headedness replaces reason and we wallow. Much or even most
of what has been popularly written about love is nonsense" (*Love:
Plato, the Bible and Freud*, Englewood Cliffs, N.J., 1964, p. 1).

country may thus attempt to "become gods" is generally recognised. But family affection may do the same. So, in a different way, may friendship.[4]

Love is a very wonderful part of life. It is exciting and fulfilling, and can enrich our lives to an unbelievable extent. But when we worship it, it becomes destructive. There is no end to the list of horrors that have been perpetrated in the name of love.

But even when we do not turn love into a demon there may be problems. Krister Stendahl argues for balance. In one sense, he points out, love is "a particularly formidable term in that it often is used to sum up the whole gospel, the whole meaning of the life, suffering, and death of Christ, the whole content of the Christian message." He protests against what he calls this "inflation," which he sees "not only in our language but also in our thoughts and feelings." But he finds another contradictory feature in modern life—the dilution of the idea of love. To many people "it seems as if true and deep theology consists in ridiculing the Golden Rule as a center of the Christian faith."[5] Stendahl warns us against this attitude. We cannot assume that the way we use the word *love* in a modern western community is the way it was used in the Bible. Nor can we assume that our current use of it gives the word its most Christian or most meaningful definition. Indeed, Günther Bornkamm says, "This word, almost more than any other, has entered into the vocabulary of Christians and—used and misused—has largely lost its meaning and force."[6]

Because the Bible has some significant and distinctive things to say about love, we must guard against assuming that we know all about love, so that we make the Bible parrot our ideas. It is important that we let Scripture speak for itself. We

---

[4] *The Four Loves,* London, 1960, p. 15. Lewis begins with a quote from Denis de Rougemont concerning *erōs:* "In ceasing to be a god, he ceases to be a demon" (*Love in the Western World,* Philadelphia, 1953, p. 295). The possibility that love may become a demon does not appear to be considered by Joseph Fletcher. He entitles Chapter III of his *Situation Ethics* (Philadelphia, 1966) "Love only is always good," and says things like, "Nothing is intrinsically good but the highest good, the *summum bonum,* the end or purpose of all ends—love" (p. 129). But this is simplistic. It does not fit the facts.

[5] *Paul among Jews and Gentiles,* Philadelphia, 1976, pp. 52f.

[6] *Paul,* London, 1971, p. 216.

must go on to ask how its ideas affect our understanding of love and our attempts to show love to others.

We begin this study with the Old Testament. Here a surprising fact emerges: there is a great deal about love in this part of the Bible. I say "surprising" because we would never gather that this is the case from the way standard works treat the Old Testament. The very important *Encyclopaedia Biblica* with its four volumes and 5,444 columns has no article on love (though it has one on "Lovingkindness"). This omission is really extraordinary in such a standard work, but it is not atypical. Until quite recently there has been a dearth of books on the theology of the Old Testament; indeed, there are still not very many. For many years the standard work in English was A. B. Davidson's *The Theology of the Old Testament*. This is a book of 532 pages, so that it cannot be accused of skimping on evidence. But the word *love* is found neither in the table of contents nor in the index.

More recently some important and extensive works on the subject have been published, but they devote little space to the subject of love. Gerhard von Rad has written a two-volume work called *Old Testament Theology* (888 pages long), yet *love* cannot be found in either table of contents, nor in the index to volume one. There are some references to *love* in the index to volume two, but never to an extended treatment of the theme. It is a little better in Walther Eichrodt's massive work, *Theology of the Old Testament*. He also has produced two volumes (520 and 529 pages respectively), and he does find a place for love. In volume one he gives us seven pages on "The lovingkindness of God" and eight on "The love of God." Volume two has eleven pages on "Love for God." It is good to see these sections, but the total space given to the theme is less than impressive. T. C. Vriezen has written *An Outline of Old Testament Theology* with no mention at all of *love* in its table of contents, while Edmond Jacob's *Theology of the Old Testament* has but six pages on "The love of God." Ludwig Koehler, author of *Old Testament Theology*, mentions *love* neither in his table of contents (five-and-a-half pages of it) nor in his index.

It cannot be said that the idea of love really grips these leading writers on the Old Testament. Of course, there is more to this matter than a counting of pages under a specific heading. And I do not wish to accuse any of these writers of not knowing that there is much about love in the Old Testament.

On examination it is clear that they interweave references to the love of God with their discussions of other topics. But I find it astonishing that so many scholars can write so much about the Old Testament with so little formal recognition of the place of love in it. They do not put it in a place of major importance to suggest that it is a leading theme: when they select the major subject headings under which they will treat the theology of the Old Testament, they find that they can dispense with love altogether, or relegate it to a very minor place.

It seems to me that this treatment is unjustified. Understanding the meaning of love is essential to understanding the Old Testament. It is essential because of the number and variety of words used to express it. And it is essential because the great, surprising truth that God loves puny and sinful man underlies almost everything that is written throughout the entire Old Testament. We do not do justice to the writings of the prophets, the lawgivers, the psalmists, and the rest if we do not recognize them as revelations about the God who loves. He loves those he has made, and his love leads to action to meet their needs.

In books about the New Testament there is, as we might expect, a greater readiness to see love as significant. Notice must be taken of explicit statements like "God is love" (I John 4:8, 16) and "The greatest of these is love" (I Cor. 13:13). It is scarcely possible to write about the New Testament without noticing that love is one of its most important topics—if not the most important of them. Yet even here some curious facts emerge. For example, Hans Conzelmann's book, *An Outline of the Theology of the New Testament,* has a detailed, six-page table of contents. But, though he lists topics like "Hope," "The Law," and "The Wrath of God," *love* does not rate a mention. W. G. Kümmel's *The Theology of the New Testament* does only a little better. His table of contents covers five pages, but in it *love* is mentioned only once. In the section on "The Johannine message of Christ in the Fourth Gospel and in the Epistles" there is the heading "Salvation and the way of salvation," under which we find the subheading "Faith and love," with seven pages assigned to it. Interestingly, this discussion is largely about faith. *Love* does not figure in the table of contents in either volume of R. Bultmann's two-volume *Theology of the New Testament,* nor in Alan Richardson's *An Introduction to the Theology of the New Testament.* And J.

Jeremias assigns only three pages of his *New Testament Theology* to "The commandment to love as the law of life under the reign of God."

I find this all very curious. Let me make it clear once again that I am not accusing these writers of not knowing that love is important. But I do find it strange that in profound and serious works on the New Testament it is possible to give such detailed lists of topics to be studied in a theological treatment and assign little or no place to love.

Accordingly, it is far from superfluous to devote time to this subject. Love is given great emphasis throughout the Bible.[7] There are many words for love that are used in a variety of ways. And love is at the core of almost all biblical events. Throughout the Bible love is at the heart of God's dealings with men, little of which can be understood if this basic fact is not recognized. And little of what is expected of men can be appreciated until we realize that the commands to love God and our neighbor are basic. Love is not to be treated as peripheral.

Though love has been essential from very early times onward, I should make it clear that I am not attempting in this study to show how the concept developed. I decided not to do so partly because it is difficult to date all of the documents, and there seems to be some difference of opinion on the subject among Old Testament experts. I do not see how a satisfactory account can be produced on the basis of present knowledge. But neither does such a treatment seem necessary for our present purpose. The basic ideas about love are quite constant. Admittedly, there are differing emphases, but from very early times onward the same basic idea has persisted: that God has chosen or "elected" certain people, which seems to imply love for them. Similarly persistent is the thought that God has given men his blessing, quite irrespective of their merit. Whether or not any of the words for love are used to describe these truths, they are nonetheless evidence of the love of God.[8]

---

[7]Cf. Douglas Morgan: "The Bible is a book of love" (*Love: Plato, the Bible and Freud*, p. 47).

[8]Viktor Warnach holds that God's love for men "is attested even in the earliest sections of the Bible. True, it is seldom mentioned *expressis verbis,* but nonetheless it is expressed clearly, though indirectly, in the numerous *narratives* of how he acted towards men" (Johannes B. Bauer, ed., *Encyclopedia of Biblical Theology,* II, Lon-

It may be profitable to draw attention to a further point. Gerhard von Rad has made the following claim:

> Scholars are even beginning to allow a scientific standing of its own to the picture of her history which Israel herself drew, and to take it as something existing *per se* which, in the way it has been sketched, has to be taken into account as a central subject in our theological evaluation.... These two pictures of Israel's history lie before us—that of modern critical scholarship and that which the faith of Israel constructed—and for the present, we must reconcile ourselves to both of them. It would be stupid to deny the right of the one or the other to exist.[9]

But in this particular study we will perhaps be more concerned with this second picture than the first. It is the teachings of the Old Testament by the biblical writers themselves that we shall seek. For some purposes it may be important to note the way one writer has built upon and advanced beyond the work of another, but scarcely for ours. We must also keep in mind that the New Testament writers read the Old Testament without the benefit of the reconstructions of modern critical scholarship. They accepted the Old Testament just as it is. If we are to understand what they believed their Bible was saying to them about the love of God and man, we must try to see the Old Testament in much the same way.

Our object, then, is to examine the Bible to see what it tells us about love. We shall investigate the principal words for love in both testaments and try to reach some conclusions about what the teaching of the Bible means for God's people today.

---

don and Sydney, 1970, 519). In contrast, Irving Singer holds that "the concept of love undergoes a complex evolution throughout the Old Testament" (*The Nature of Love*, New York, 1966, p. 246), though he does not document this idea.

[9] *Old Testament Theology*, I, Edinburgh and London, 1962, 107.

CHAPTER ONE

Loved with Everlasting Love

"*I* HAVE loved you with an everlasting love; therefore I have continued my faithfulness to you" (Jer. 31:3).

It is possible to read these words too quickly, as though the prophet Jeremiah were enunciating a truism. But in fact this declaration stands in marked contrast to all that he says elsewhere about love. He tells us that God said, "I remember the devotion of your youth, your love as a bride" (Jer. 2:2). But this love was short-lived, as Jeremiah points out when he replaces this beautiful picture with one that paints Israel as an adulteress: "How well you direct your course to seek lovers! So that even to wicked women you have taught your ways" (Jer. 2:33).[1] He puts words of betrayal into the mouth of Israel: " 'I have loved strangers, and after them I will go' " (Jer. 2:25; the strangers, of course, are the strange gods, the idols that so fascinated the unstable nation). The people have "loved," "served," "gone after," "sought," and "worshipped" the "sun and the moon and all the host of heaven" (Jer. 8:2). They love it when prophets prophesy falsely and priests rule accordingly (Jer. 5:31); they love to wander (Jer. 14:10). But the false

---

[1] J. Skinner translates verse 20 this way: "From of old thou hast broken thy yoke, and burst thy thongs; and said 'I will not serve': while on every high hill, and 'neath every green tree, thou sprawledst, a harlot." He comments, "The same idea is still more drastically expressed in the comparison of the nation to a domestic animal—a young she-camel or a heifer—running wild in the heat of sexual desire, utterly beyond the control of her owner, but easily approachable by the males who seek her (*vv.* 23*b*, 24). The text of these verses is very uncertain, and the combination of metaphors embarrassing" (*Prophecy and Religion,* Cambridge, 1940, p. 68 and n.1). L. Elliott Binns comments on verse 20: "The term would receive greater force from the immoral practices which were carried on in connexion with such worship" (*The Book of the Prophet Jeremiah,* London, 1919, p. 23).

gods Judah worships, her "lovers," turn out to be a pretty poor lot. Twice it is said that they will be destroyed (Jer. 22:20, 22). They are numerous, as Jeremiah indicates: "You have played the harlot with many lovers" (Jer. 3:1). But among them all there is none that really cares about the fickle nation: "All your lovers have forgotten you; they care nothing for you" (Jer. 30:14); "Your lovers despise you" (Jer. 4:30).[2]

And that is it. These are all of the passages in which Jeremiah uses the word *love*.[3] There is nothing to alleviate the picture, nothing to indicate that deep down Judah may harbor a

---

[2]The prophet paints a pathetic picture as he sees the nation vainly seeking to attract the favors of the idols: "And you, O desolate one, what do you mean that you dress in scarlet, that you deck yourself with ornaments of gold, that you enlarge your eyes with paint? In vain you beautify yourself. Your lovers despise you; they seek your life" (Jer. 4:30).

[3]His verb is *'āhēbh* (*'āhabh*). The statistics are complicated a trifle owing to problems with such forms as the infinitive absolute (this is sometimes taken as part of the verb and sometimes read as the noun *love*). But, if we follow the classification in B. Davidson's concordance, the verb occurs 208 times in the Old Testament: 72 occurrences refer to the love of people for people, 27 to the love of men for God, 29 to God's love, 33 to men's love for things, 46 to their love for evil, and one to love in general ("a time to love"). Of the love of people, 31 times there is a reference to sexual love, 24 times to love of friends, 8 times to love of members of the family, 3 times to loving enemies, 2 times to love for a master, while we may classify four occurrences as miscellaneous. The cognate noun *'ahⁿbhāh* is found 40 times: 27 occurrences refer to love of people (15 to sexual love and 12 to love of friends), 10 to God's love and one each to love for God, for good, and for evil. The forms *'ⁿhābhiym* and *ᵒhābhiym* are also found occasionally (twice and once respectively). The most frequent use of the words from this root is thus for love between the sexes. G. Quell speaks of "the natural basis residing in sexuality" and adds a footnote: "For lack of any sure indication of its etymology, this may be concluded in the case of *'hb* from its more extended use in the erotic sense" (*TDNT*, I, p. 23 and n. 14). E. M. Good says of the verb, "Its primary connection with sexual love is suggested, but not proved, by the nominal adjectives *'āhabh*, 'carnal love' ... and *'ōhabh*, used only in Hos. 9:10 of 'idolatrous love'" (*IDB*, III, 165). D. Winton Thomas thinks the verb derives from a root with a meaning like "breathe, pant" and thus means "pant after, desire" (*ZAW*, XVI, N.S., 1939, 57–64; he points out that the verb "is peculiar to Hebrew, the usual words for 'love' in the other Semitic languages being quite different"; p. 58).

lingering affection for Yahweh. The nation is wholly set on her dalliance with the idols. It is quite clear that when Jeremiah uses the terminology of love, the thought that springs naturally to his mind is that the nation loves false gods—it knows nothing of true love. Despite the multitude of blessings God has given her, despite his constant goodness and lovingkindness, Judah has consistently played him false. In an impressive number of places Jeremiah castigates the sin of the nation as adultery or harlotry (Jer. 3:2, 6–10; 5:7; 9:2; 13:27; 23:10, 14) or likens the people to a "faithless wife" (Jer. 3:20; 5:11). Judah has lavished her love on the gods of the heathen, gods that are completely impotent, that have never given her anything, and that in due time will certainly be destroyed by the Lord.

There is nothing in all this to prepare us for God's resounding declaration—"I have loved you with an everlasting love." But this love is not to be taken as a matter of course, as though it welled up naturally from all that Jeremiah has been saying about love. Nothing of the sort. It cuts right across what the prophet has been saying. In fact, the certainty of judgment pervades his prophecy with such strength that we would not be at all surprised if he announced that God had utterly rejected the nation, that he had cast them off and ceased to care for them.

Instead we have this tremendous affirmation of love—and everlasting love at that. Despite all that they have done, God still loves his people and will love them forever. This is a deeply held conviction that means much to the prophet, though he does not usually employ the word *love* to express it. He usually speaks of God as never forsaking his people, no matter what they have done. His entire prophecy proceeds from the conviction that God is concerned for his people, and his anguish arises from the fact that God's "everlasting love" is directed towards a completely unworthy people.

Judah's conduct is indefensible. In due time it will certainly reap inevitable consequences. Indeed, if C. F. Keil's understanding of the passage is correct, the nation had already received her punishment: he sees a reference to Israel in exile in the phrase "the Lord had withdrawn from him." He thinks that "from afar" in this verse means that the Lord, speaking from Zion, addresses Israel in a place of exile where the nation is being punished for its sins. (But the people are not annihilated, as Keil points out: "Because He loves His people with everlasting love, therefore He has kept them by His grace, so that they were not destroyed."[4]) Jeremiah is well aware that this is a universe in which, in the end, "debts must be paid." Whatever a man or a nation sows, that and that alone will be reaped (cf. Gal. 6:7). God's love does not mean that the nation can sin with impunity, leaving it to him to avert the natural consequences of their sin. That is not the way life works out. The man who chooses to live selfishly cannot avert the consequences and know the joys of being unselfish. Similarly, the nation that worships moral-sapping idols cannot but be morally frail; there is no way it can have the blessing of uprightness. Hosea proclaimed that they who sow the wind will reap the whirlwind (Hos. 8:7), and Jeremiah was well aware of this truth. His prophecy contains many chapters of fierce denunciation of evil accompanied by clear prophecies of the consequent disaster. He left the people in no doubt that God disapproved of their sin and in due course would punish it.

But in the face of all this God still loves Judah. He does not simply tolerate the people—he loves them with all the fervor of his holy nature. That is the extraordinary message Jeremiah brings about God's love. When everything else leads us to expect that God will abhor these sinful people, we find that instead he loves them, loves them with an everlasting love. It is true that the prophet speaks of judgment. But even in the judgment passages there is often a note of hope, notably when Jeremiah proclaims exile but also return from exile after seventy years (Jer. 29:10f.; cf. 30:3, 8ff.; 46:27). He also appeals to the sinful nation with moving words of forgiveness: "Return, faithless Israel, says the Lord. I will not look on you in anger, for I am merciful, says the Lord" (Jer. 3:12; cf. v. 15). Yahweh is "a father to Israel" (Jer. 31:9) who can ask, "Is Ephraim my dear son? Is he my darling child?" and go on to say, "My heart yearns for him; I will surely have mercy on him" (Jer. 31:20).[5] This leads to the prophecy of the new cov-

---

[4]*The Prophecies of Jeremiah*, II, Grand Rapids, 1950, 17f.

[5]On this verse W. Eichrodt comments, "He sees the father-relationship as an image of undying love, the kind of love which will take the lost son to its arms again with fervent emotion, whenever that son returns in penitence; and this despite the fact that even the love itself cannot give a reason for the triumph of such compassion over the most justifiable indignation, but is aware of its own behaviour only as an inner but incomprehensible imperative" (*Theology of the Old Testament*, I, London, 1961, 238).

enant with its assurance of forgiveness, a covenant in which
God will write his law on their hearts and they will all know
him (Jer. 31:31ff.; 32:40). God's constancy to Israel is as sure
as the sequence of day and night; his blessing will make the
nation as immeasurable as heaven and earth (Jer. 31:35ff.; cf.
33:19–26).

The words for love in the passages we have been considering are the verb *'āhēbh* and its cognate noun *'ah*ᵃ*bhāh*. These
words appear to signify love freely given, love given when there
is no sense of obligation.[6] When used to refer to God they imply
his grace. God's love is freely given to sinners, not irresistibly
drawn from him by the virtues of a group of attractive people.
God loves not because the objects of his love are upright and
winsome, but because he is a loving God.[7] Again and again the
Old Testament draws attention to the absence of merit in those
God loves. The constancy of his love depends on what he is
rather than on what they are.

OTHER PROPHETS

Jeremiah is not the only prophet to speak of God's love.
Indeed, that love is one of the most significant topics in the
prophetic writings. Sometimes the statement is simply that
God loved the nation (Isa. 43:4; 48:14; Hos. 3:1; 11:4). This is a
love in which God's people may safely rest (Zeph. 3:17).
Hosea sees God's love freely expressed in the past, when the
Lord brought his people out of Egypt (Hos. 11:1). And in what
is almost his last word, that prophet tells us that God says, "I
will love them freely" (Hos. 14:4), affirming that God's love
will continue. Like Hosea, Isaiah looks back to the way God's
love operated in the past: "In his love and in his pity he re-

---

[6]G. Wallis sees love as "the passionate desire to be intimately
united with a person (in all of life's relationships, not only inwardly,
but also outwardly) with whom one feels himself united in his affections"; "the Hebrew of the OT has filled the concept of *'ahabh(ah)*
with an entirely independent meaning" (*TDOT*, I, 103).

[7]Cf. F. H. Palmer's idea: "Being rooted firmly in the personal
character of God Himself, it (i.e., God's love) is deeper than that of a
mother for her children (Is. xlix.15, lxvi.13). . . . Israel's unfaithfulness can have no effect upon it, for 'I have loved thee with an everlasting love' (Je. xxxi.3)" (*NBD*, p. 752).

deemed them" (Isa. 63:9). He also says that God speaks of Abraham as "my friend" (Isa. 41:8; the Hebrew has the participle of the verb "to love"—i.e., "him whom I loved"[8]). And Malachi begins his prophecy with a threefold reference to God's love (Mal. 1:2). Evidently he was confronted by people who doubted whether God loved them, and the prophet in his argumentative way refutes them. For him the first and fundamental thing is God's love—in fact, his entire prophecy proceeds from this premise.

---

[8]The term is *'ōhᵃbhiy*, which some interpret to mean "him who loved me." For example, Edward J. Young says, "Actually, the word means *he who loves me,* the suffix being objective" (*The Book of Isaiah,* III, Grand Rapids, 1972, p. 83, n.17). Similarly, Claus Westermann points out, "In the Hebrew there is an active verb in the perfect with a suffix—i.e., 'who loves, or loved, me'" (*Isaiah 40–66,* Philadelphia, 1969, p. 70). Reuben Levy's translation is "Abraham that loved me"; he sees the words as "expressing the people's love for God as the return for being chosen out of all the nations." He goes on to say that the Hebrew, "my lover, may also be an attempt to express 'my friend,' though the idea of reciprocity contained in the latter does not exist in Hebrew" (*Deutero-Isaiah,* London, 1925, pp. 133f.). Against that is the conjecture (which Levy reports) that in Isaiah 48:14 "my friend" be read, referring to Cyrus. Whatever the solution of the textual problem, this suggestion points to God as the loving one, for it cannot be said that Cyrus loved Yahweh. The suffixed participle in the plural, "my lovers," describes people who love God (e.g., Ex. 20:6; Deut. 5:10; 7:9; etc.). But other than in the similar reference to Abraham as "thy friend" (II Chron. 20:7), the term does not seem to be used with the singular suffix on the singular participle. LXX takes the expression to mean "loved by God." C. Spicq remarks, "The Septuagint always avoided writing *philos,* perhaps to put more stress on the religious and honorable characteristics included in being *ēgapēmenos,* the preferred of God. What is certain is that Abraham is the object of the divine charity" (*Agape in the New Testament,* III, St. Louis and London, 1966, 229). The context lends support to this view, referring as it does to God's activity rather than man's: God speaks of "Jacob, whom I have chosen" and after "my friend" says, "you whom I took from the ends of the earth." Christopher R. North supports the view that the expression points to God's love for Abraham. He also holds that it "implies a more intimate relationship than *rēʿî,* the usual word for 'my friend/companion'" (*The Second Isaiah,* Oxford, 1964, p. 97). Many point out that in the Koran Abraham is called the Friend of God. J. B. Mayor cites Plumptre for the information that among the Arabs "the name of

Much the same could be said about other prophets. That God loved the people is a truth that mattered greatly to them all. The idea is, of course, more pervasive than the terminology: often the idea of God's love is present even though the actual word is not used. Take as an example Isaiah 44:1-5. God does not specifically say that he loves the people. But God does say that he made them, formed them from the womb, and twice he says he has chosen them. He also says that he will help them, and he calls on them not to be afraid. He promises the gift of water in dry places, and the gift of his Spirit, his blessing. He says that they will "spring up like grass amid waters" (v. 4) and call themselves by his name. What does all this mean but divine love?

Love, then, is a basic concept for the prophets. It is used widely and in a variety of ways. But we must give particular attention to the marriage imagery used in a number of the prophetic books. The language that Jeremiah adopted is used by other prophets as well.

THE BRIDE OF YAHWEH

Words from the '*hb* word group are most commonly used to indicate sexual love, the love of man and wife. Because it is so beautiful and so important, this kind of love became a useful illustration for the writers of the Old Testament who wanted to stress some significant aspects of the relationship between God and Israel. We have already noticed that Jeremiah and other prophets speak powerfully of Israel's bride-like love for God in the early days of their "marriage," and then poignantly go on to show how this highlights her subsequent unfaithfulness.

The first and outstanding example of a prophet who

Khalil Allah (the friend of God), or more briefly El Khalil, has practically superseded that of Abraham" (*The Epistle of St James,* Grand Rapids, 1954, p. 105; James 2:23, of course, says that Abraham was called "God's friend"). E. Nestle argued from Philonic usage: "This passage proves at the same time that 'friend of God' in James is not to be explained as he 'who loved God,' but 'whom God loved,' who is beloved by God" (*ET,* XV, 1903-04, 47; the passage is i.401 in Mangey's edition). There are thus good arguments on both sides, but at least we can say that there are reasonable grounds for seeing a reference to God's love for Abraham.

chooses this imagery is Hosea.[9] His own marriage was clearly an unhappy one, so when he uses the terminology it is with the painful accuracy of experience. It is unclear whether Gomer had a bad reputation before Hosea married her. Some scholars think she did, because the first words of God to the prophet were, "Go, take to yourself a wife of harlotry and have children of harlotry" (Hos. 1:2). They think this command indicates that the prophet was to marry a woman who was a prostitute.[10] Most, however, think the words refer to what she would become rather than to what she was, assuming that Gomer must have been chaste at the time of the marriage.[11] They find it unthinkable that a servant of God like a prophet should have consorted with a woman of evil repute. They argue, further, that part of the imagery used so forcefully in this prophecy depends on initial faithfulness, the kind of faithfulness Israel showed at the beginning.[12] Another suggestion is that of H. W. Wolff, who takes note of "the inroads of a Canaanite sexual rite into Israel in which young virgins offered themselves to the divinity and expected fertility in return. They surrendered themselves to strangers inside the holy precincts." Thus he

---

[9]W. G. Cole begins his book, "Any discussion of love in the Old Testament must begin with Hosea, the prophet who married a whore." This is so because "all the developments in early Hebrew thought are in some sense preparatory to and gathered up in the career and the message of this wronged husband" (*Sex and Love in the Bible,* New York, 1959, pp. 15f.).

[10]T. H. Robinson accepts this view in *Prophecy and the Prophets in Ancient Israel,* London, 1941, pp. 75f. So does G. Quell, who says, "The prophet is to take a harlot to wife, for only a marriage which is nonsensical in the eyes of men and dishonouring to the husband can really give a faithful picture of the relationship of Yahweh to the land of Israel" (*TDNT,* I, 31).

[11]This view is held by W. R. Harper in *A Critical and Exegetical Commentary on Amos and Hosea,* New York, 1905, p. 207. Also supporting this view is Charles F. Pfeiffer in *The Wycliffe Bible Commentary,* ed. Charles F. Pfeiffer and Everett F. Harrison, Chicago, 1962, p. 801.

[12]David Allan Hubbard, however, points out that "Hosea's marriage with Gomer was not meant to recapitulate God's dealings with Israel but to thrust into sharp relief Israel's present degeneracy. Its purpose was to highlight the bleakness of the times, to testify against the degradation of the hour in which he was living" (*With Bands of Love,* Grand Rapids, 1968, p. 52).

thinks that "wife of whoredom" means "any young woman ready for marriage (as in 4:13f.) who had submitted to the bridal rites of initiation then current in Israel. The cultic symbols made her easily recognizable as an average, 'modern' Israelite woman."[13] But this idea is very speculative.[14]

However the question is resolved, it is clear that Gomer became unfaithful after marriage and that this caused Hosea untold anguish because he still loved her. Even when she became a slave as well as an adulteress, Hosea bought her back for a sum of money and some grain (Hos. 3:2). Despite everything, Hosea's love remained pure and strong and constant. He did not condone her faithlessness (Hos. 3:3), but he loved her. As T. H. Robinson points out:

> He was a man possessed and dominated by his love. It went to the very roots of his being, and so fully did it absorb him that no sin or folly on her part could shake it. It was no mere explosive flash of strong emotion that had kindled in his life, it was a consuming fire shut up in his bones, which no rejection could weaken and no suffering quench. In all the world's literature there is no record of human love like his.[15]

And in his constant love for his unworthy wife Hosea saw a small picture of God's great love for his unworthy people.[16] If it was possible for Hosea's love to remain pure and strong despite all that Gomer had done to him, certainly it was much more possible—nay, certain—that God's love would not waver. Constant and deep, his love would not change no matter how his people might sin—and sin they did. Hosea speaks of their conduct as adultery or harlotry on several occasions (Hos. 2:2; 4:12–15, 18; 5:3f.; 6:10; 7:4; 9:1). Because his own

---

[13]H. W. Wolff, *Hosea,* Philadelphia, 1974, pp. 14,15. J. L. Mays points out, however, that "serious objections to the hypothesis have been raised which leave it in a precarious position" (*Hosea,* Philadelphia, 1969, p. 26).

[14]There is an excellent account of the various views in H. H. Rowley, *Men of God,* London, 1963, pp. 66–97.

[15]*Prophecy and the Prophets in Ancient Israel,* p. 77.

[16]E. W. Heaton says that Hosea "had suffered the conflict between the love which must express itself in judgement and the love which demands mercy, and had boldly identified his own pathos with the pathos of Yahweh himself" (*The Old Testament Prophets,* Harmondsworth, 1961, p. 49).

tragic marriage brought home to him the repulsiveness of adultery, he saw with horror how unfaithfulness must appear to God.[17]

God's continuing love does not mean that sin will have no consequences.[18] Hosea saw clearly that there is a necessary punishment of sin. Part of the punishment lies in sin's effect on the sinner. To respond to God's love with an answering love is to enter a life of peace and joy, but to reject it is to shut oneself up with unhappiness in a variety of forms. The other part of punishment lies in physical consequences. Israel was threatened by strong enemies, the Assyrians. To stand firm in the day of attack, the nation would need all the resources it could muster—material resources like horses and chariots, but also spiritual resources like courage and constancy and the trust that makes men turn confidently to God and look to him for needed strength. But because the people refused to return God's love, they forfeited these resources, and Hosea foresaw that they would fall, just as Gomer had. The poignancy of Hosea's prophecy arises from his certainty that the sinning nation, though deeply loved, would suffer for its sins just as certainly as his beloved but unworthy wife had suffered for hers. He relays this word of grief from God: "Like grapes in the wilderness, I found Israel. Like the first fruit on the fig tree, in its first season, I saw your fathers. But they came to Baal-peor, and consecrated themselves to Baal, and became detestable like the thing they loved" (Hos. 9:10).

It is Hosea's consistent lament that the people failed to

---

[17]H. Wheeler Robinson sees Hosea's suffering as important: "Thornton Wilder in his little play, *The Angel that Troubled the Waters*, gives the plea of one who seeks for healing in vain, saying: 'It is no shame to boast to an Angel of what I might still do in Love's service were I freed from his bondage.' To this the Angel's reply is: 'Without your wound, where would your power be? The very angels themselves cannot persuade the wretched and blundering children on earth as can one human being broken in the wheels of living.' Hosea's power was in his wound" (*Two Hebrew Prophets*, London, 1948, pp. 28f.). Apart from his suffering Hosea could not have given us such a wonderful picture of God.

[18]Cf. James Moffatt: "Hosea's interpretation of the character of God is reached through the tender, chivalrous love of an injured husband for his wife, a love which magnanimously survives the offence, though it by no means condones it" (*Love in the New Testament*, London, 1932, p. 16).

respond to God's love as they should have, and he uses the
language of unfaithfulness to express it: "For she said, 'I will
go after my lovers, who give me my bread and my water, my
wool and my flax, my oil and my drink'" (Hos. 2:5). In her
folly she ascribed her bread and water and the rest to the false
gods she served, not realizing that it all came from the Lord (v.
8). The very gifts she gave to Baal came from the Lord. She
"went after her lovers, and forgot me, says the Lord" (Hos.
2:13). In her unfaithfulness she hired her lovers (Hos. 8:9).

Hosea is saddened to see this behavior invite inevitable
judgment. Love is never harsh, but it can be stern.[19] God says,

> Now I will uncover her lewdness in the sight of her lovers,
> and no one will rescue her out of my hand.... And I will
> lay waste her vines and her fig trees, of which she said,
> "These are my hire, which my lovers have given me." I
> will make them a forest, and the beasts of the field shall
> devour them. And I will punish her for the feast days of the
> Baals when she burned incense to them and decked herself
> with her ring and jewelry, and went after her lovers, and
> forgot me, says the Lord (Hos. 2:10–13).

Hosea uses vivid imagery to picture God's hostility toward the
sinful nation. He likens God to what the RSV renders "a moth"
and "dry rot," but which most scholars think more probably
signifies pus and rottenness (Hos. 5:12).[20] Using nature imagery, he describes God as a lion, a leopard, and a bear robbed of
her cubs (Hos. 5:14; 13:7f.). He pictures God as building a
hedge of thorns about the people (Hos. 2:6), as bringing them
down like trapped birds (Hos. 7:12). Yahweh will send fire on
their cities (Hos. 8:14), bereave them of their children (Hos.
9:12), drive them out and love them no more (Hos. 9:15). There
will be terrible destruction (Hos. 10:14f.); they will be lost in
Sheol (Hos. 13:14). Well may Walther Eichrodt remark,
"Hosea is outdone by hardly any other prophet in the ferocity

---

[19]Martin Buber points out that "Hosea does not use the precious
word 'love' lavishly." According to Buber, the prophet uses the word
in order to say three principal things: "First, it is a demanding
love.... Second, it is a wrathful love. ... And third, it is a merciful
love" (*The Prophetic Faith,* New York, 1949, p. 113).

[20]H. W. Wolff agrees (*Hosea,* p. 115). Cf. J. L. Mays: "The
metaphors used for the work of Yahweh are shockingly bold and
abrasive, even for Hosea. God is putrefaction and bone rot in the
body of both peoples" (*Hosea,* p. 90).

of his threats and the savagery of his proclamation of punishment."[21]

Not only does Hosea speak of God as punishing a sinful people, but he also describes sin as having its own built-in punishment. To spurn God's love and bestow one's affections elsewhere is to bring down on oneself an inevitable judgment. Hosea speaks of the people as having become "detestable like the thing they loved" (Hos. 9:10). He says, "Their deeds do not permit them to return to their God. For the spirit of harlotry is within them" (Hos. 5:4); "there is swearing, lying, killing, stealing, and committing adultery; they break all bounds and murder follows murder. Therefore the land mourns, and all who dwell in it languish" (Hos. 4:2f.). In his analysis of Hosea's pronouncements, H. Wheeler Robinson quotes some words of a poem by Whittier:

> *Forever round the Mercy-seat*
> *The guiding lights of Love shall burn;*
> *But what if, habit-bound, thy feet*
> *Shall lack the will to turn?*
>
> *What if thine eye refuse to see,*
> *Thine ear of Heaven's free welcome fail,*
> *And thou a willing captive be,*
> *Thyself thy own dark jail?*

He proceeds, "Does Hosea, then, say this? Not in so many words, but it is implicit in some of his sayings."[22] Hosea saw with crystal clarity the inevitable consequences of Israel's sin, and it grieved him.

But what he saw with equal clarity was that, though Israel was steadily destroying herself with her harlotries, she was not destroying God's love for her. She could not. God's love is firm and sure and steadfast, continuing no matter what happens.[23] Hosea paints a tender picture of a loving God bringing her back to the wilderness. He will "allure her... and speak tenderly to her," and she will "answer as in the days of her youth"; she will call God "my husband" (Hos. 2:14–16).[24]

---

[21] *Theology of the Old Testament,* I, 252.

[22] *Two Hebrew Prophets,* p. 40.

[23] Cf. Hugh Thomson Kerr, Jr.: "The love story of the Bible is the story of God's unrequited love" (*IB,* V, 141).

[24] Cf. W. O. E. Oesterley and T. H. Robinson: "There is a love so great, passionate, and intense, that it cannot abandon the hope of

The classic passage is chapter 11, in which the prophet contemplates the certainty of the disaster that would overtake the people. He begins on a note of tenderness as he looks back to the deliverance from Egypt and pictures God as saying, "When Israel was a child, I loved him, and out of Egypt I called my son."[25] He speaks of the nation's faithlessness and goes on, "Yet it was I who taught Ephraim to walk, I took them up in my arms..." (Hos. 11:1, 3). Hosea continues by delivering God's ominous proclamation; he says that the sword "shall rage against their cities," and goes on, "My people are bent on turning away from me; so they are appointed to the yoke, and none shall remove it" (Hos. 11:6-7). But immediately God says, "How can I give you up, O Ephraim! How can I hand you over, O Israel! How can I make you like Admah! How can I treat you like Zeboiim! My heart recoils within me, my compassion grows warm and tender. I will not execute my fierce anger, I will not again destroy Ephraim; for I am God and not man, the Holy One in your midst, and I will not come to destroy" (Hos. 11:8f.).[26]

LOVE IN EZEKIEL

This magnificent picture of a love that never fails has its parallels elsewhere. Ezekiel uses the same kind of imagery that Hosea employs. He develops a full-scale treatment of the subject, starting with the birth of the nation, which he sees as an unsavory origin: "Your father was an Amorite, and your mother a Hittite" (Ezek. 16:3). He goes on to point out some distressing aspects of the birth in question and the repulsiveness of the newborn child. But God says, "And when I passed by you, and saw you weltering in your blood, I said to you in your blood, 'Live, and grow up like a plant of the field' " (vv.

---

restoration, even when men and nations have reached the limits of sin and suffering. It was incredible to Hosea that Yahweh should be defeated in the long run. His love was bound up with a patience which could endure to the uttermost, and still would leave room for a fresh start" (*Hebrew Religion*, London, 1944, p. 239).

[25]Hosea "explains Israel's call in terms of divine love and grace" (C. F. Whitley, *The Prophetic Achievement*, London, 1963, p. 50).

[26]On Hosea 11:9, C. E. B. Cranfield comments, "The OT comes very near to saying that God *is* love" (*TWBB*, p. 132; Cranfield's italics).

6f.).[27] There was nothing attractive about the people in their natural state. But God took pity on them and made them live. It was his initiative, not theirs.[28]

The prophet continues the metaphor, describing the nation as a maiden growing up and eventually marrying.[29] The bridegroom is God, her Savior (v. 8), and the marriage one in which the bridegroom provided the bride with many wonderful gifts (vv. 10-14). But the marriage did not turn out well because of the bride's unfaithfulness, which Ezekiel points out: "You trusted in your beauty, and played the harlot because of your renown, and lavished your harlotries on any passer-by" (v. 15). The prophet sadly records that "the like has never been, nor ever shall be" (v. 16). He goes on to detail the nation's idolatries, the way she took God's gifts and used them in the idol worship she practiced. "Men give gifts to all harlots," he points out, "but you gave your gifts to all your lovers, bribing them to come to you from every side for your harlotries. ... None solicited you to play the harlot; and you gave hire, while no hire was given to you; therefore you were different" (vv. 33f.).

The prophet makes it clear that the nation will suffer for her waywardness: "I will judge you as women who break wedlock and shed blood are judged" (v. 38). The punishment will fit the crime, for God says, "I will give you into the hand of your lovers" (v. 39), and it is they who will inflict the punishment. Sodom and Samaria were punished for their sins (vv. 48ff.); Judah, their "sister," cannot expect to escape.

But the result is not that God ceases to love his people. That is impossible. It is true that justice will be done, that the

---

[27]There is a textual problem with verse 7, and John W. Wevers comments, "RSV correctly presupposes the omission of *nttyk*, 'I gave you,' and the change of *rbbh*, 'a myriad,' to the infinitive *rbby*, 'grow up'" (*Ezekiel*, London, 1969, p. 121). John B. Taylor accepts the amendment (*Ezekiel*, London, 1969, p. 135).

[28]Cf. C. F. Whitley: "Any relationship that subsisted between Israel and Yahweh rested entirely on Yahweh's initiative in approaching and defending her when she was but an insignificant outcast among the nations of the world" (*The Prophetic Achievement*, p. 52).

[29]Cf. C. E. B. Cranfield: "*Aheb* and the figure of marriage point behind and beneath the covenant to its motive and origin in the innermost personal being of Yahweh. His love is part of the mystery of his personality" (*TWBB*, p. 132).

sinful nation will be punished. But this is not the last word.[30] Ezekiel looks forward to a day when God will restore wicked nations like Sodom and Samaria, and Judah is among them (16:53). He has written some noteworthy passages about the certainty and severity of the punishment for sin, so it is worth noticing that the promise of restoration pervades his writing (e.g., 11:17; 20:33ff.; 36:33ff.; 39:25). This promise also underlies the prophecy of the dry bones (chapter 37) and the overthrow of Gog and Magog (chapters 38, 39). It is also suggested in the vision of the new temple (chapters 40–47) with the cleansing waters flowing from it (47:1), which would enable the trees to grow and produce fruit for food and "leaves for healing" (47:12). In chapter 16, the prophet refers to this promise as a covenant: "Yet I will remember my covenant with you in the days of your youth, and I will establish with you an everlasting covenant" (v. 60; Ezekiel comes back to the everlasting covenant, "a covenant of peace," in 37:26, and he refers to something very much like it in 11:19f. when he speaks of God as putting a new spirit and a new heart in them so that they will do his will and become *his* people).[31] The chapter finishes with a reference to the time "when I forgive you all that you have done, says the Lord God" (v. 63).

Ezekiel uses the sexual theme a number of times—for example, when he complains of adultery (33:26) or looks for a day when the nation will abandon its harlotry (43:7). In chapter 23 he has a frank[32] and sustained treatment of the theme as he

---

[30]Cf. Elizabeth Achtemeier: "Israel's hope, in the Old Testament, rests not on the wrath of God but on his love, and Israel has a future, according to the prophets, not because of what she may become but because of what Yahweh will do"; "the overflowing love and compassion of Yahweh for his own manifests itself not only in a new life but in a recovery and fulfillment for his people of all the promises from the past" (*The Old Testament and the Proclamation of the Gospel,* Philadelphia, 1973, pp. 69, 70).

[31]"In attributing Israel's spiritual regeneration to the atoning activity of God, Ezekiel, accordingly, makes a notable contribution to the theology of grace and forgiveness" (C. F. Whitley, *The Prophetic Achievement,* p. 171).

[32]C. G. Howie speaks of this part of the prophecy as "this remarkable and somewhat shocking chapter" (*Ezekiel, Daniel,* London, 1961, p. 54). G. A. Cooke sees it as following the lines of chapter 16, but "with even more repulsive detail" (*A Critical and Exegetical Commentary on the Book of Ezekiel,* Edinburgh, 1936, p. 247).

compares sinning Judah (Oholibah) to sinning Samaria (Oholah). He shows that Judah is worse than her sister in her continuing harlotry. This time he makes the point that the nation will be destroyed at the hands of her paramours, but adds that she has become disgusted with them: "Behold, I will rouse against you your lovers from whom you turned in disgust, and I will bring them against you from every side"; "I will deliver you into the hands of those whom you hate, into the hands of those from whom you turned in disgust" (23:22, 28). But though the sinning nation had become disgusted with its sin, it did not abandon its evil ways—it simply chose new partners and continued to sin. And Ezekiel says that it is obvious to good men that the nation must suffer the penalty: "Righteous men shall pass judgment on them with the sentence of adulteresses, and with the sentence of women that shed blood; because they are adulteresses, and blood is upon their hands" (v. 45).

The truth that God loves the people is brought out elsewhere in Ezekiel's prophecy when he uses metaphors other than those of the marriage bond. God's majesty is insisted on (cf. the awe-inspiring visions of chapters 1 and 10), so that sin against him is terrible and necessarily invites punishment. Consequently, the people were exiled, but even when that happened God was a "sanctuary" to them (11:16).[33] A loving God, he takes no pleasure in the death of the wicked and asks, "Why will you die, O house of Israel?" (33:11). Clearly God is ready to save the people, but they insist on following the course that leads to death. God is also displeased when the prophets fail the people: "You have not gone up into the breaches, or built up a wall for the house of Israel, that it might stand in battle in the day of the Lord" (13:5). In chapter 34 he castigates the "shepherds" of Israel who have not taken care of their flock. But note the tender conclusion: "You are my sheep, the sheep of my pasture, and I am your God, says the Lord God," v. 31. Clearly Ezekiel is not in doubt about God's love and tender concern for Israel.

Perhaps the point is not made as poignantly as it is in Hosea, but its emphasis is essentially the same. As any right-minded person can see, the people have sinned grievously.

---

[33]John B. Taylor explains that in this way God is "making up to them for the lack of a temple and sacrifices by being their protection and their source of strength" (*Ezekiel,* p. 111).

And sin has a way of reaping a dreadful crop. The nation's consistent idolatry and abandonment of the Lord will necessarily be judged and punished.[34] But this does not mean that God has stopped loving the people.[35] He loves them despite all they have done amiss, and Ezekiel emphasizes the point that this love will certainly continue.

GOD'S SANCTUARY

Malachi is another prophet who uses the marriage imagery, though with a difference. He describes the Israelites as marrying idol-worshippers, and makes an interesting reference to God's love for his sanctuary: "Judah has profaned the sanctuary of the Lord, which he loves, and has married the daughter of a foreign god" (Mal. 2:11). Though the prophet says that "Judah" has married, the context shows that he is referring to marriages between worshippers of God and idol-worshippers, not between God and his people (the metaphor of Hosea and others). These marriages violate God's love. Malachi's declaration of God's love for the sanctuary appears to be the only specific affirmation of this love (though his love for Mount Zion, expressed in verses like Psalm 78:68, amounts to much the same thing). God's love for his people (1:2) is implied in the reference to him as father and creator (2:10), and it is this that makes the profanation of the sanctuary so serious—it is a sin against love.[36]

---

[34]Cf. "I the Lord love judgment [mishpāṭ]" (Isa. 61:8). The context shows that the judgment exercised by God's people is primary here. But the expression tells us something about God, too. D. R. Jones introduces his comment on this passage with, "The source of confidence is in the character of God himself" (Isaiah 56–66 and Joel, London, 1964, p. 79).

[35]Cf. T. C. Vriezen: "These two strands of judgment and salvation are interwoven closely and wonderfully in his preaching. Even in the midst of the worst catastrophe that befell his people he remains confident of God's love and justice" (An Outline of Old Testament Theology, Oxford, 1962, p. 64).

[36]The word rendered "sanctuary" in the RSV is qōdhesh. The AV rendered it "holiness," an interpretation accepted by E. B. Pusey (The Minor Prophets, II, Grand Rapids, 1950, 482). This is quite possible, but most see a reference to the place of worship, as does J. M. P. Smith: "The presence of sinful people within the sacred pre-

DISCIPLINE

Certainly a sin against love has its consequences. The classic expression of this truth is given in Proverbs, where we read: "My son, do not despise the Lord's discipline or be weary of his reproof, for the Lord reproves him whom he loves, as a father the son in whom he delights" (Prov. 3:11f.). But the prophets see equally clearly that a God who really loves his people will discipline them from time to time. In modern times we often confuse love with sentimentality, and we do not always see as clearly as the prophets did that there is a stern side to real love. An easy sentimentality will decline to take stern action when the beloved does what is wrong. But this leaves the beloved secure in his wrongdoing, unfairly confirming the very action that makes him less of a person. Because sentimentality refuses to do what is distasteful, it ignores the long-term benefits of reproving the beloved because it sees that he will dislike the immediate unpleasantness. Sentimentality thus takes the easy way out.

But the more one loves, the more one hates the things that prevent the beloved from enjoying the fullest and most abundant life. And if these things are really hated, then every effort will be made to see that they are put away. If the loved one is subordinate, that may mean taking strong disciplinary measures, and the Bible assures us that God does take such strong measures. He sees more clearly than we ever can that the sins we pursue so resolutely cut us off from the fullest life that we might have: "Your sins have kept good from you" (Jer. 5:25); "their land will be stripped of all it contains, on account of the violence of all those who dwell in it" (Ezek. 12:19). When there is no peace the false prophets may mislead the people with their cry of peace, but the sham on which they rely will inevitably be found wanting in the time of testing. It will be seen for the whitewash it is—the whitewash that will disappear

---

cincts contaminates the whole place" (*A Critical and Exegetical Commentary on the Book of Malachi,* Edinburgh, 1961, p. 49). Robert C. Dentan agrees: "The RSV is undoubtedly right in understanding *qôdhesh* to mean concretely 'the sanctuary.' Since it was believed that in some way God actually dwelt in the temple, the presence in its vicinity of anyone or anything unconsecrated to him, such as a woman of heathen religion, 'the daughter of a foreign god,' could be regarded as a profanation" (*IB,* VI, 1134f.).

in the rain (Ezek. 13:10ff.). Hosea speaks of the sinners he knows: "Like an oven their hearts burn with intrigue; all night their anger smolders; in the morning it blazes like a flaming fire. All of them are hot as an oven, and they devour their rulers" (Hos. 7:6f.). Examples like these are many. God, who loves his people, will have none of these sins, these self-destructive practices of his people.

True love will lead the beloved to the best possible path. And that will mean that from time to time disciplinary measures will be taken. The Bible clearly points out that God disciplines his people to deter them from destructive sin. The Old Testament saints did not doubt that the sufferings and trials of this life are meaningful. They are evidence not that God does not love his people, but that he does. They are his way of bringing his people out of their petty sins and leading them along the way of right into the place of blessing.[37]

GOD'S LOVE IS ACTIVE

And there is no doubt that God blesses his people; in fact, the prophets see him as ceaselessly active on their behalf. He is ready to save them at great cost: "Because you are precious in my eyes, and honored, and I love you, I give men in return for you, peoples in exchange for your life" (Isa. 43:4). The metaphor of redemption brings out the depth of God's concern. The basis of the redemption in question is payment for the captives' release. It is, of course, impossible to envisage God as paying a literal price to anyone. But the metaphor is not without point, because it indicates that God saves his people with the "payment" of loving effort.[38]

---

[37]Cf. C. E. B. Cranfield: "God's punishment of sin is no contradiction of his love; it was precisely because he loved that he took Israel's sin so seriously (cf. the 'therefore' in Amos 3.2). His love was love in deadly earnest and could be severe. It was willing to hurt in order to save, to shatter all false securities and strip Israel of his gifts, if so be that in the end, in nakedness and brokenness, they might learn to know their true peace. But the severity was never separated from tenderness" (*TWBB*, p. 132).

[38]Cf. B. F. Westcott: "The idea of the exertion of a mighty force, the idea that the 'redemption' costs much, is everywhere present. The force may be represented by Divine might, or love, or self-sacrifice, which become finally identical" (*The Epistle to the Hebrews,* London and New York, 1892, p. 296).

By contrast the might of the nations is sometimes dismissed as of no more account than a drop in a bucket or the fine dust that the merchant does not bother to wipe off the scales (Isa. 40:15). But the redemption terminology is not used in such comparisons. When the prophet does talk about redemption, the idea of cost is also introduced—a price God pays because he loves. So we read, "In his love and in his pity he redeemed them" (Isa. 63:9), a verse in which redemption is explicitly linked with God's love, that love that constantly gives on behalf of his people.

God's purposes are clearly a direct result of his love: "The Lord loves him; he shall perform his purpose on Babylon" (Isa. 48:14). The people who put their trust in the Lord need not fear that he will let them down. He is infinitely powerful and ceaselessly active, working out his purposes in this world that he has created. Because he loves his people, he will take whatever action is needed on their behalf. They are included in the scope of his loving purpose.

UNMERITED LOVE

That God loved the people is a truth insisted upon in many places besides the prophetic books. Usually no reason is given for God's selectivity. A. B. Davidson remarks, "We can see, indeed, why He should love some one people, and enter into relations of redemption with them, and deposit His grace and truth among them; but we cannot see why one and not another."[39] Certainly Israel was not chosen for its great size, as Moses points out: "For you were the fewest of all peoples" (Deut. 7:7). It is often said that God loved the fathers and sometimes that he loved Israel because he loved the fathers. But no reason is provided for God's love for the patriarchs, either, though the strength of it is obvious: the Exodus from Egypt[40] and the expulsion of the nations before Israel in the

---

[39] *The Theology of the Old Testament,* Edinburgh, 1904, p. 171. He finds it a help that the choice of the people "was only temporary, and for the purpose of extending His grace unto all," and he goes on to point out that "we are assured that His love is not arbitrary, nor a mere uncalculating passion; but, seeing it is said that God is love, His love is the highest expression of His ethical being, the synthesis and focus of all His moral attributes" (p. 171).

[40] Gabriel Hebert notes that the Exodus is often referred to in the Old Testament. (The expression "I am the Lord thy God who brought

promised land are ascribed to God's love for the fathers (Deut. 4:37f.).[41] Indeed, God's love and care for the people is linked to an oath he made to the fathers (Deut. 7:8). In the same spirit God declined to listen to the curse of Balaam and turned the curse into a blessing, "because the Lord your God loved you" (Deut. 23:5). In Deuteronomy 10:15 we read that "the Lord set his heart in love upon your fathers and chose their descendants after them." Here again God's love for the fathers is stressed, but again God seems to have no reason that men can discern for loving them. Once in Deuteronomy merit is linked with love in a prophecy: "Because you hearken to these ordinances, and keep and do them, the Lord your God will keep with you the covenant and the steadfast love which he swore to your fathers to keep; he will love you, bless you, and multiply you . . ." (Deut. 7:12f.). But notice that even here the covenant[42] and the "steadfast love" of the Lord come first. It is expected that Israel will keep the commandments, but this proceeds from the fact that the people are already included in the covenant, that covenant that proceeds from the love of God.[43] Of course, God's love for Israel is the source of blessing to the people (Deut. 7:13; 23:5; cf. 10:18).

---

thee out of the land of Egypt" occurs with minor variations about a hundred times.) He quotes Micah 6:3-5 and comments, "The Exodus-faith is no mere formal creed, but expresses the personal love of the Deliverer" (*When Israel Came out of Egypt,* 1961, p. 23; cf. p. 26).

[41]Cf. W. Eichrodt: "As distinct from the prophetic conception, in which the love of God is pressing forward to a completely new world order, that love is here (i.e., in Deuteronomy) understood as *the power which upholds the present order*" (*Theology of the Old Testament,* I, 256; Eichrodt's italics).

[42]William L. Moran sees love in Deuteronomy as connected with the covenant: "It is, in brief, a love defined by and pledged in the covenant—a covenantal love" (*CBQ,* XXV, 1963, 78). Deuteronomy does not depend on Hosea for its concept of love (it does not use the marriage bond as its illustration): "The deuteronomic love of service is older, probably as old or almost as old as the covenant itself" (p. 87). Norbert Lohfink argues from Hosea 9:15 that Hosea's concept of love "is also related to covenantal love, even though he gives this love in all other texts a new and different accent" (p. 417).

[43]R. E. Clements sees the appeal to the patriarchs as important: "In the Deuteronomic view, the patriarchal and the Horeb covenants were not two separate institutions, but were seen to be parts of the

There are not many references to God's love in the historical books. But about the baby Solomon, Samuel writes that
"the Lord loved him" and gave him the name "Jedidiah" to
signify that love (II Sam. 12:24f.; Jedidiah means "beloved of
the Lord"). Because Solomon was just a baby, there can be no
question of merit or the lack of it—God simply loved him. It is
not impossible to imagine that something in David or
Bathsheba elicited God's love for their child. But if we make
this assumption we should realize that the connection is in our
imagination; there is nothing in the context to substantiate it.
As we have it, the narrative indicates that God's spontaneous
love—born of his loving nature—is the decisive factor. There
is another reference to God's love for Solomon at a much later
time. It emphasizes the enormity of Solomon's sin in the face
of the fact that "there was no king like him, and he was beloved by his God" (Neh. 13:26). Once more it is God's spontaneous love that is in mind. There is no indication given that
there was anything especially attractive in Solomon to win
God's love.

A third relevant passage is the one that records
Jehoshaphat's prayer, in which he refers to "Abraham thy
friend" (II Chron. 20:7). This probably means that God loved
Abraham, though the possibility cannot be excluded that the
speaker had in mind Abraham's love for God.[44]

In the historical books God's love for Israel is mentioned
twice—both times, interestingly enough, by heathen rulers.
The Queen of Sheba was impressed by Solomon and recognized that God "delighted" in him and made him king. She
noted, "Because the Lord loved Israel for ever, he has made
you king" (I Kings 10:9; a similar verse is II Chron. 9:8). And
Huram, king of Tyre, drew the same conclusion from the fact
that Solomon was Israel's king (II Chron. 2:11).

When we turn to the Psalms we find references to God's
love for Jacob (Ps. 47:4),[45] for Zion (Ps. 78:68), and for the

---

one great mystery of God's choice of Israel to be his holy people.
Grace and law were as inseparable as promise and fulfillment." (*God's
Chosen People*, London, 1968, p. 49).

[44]For a discussion of the meaning of the Hebrew expression, see
above, pp. 13f., n.8.

[45]Derek Kidner comments, "The phrase *Jacob whom he loves*
may provoke the question 'Why?'—which is equally unanswerable

gates of Zion (Ps. 87:2). These verses all attest to God's tender
concern for his people Israel. He loved the people as he loved
their ancestors, and he loved the place where he had settled
them. The Psalmist also indicates that God is a righteous God
who loves righteousness (Ps. 11:7; 33:5) and righteous people
(Ps. 146:8). Similarly, the wisdom literature notes God's love
for "him who pursues righteousness" (Prov. 15:9). Related to
God's love of righteousness is his love of judgment (Ps. 33:5;
37:28). And it is said he reproves those he loves (Prov. 3:12).
Once again, no reason is given for this love. We are told only
that the man God loves is the recipient of his reproof (which
points to God's concern for the man's moral well-being).

One fact that emerges from all this is that it is usually the
people as a whole who are the objects of God's love. There are
a few references to God's love for individuals, but these are
not prominent. In fact, T. W. Manson claims, "It is remarkable how little the Old Testament uses expressions implying
that God loves any particular person. There are not more than
half a dozen in the whole Old Testament."[46] This is something of an overstatement, because there are certainly more
than half a dozen such passages.[47] It is also true that God's
love for individuals isn't always expressly stated, but is
nonetheless implied. The trustful attitude of Old Testament
saints shows that they were quite confident of God's love for
them. Edmond Jacob draws attention, for example, to the significance of the invocation "my God." This is "frequent in
hymns and lamentations, by which individuals committed their
faith into the hands of a God with whom they knew themselves
to be in personal contact and by whom they knew themselves

---

whether the object of the love is 'Jacob' or 'me' or 'the church' or 'the
world'.... The Bible's concern is, instead, to deal with our wrong
answers (Dt. 7:7), doubts (Mal. 1:2ff.), and betrayals (Ho. 11:1f.)"
(*Psalms 1–72*, London, 1973, p. 177).

[46]*On Paul and John*, London, 1963, p. 97.

[47]Manson notes Psalm 127:2, Deuteronomy 33:12, II Samuel
12:24, and Nehemiah 13:26, and includes Isaiah 48:14 as a possibility.
But to these we should add passages like those referring to Abraham
(II Chron. 20:7; Isa. 41:8) and those referring to Daniel as "greatly
beloved" (Dan. 10:11, 19). Edmond Jacob sees only three such references (II Sam. 12:24; Neh. 13:26; Isa. 48:14), and in all three "royal
personages are concerned, which gives the use of the verb 'to love' a
significance it is impossible to extend to all men" (*Theology of the
Old Testament*, London, 1958, p. 109).

to be loved."[48] Nevertheless, it is certainly the case that the emphasis is on God's love for the people as a whole, because the Old Testament writers concentrate on God's love for an unworthy nation. But this emphasis should not be interpreted to indicate any doubt about God's love for individuals;[49] this love simply was not the center of Old Testament interest.

OBLIGATIONS

God's love for his people is very reassuring. We all like to think that we have a powerful protector and that, no matter what we do, we are still the objects of his love. This is certainly the teaching of the Old Testament. God's love is continually operative, independent of the merits of his people. But we must not miss the other truth that this love places obligations on the people of God to live righteously. While it cannot be said that their good conduct is the cause of his love for them, it can be said that God expects such conduct to follow from his love for them. The Lord's beloved must live as the beloved of the Lord. If they do not, they cut themselves off from the blessing that God's love is always offering. The fate of Old Testament Israel gives ample proof of that.

We must clearly recognize that God's love is unconditional. But it is also true that the God who loves his people loves certain qualities—for example, righteousness. "The Lord is righteous," the psalmist sings. "He loves righteous deeds." The consequence is that "the upright shall behold his face" (Ps. 11:7).[50] This verse conveys a precious truth, but it also conveys a solemn warning. Because God is righteous himself, he loves righteousness in his people. Just as the verse suggests that God favors the upright, it also implies that those

---

[48] *Theology of the Old Testament,* p. 112.

[49] G. Quell notes the rarity of expressions showing God's love for individuals. He also says, "The message of the love of God takes on a national and an individual form in the OT. If chronological priority must be ascribed to the former, the nature of love finds purer and more instructive expression in the latter" (*TDNT,* I, 30). ˙

[50] "If the first line of the psalm showed where the believer's safety lies, the last line shows where his heart should be. God as 'refuge' may be sought from motives that are all too self-regarding; but to *behold his face* is a goal in which only love has any interest" (Derek Kidner, *Psalms 1–72,* p. 74).

who are not upright place themselves outside the sphere of his blessing. In fact, Psalm 33:5 says that the Lord "loves righteousness and justice" (or judgment; the Hebrew is *mishpāṭ*), a declaration that carries a similar implication. In Psalm 99:4 God seems to be called "Mighty King, lover of justice" (*mishpāṭ* is used again). Scholars don't agree about the meaning of this verse,[51] some holding that the translation should be, "The king's strength also loveth justice" (ASV). But if this is so, "what is meant is the theocratic kingship, and ver.4c says what Jahve has constantly accomplished by means of this kingship."[52] The expression may rightly be understood to express God's concern for justice. He has a special regard for those who do right: he "loves him who pursues righteousness" (Prov. 15:9),[53] or, as the psalmist puts it so simply, "The Lord loves the righteous" (Ps. 146:8). Certainly he loves his own people, but he also loves "the sojourner," the "resident alien" (Deut. 10:18), the one who has left home to cast in his lot with God's people.[54]

*   *   *   *   *

There is, then, a considerable number of passages in which the term *love* is specifically used to refer to God, passages that teach significant truths about the nature of God and of God's

---

[51]Derek Kidner has an excellent summary of the position: "In the standard Heb. text, 4a reads 'And the king's strength loves justice' (cf. AV, RV)—an abrupt but intelligible statement of the union of might and right. But RSV and most modern versions revocalize '*ōz* (strength) as '*āz* (strong, mighty), and either append it to 3b ('He is holy and mighty,' cf. JB, NEB) or make it qualify 'king' by changing the Heb. word-order ('Mighty King,' RSV, TEV)" (*Psalms 73–150*, London, 1975, p. 354). The NIV renders, "The King is mighty, he loves justice." But most see a reference to Yahweh in this verse.

[52]F. Delitzsch, *Biblical Commentary on the Psalms*, III, Grand Rapids, 1949, 100.

[53]Edmond Jacob sums up the teaching of the Old Testament about wisdom in this way: "The wise man shows and teaches still more that there is no happiness possible outside God's love" (*Theology of the Old Testament*, pp. 253f.). This is the thrust of the wisdom literature, not merely the teaching of a few isolated passages.

[54]S. R. Driver says, "The term is really a technical one, and denotes the protected or dependent foreigner, settled for the time in Israel" (*A Critical and Exegetical Commentary on Deuteronomy*,

activity. But this is far from being the whole story. Biblical writers use other words that bring out other facets of love, and there are many passages that do not use any of the words for love but that are nevertheless important, because they describe occurrences that indicate God's love. This point must be insisted upon in the face of the contention sometimes made that the idea of God as a loving God is far from characteristic. T. H. Robinson is one who makes this assertion; he writes, "We have already had occasion to note what must indeed be obvious to every reader of the Old Testament, that the conception of a loving God is comparatively late, and even in the preexilic Prophets by no means universal."[55] But this is true only if we are dealing with specific occurrences of the one verb and its corresponding noun. G. Ernest Wright gives a truer assessment of Old Testament teaching when he writes,

> The belief in the grace of God, in the continual flow of unmerited kindness to man, can be seen throughout the literature of Israel. It began with the dawn of history and was especially clear in the pity of God for the oppressed Hebrews in Egypt and his deliverance of them from slavery. God's gracious action in history is so constantly affirmed that a stereotyped sentence was used over and over: "God is gracious and merciful, slow to anger, and plenteous in *hesed* ('Faithfulness to the covenant')." That sentence is not confined to the later literature alone but appears as early as the prophetic histories of the ninth and eighth centuries (Exod. 34:6–7). The prophets became so denunciatory of the upper classes precisely because of the latter's wilful disregard of God's action.[56]

Edinburgh, 1973, p. 126). Peter C. Craigie provides a similar definition: "The resident alien was a foreigner who resided with the Israelites under their protection, and though he was not equal in all respects to the Israelites, under the law he was treated as they were" (*The Book of Deuteronomy*, Grand Rapids, 1976, p. 98).

[55] *Prophecy and the Prophets in Ancient Israel*, p. 153.

[56] *The Challenge of Israel's Faith*, Chicago, 1944, pp. 6]f. He has earlier said, "One cannot learn about the true nature of the God of Israel by the concordance method of study alone"; and again, "The two anthropomorphic words 'grace' and 'love,' when applied to God... mean precisely the same thing" (pp. 60, 61). W. Eichrodt is another to notice that the concept of love is much wider than the use of the love terminology (*Theology of the Old Testament*, I, 250f.).

What gives color to Robinson's assertion is the fact that the prophets make such obvious use of the love terminology. As Larry L. Walker says,

> The prophets, utilizing a rich religious heritage, proclaimed a manifold love of God. The entire range of Hebrew vocabulary for love, loyalty, mercy, kindness, and grace is used in preaching the message of God to the heirs of the covenant promises. It is in the prophetic books that the love of God is made vivid, being preached with great force and conviction.[57]

But this does not mean that the idea of God's love did not emerge until the coming of the prophets. It was there before them, but simply expressed less vividly and in other terms.

God's wholehearted care for his people that the Old Testament continually brings out is important and relevant to our inquiry. That God called this one or that, that he sent his prophets, his lawgivers, and a host more, that he intervened in the history of his people—these things and many more are inexplicable unless we accept the supposition that God loves. How are we to explain such things otherwise? Whether or not we refer specifically to the love terminology, it is not an overstatement to say that the love of God underlies the whole of our Old Testament.[58] If we don't recognize that as the foundation, nothing in the Old Testament makes much sense.

---

[57]Gerald F. Hawthorne, ed., *Current Issues in Biblical and Patristic Interpretation,* Grand Rapids, 1975, p. 284.

[58]J. E. Fison is another to recognize that the idea of love is much more pervasive than the express use of the love terminology. He finds it even in the notion of exclusiveness we find in parts of the Old Testament, "for it is the prerogative of love to work towards ultimate inclusion by way of proximate exclusion." Then he goes on, "No grander vision of this inclusiveness is given in all scripture than the unbelievable word of Yahweh through his prophet: 'Blessed be Egypt my people, and Assyria the work of my hands, and Israel mine inheritance'" (*The Faith of the Bible,* Harmondsworth, 1957, p. 66; the quotation is from Isaiah 19:25).

CHAPTER TWO

Man's Love

I *HAVE* maintained that the Old Testament writers primarily emphasize God's love. God's love is not a response to man's attractiveness, nor the result of man's obedience to God. Nor does anything else in man "extract" love from an unwilling or a neutral deity. Men do not persuade God to be loving and gracious—he *is* loving and gracious by nature. He loves because he is a loving God.

Now this primary fact about love has important consequences. We noticed some of them in the preceding chapter. Here we notice further that God's love draws from men an answering love[1] and it requires men to love their brothers. Twenty-seven times in the Old Testament we read of men loving God,[2] a fact which makes it difficult to accept the contention of some writers that the verb normally denotes the love

---

[1]G. Ernest Wright sees this as an example of a type of relationship which he describes in these terms: "If the relationship began through some undeserved act of kindness, an act which sought no reward, nor did it require any reciprocal action; if someone goes out of his way to do something for me, particularly at a time when I am in need of help; if any of these happen, a special relationship is established between me and that person. I cannot pay him back. To reduce this act of kindness into a matter of bookkeeping so that I could easily repay what has been done is to annul the relationship. Nothing that I have done deserves what I have received. I am thus tied to the person in question by a bond that is stronger than any mutual agreement involving mutual obligations" (G. Ernest Wright and R. H. Fuller, *The Book of the Acts of God,* New York, 1960, p..81).

[2]Love for the "name" of God (Isa. 56:6) is included under this heading, because the name stands for the whole person; to love the name of God means to love all that God is and means. The figures refer to the verb. In addition, the noun is used once to refer to men's love for God.

of a superior for an inferior.[3] In addition to denoting men's love for God, the word is used to denote a slave's love for his master (Deut. 15:16). And, in view of the ideas of the time about feminine inferiority, it is worth noticing that it is used to indicate a woman's love for her future husband (I Sam. 18:20). Clearly, then, love is not concerned with gradations of rank.

Johannes Pedersen sees love as the natural, healthy response from men made as they are:

> In love the soul acts in accordance with its nature, because it is created to live in connection with other souls, with the family and those whom it receives into the peace of the family. The commandment to love is thus not a dogmatic invention, but a direct expression of the character of the soul and the organism of family and people. It means that the individual acts for the whole, and the whole for the individual, and this is not an abstract or an unnatural claim, but only the substance of normal life. He who keeps the law of love shows that his soul is sound.[4]

The Old Testament writers see the failure to live in love as unnatural. God created men for community, for one another.

---

[3]For example, N. Snaith argues with reference to '*hb* "that when the root is used of loving persons, it is used of the attitude of a superior to an inferior. Secondly, where it is used (rarely) of an inferior to a superior, it is a humble, dutiful love" (*The Distinctive Ideas of the Old Testament*, London, 1953, p. 132). But that the verb is used twenty-seven times to indicate men's love for God and twenty-three times to indicate God's love for men shows that it is incorrect to say that the root is "rarely" used of the love of an inferior for a superior. And sometimes at least references to the love of friends indicate no notion of superiority and inferiority. L. Koehler holds that "'*āhēbh* is love because of pleasure and is between equals: a man loves a woman and a friend because they attract him. *rāham* can therefore mean pitying love but '*āhēbh* cannot. God is therefore *rāḥûm* and *ḥannûn* but not '*ōhēbh*" (*Old Testament Theology*, London, 1957, p. 240, n.24). But it is more than doubtful that the men of the Old Testament would have regarded women as equals. Koehler holds that Deuteronomy 10:18 and Hosea 11:1 do not contradict his position. But he gives no reason for this assertion, so I cannot follow his logic. Moreover, he overlooks the fact that the participle '*ōhēbh* is used to refer to God in the expression "The Lord loves the righteous" (Ps. 146:8). Nor does he reckon with the many passages where the verb is used to indicate divine love, apart from the participle.

[4]*Israel: Its Life and Culture*, I–II, London and Copenhagen, 1954, 310.

Because he loves men himself, he looks for men to respond in kind by loving both him and each other. Undeniably, love is central.

LOVE AMONG THE PATRIARCHS

In the Pentateuch the word *love* usually means love among people. Twenty times it refers to people's love of other people. (The verb form is used nineteen times; the noun form, once.) Thirteen times it refers to love for God (the verb is always used; except for Exodus 20:6 this usage is confined to Deuteronomy); and three times it refers to a love for food (Isaac's love for "savory food," Gen. 27:4, 9, 14). The most frequently mentioned kind of human love is sexual love, the love of man for maid and of husband for wife. For example, the verb is used to express Isaac's tender affection for Rebecca, a love which comforted Abraham's son after the death of his mother (Gen. 24:67). And it is recorded in another passage that Jacob, the offspring of the love match we have just noted, fell in love with Rachel (Gen. 29:18). He agreed to serve Laban for her for seven years, "and they seemed to him but a few days because of the love he had for her" (Gen. 29:20; cf. also v. 30). This story has instant and abiding appeal, although Jacob's character had many unattractive features, especially in those early years. It is impossible, for example, to condone his theft of the birthright from his older brother Esau or his deception of his old father, with which he secured the aged patriarch's blessing. And his years with Laban were a constant and unedifying struggle, a time when he matched his wits with a schemer as unscrupulous as he, repeatedly deceiving Laban in his unholy determination to succeed in his pursuit of wealth. Clearly, there is little to admire and much to condemn. But there is one redeeming feature of those troubled years: the beautiful love he had for Rachel.[5] Even this had its selfish element, because he certainly wanted to possess the object of his affection. But at least there is something beautiful there that softens his fierce determination to get the girl he loved.

There is a certain wistfulness about Leah's use of the word for love. Tricking a man into marrying a girl is not the ideal

---

[5]W. Zimmerli sees this as an outstanding instance of what he calls "the basic power of love" (*The Old Testament and the World*, London, 1976, p. 33).

way to make him love her, and Jacob did not love Leah—he hated her (Gen. 29:31). But the beloved Rachel bore him no son, whereas Leah gave birth to Reuben, whereupon she exclaimed, "Because the Lord has looked upon my affliction; surely now my husband will love me" (Gen. 29:32). Did Jacob ever come to love her? If so, we have no record of it. As far as we know Leah looked for love in vain.

Jacob's home life brings before us a problem that must have developed from time to time in a polygamous culture. An aspect of this problem is explored in Deuteronomy in the passage that describes a predictable situation: a man has two wives, one of whom he hates and the other of whom he loves. This man cannot make the son of the loved wife his heir if the son of his hated wife is the firstborn (Deut. 21:15–17). In this instance love might easily lead to injustice, but the law steps in to preserve the rights of the son of the unloved.

So far, all of the examples have been of marital love. But if the term is used to indicate admirable marital love, it is also used to speak of less worthy loves. For example, it is used to express Shechem's love for Dinah, a passion which resulted in fornication (or rape; Gen. 34:2f.).[6] The term refers to the emotion, the attitude, and not to its rightness or wrongness.

But our word may be used to express love other than sexual love. In Genesis there are half a dozen passages where it is used to indicate love for children, mostly the love of fathers for sons. For example, it is used to express Abraham's love for Isaac (Gen. 22:2), Isaac's love for Esau (Gen. 25:28), and Jacob's love for Joseph (Gen. 37:3, 4) and for Benjamin (Gen. 44:20). Once, in Genesis 25:28, it denotes the love of a mother for her son—namely Rebecca's love for Jacob. On each occasion it is the special love for a son preferred above another (or others): it is not simply love for "a son" or love for an only son.[7] Similarly, in a closely knit household a slave may love his

---

[6] G. von Rad speaks unequivocally of rape (*Genesis*, London, 1961, pp. 326ff.), but Derek Kidner says, "Whether it was rape or fornication is not clear" (*Genesis*, London, 1967, p. 173).

[7] It is true that Isaac is called "your son, your only son Isaac, whom you love" (Gen. 22:2). But "only" here means "unique"; Abraham was also the father of Ishmael (Gen. 16:15). E. A. Speiser translates the phrase as "your son, your beloved one," and comments that the Hebrew "uses a term that is not the regular adjective for 'one,' but a noun meaning 'the unique one, one and only' " (*Genesis*,

master so intensely that he would refuse the gift of release (Ex. 21:5; Deut. 15:16). Freedom would take him away from the household, and love might be stronger than his desire to be free.

Even when we leave the family circle altogether, the obligation to love is still binding. The Israelite is to love his neighbor (Lev. 19:18).[8] This did not mean merely that he was to love his fellow countrymen and feel free to dislike everyone else. He was also enjoined to love the stranger or resident alien (Lev. 19:34; Deut. 10:18f.). There would be every temptation to take advantage of men without rights of citizenship who presumably were not well off. (If they were, why would they have left their own country?) But the servant of God must resist such temptations. Because he has received much love and many blessings from God, he must accordingly show love to others.

Jesus said that this command and the command to love God sum up all that the law and the prophets require (Matt. 22:37–40). His follower Paul likewise saw the command to love one's neighbor as fulfilling the law (Rom. 13:8–10). Love is thus central to a proper understanding of the Old Testament.[9] Does this mean that a man should love even his enemies? The Old Testament does not say this in specific terms. "Love your enemies" is a New Testament precept, not an Old Testament one. But at least the way is prepared for it in the Old Testa-

---

New York, 1964, pp. 161, 163). S. R. Driver cites A. Dillmann, who claims that Isaac "alone remains to Abraham after the dismissal of Ishmael (xxi. 14ff.), and has the whole of his father's love" (*The Book of Genesis*, London, 1916, p. 217).

[8]G. Quell points out that this is not to be taken in a juristic sense because the attitude required is not one which can be legally directed: "All claim to legal competence must be renounced, and we are not to see in the legal form any more than an oxymoron designed to make the reader sharply aware that the ultimate concern of social legislation is to protect, foster and sometimes awaken the sense of brotherliness" (*TDNT*, I, 25). W. Eichrodt understands the passage to mean that we can derive "the social law from love as the highest force in'personal and moral life" (*Theology of the Old Testament*, II, London, 1967, 253).

[9]Cf. P. E. Hughes: "In a single word, 'love' is what the law is all about"; "in itself, indeed, the law is a principle of life, not of death. It prescribes the divine standard, which is the standard of total love" (*Interpreting Prophecy*, Grand Rapids, 1976, p. 67).

ment. In addition to the commands to love the neighbor and the "resident alien," we find a requirement that a man return his enemy's straying cattle rather than let them roam. He should also bring back his enemy's ass if it strays and help him lift it up if it is lying under its burden (Ex. 23:4f.). And in the wisdom literature he is instructed to give food and drink to his needy enemy, even if only from motives of prudence (Prov. 25:21f.). For such reasons Walther Zimmerli calls the Old Testament "the true pathfinder to the gospel of the New Testament." He goes so far as to say, "The demand 'Love your enemies' certainly occurs in the Old Testament," though he admits that it is "not at the very centre of belief as it is in the New Testament."[10]

Love for God

In Deuteronomy, Israel is repeatedly commanded to love God (Deut. 6:5; 10:12; 11:1, 13, 22; 19:9; 30:6, 16). The command to love is also implied in such passages as that in which Moses explains that the people can choose between good and evil, and exhorts them to choose good, "that you and your descendants may live, loving the Lord your God" (Deut. 30:19f.). Love for God is part of the alternative he is urging the people to choose. It is implied also in the commendations of those who love God and keep his commandments (Deut. 5:10; 7:9). In short, love for God is clearly at the heart of religious life as it is envisaged in Deuteronomy, and this love should be echoed in one's love for his fellowman (Deut. 10:19; cf. Lev. 19:18, 34). Love is certainly no minor emotion.

The command to love gives us food for thought, because in the way we commonly use the term *love* the response cannot be commanded. It is drawn from us by the attractiveness of the loved one, something that cannot be ordered. We "fall in love"; we do not think of ourselves as in charge of the process. In another way a mother may love her child, however unworthy of that love he may be. But this love is not given in response to a command, either. It arises from the nature of the relationship between the two: he is *her* son. We could probably describe every kind of human love this way, because we

---

[10] *The Old Testament and the World*, p. 65. The passages on which he relies for the demand "Love your enemies" in the Old Testament are Exodus 23:4ff.; Deuteronomy 22:1–4.

are apt to see love as spontaneous, called forth by some quality of attractiveness or some natural tie.

But we should not understand our love for God in this way. It is different because it is always a response.[11] As C. E. B. Cranfield puts it, man's love for God "is not something independent, not the mystical quest of the religious *eros,* the upward striving of the human spirit towards the divine, such as is prominent in Plato, Plotinus, etc., but rather something dependent on God's prior love, the response of man to God's love, his gratitude. The initiative remains God's."[12] Indeed, sometimes God is even said to produce love in man: "The Lord your God will circumcise your heart and the heart of your offspring, so that you will love the Lord your God with all your heart and with all your soul, that you may live" (Deut. 30:6). Thus even wholehearted human love for God is not a purely human product, springing from unaided human resources. It is a result of God's love working in men's hearts.

In Deuteronomy it is clear that God's love is the great, basic fact, and that this love awakens a response in those who accept it. While it is true that God is the supremely attractive being and that men ought to love him for what he is, it is also true that the Old Testament does not simply cite God's attractiveness to explain man's love for him. It emphasizes the important truth that God loves first, that the love which men have for God can never be other than a response. Men may come to appreciate God's wonderful attractiveness, but that response is second to their initial response to God's great love for them. And because God loves men as they are, they ought to make the appropriate response, the response of love to love. Because that is the correct response, it can be commanded[13]—

---

[11]Cf. G. von Rad: "All the commandments are simply a grand explanation of the command to love Jahweh and to cling to him alone (Deut. VI.4f.). And this love is Israel's return of the divine love bestowed upon her" (*Old Testament Theology,* I, Edinburgh and London, 1962, 230).

[12]*TWBB,* p. 133.

[13]Cf. E. M. Good: "The love which Yahweh has shown is a love which initiates and sustains the covenant, and Israel's life in the covenant can properly be only a life of love to Yahweh. Therefore, the commandment of love is not the contradiction in terms which it might seem. It is a description of covenantal life, as well as an exhortation to responsibility in the covenant" (*IDB,* III, 167).

as it is in Deuteronomy: "And now, Israel, what does the Lord your God require of you, but to fear the Lord your God, to walk in all his ways, to love him" (Deut. 10:12; cf. also 11:1, 13). Once we read that the utterance of the false prophet or the dream of a false seer is a test God gives "to know whether you love the Lord your God with all your heart and with all your soul" (Deut. 13:3). God is concerned that men make the right response to his love, and he blesses those who do.

Love leads to action; it is impossible to love someone deeply and not do things for him. Love is eager to serve, to give. So it is that the Old Testament writers link love with keeping God's commands. In fact, this is a relationship that God himself establishes: in the second commandment he speaks of "those who love me and keep my commandments" (Ex. 20:6). Love and obedience go together. As Walther Eichrodt puts it, "Love, as the answer to God's act of election, cannot but lead to the unqualified affirmation of his will as this is to be known in the word of the law and the prophets."[14]

Thus the Old Testament in general and Deuteronomy in particular stress that God's people should not only receive his love but also actively return it. Both are important; indeed, this mutual love can be seen as the distinctive quality of the Israelites' view of God and man. G. G. Findlay says, "The unique place which love holds in the Israelite, as compared with other religions, is due to its insistence on a *reciprocal affection of God and people*."[15] The primacy of God's love is not in doubt, but neither is the importance of a proper response.

Eichrodt finds very significant the repeated stress on love in the Deuteronomic teaching of the law: "By the derivation of the whole law from the command to love, the basic demand of the divine will for the surrender of the whole person to the divine Thou was brought within the comprehension of the simplest citizen." It does not take a profound intellect or a

---

[14]*Theology of the Old Testament*, II, 298. He goes on to say, "Hence *the law is not an element of the divine sovereignty alien to love, but a direct proof of love*" (Eichrodt's italics). Similarly, G. Wallis says, "Not only does love presuppose a concrete inner disposition which is strengthened by experiences and events, but it includes a conscious act in behalf of the person who is loved or the thing that is preferred" (*TDOT*, I, 105).

[15]*Dictionary of the Bible*, ed. J. Hastings; rev. ed. by F. C. Grant and H. H. Rowley, New York, 1963, p. 593.

univer;ity degree to know what love is and to understand that
men rust love their God. Eichrodt goes on to point out that
this m ikes significant every requirement of the law (even one
"not immediately transparent"), "because it derives from the
counsel of the love of God, who has ordered all things for the
sake of his people's salvation, and who accepts no keeping of
the commandment just for the commandment's sake, desiring
rather to see in each fulfilment of the law the living effect of a
single-minded profession of love for God."[16] The requirement
of love is not to be pushed into the background, as though it
were of minor importance. It is central to the way of life envisaged in these Old Testament writings.[17]

THE HISTORICAL BOOKS

As in the Pentateuch, the love referred to in the historical
books of the Old Testament is usually love among people. Five
times these books refer to love for God and once to Uzziah's
love for his hobby of farming (II Chron. 26:10), but thirty-three
times they mention love among people (the verb is used
twenty-seven times; the noun, six times). The most frequent
use of the word under this heading indicates love between the
sexes.

For example, Saul's daughter Michal loved David (I Sam.
18:20), and in due course they were married (I Sam. 18:27).
The marriage had an unpromising genesis, because Saul promised Michal to David only in the hope that this would lead the
Philistines to kill the prospective bridegroom (I Sam. 18:25).
But Michal saved David's life, cleverly deceiving his would-be
murderers and lying convincingly to her father (I Sam. 19:11–

---

[16]*Theology of the Old Testament,* II, 372. Similarly, T. C. Vriezen says of Deuteronomy 6:5, "The love of God becomes the dominating idea of life; the emphasis on the heart of man proves that the
author demands man's absolute personal surrender in religious life"
(*An Outline of Old Testament Theology,* Oxford, 1962, p. 215).

[17]A. S. Peake long ago pointed out that, in Deuteronomy,
"whole-hearted love of God and devotion to Him is made the spring
of all action. This is to control the life of society and the home, as well
as the relation of man to God and the performance of the strictly
religious duties. Love of others is made secondary only to the love of
God" (*The Religion of Israel,* London, 1908, p. 86).

17).[18] Despite her intervention, those were troubled days, and a marriage like this one was not easy to maintain. In fact, David had to flee from the king and leave Michal behind. In due course he took other wives (I Sam. 25:42f.), and in his absence Saul gave Michal to a certain Palti (I Sam. 25:44; he was apparently also called Paltiel, II Sam. 3:15). She lived as this man's wife for several years until David, when he was king over Judah, demanded her return (II Sam. 3:14).[19] What did all this do to Michal's love for David? We do not find out. True, we are told that Palti was grieved when forced to give her up (II Sam. 3:16), which suggests that this second "marriage" was one marked by tenderness and affection. But we are told neither what Michal felt for Palti nor how she felt about being taken back into David's harem.

We are given one more glimpse of this lady, when she saw her royal husband leaping and dancing before the Lord, apparently in a naked or near-naked condition (II Sam. 6:16, 20). She despised him for this and said so,[20] thus initiating an unedifying domestic squabble (during the course of which David reminded her that he had been preferred to her father, II Sam. 6:21). We also learn that Michal was childless (II Sam. 6:23), which must have grieved her, given the accepted ideas of the day. Did her early love for David last through these turbulent, disappointing years? We have no way of being sure. Such evidence as we have seems to indicate that it did not, for the last word we have about Michal's attitude toward David is that she despised him in her heart. It seems, then, that 'hb can be used for a love that is real, resourceful, reckless—but not necessarily lasting.

There are many references to marital love. For instance, we learn about Elkanah, who loved his wife Hannah and did what he could to make up for her childlessness (I Sam. 1:5, 8).

---

[18]William McKane speaks of her as "a devoted wife possessing courage and resourcefulness and ready to expose herself to danger in order to secure David's escape" (*I & II Samuel*, London, 1963, p. 121).

[19]John Mauchline thinks that by this demand David was planning to secure a claim to the throne of Israel (*1 and 2 Samuel*, London, 1971, p. 210). H. W. Hertzberg (*I and II Samuel*, London, 1964, pp. 258f.) and others agree.

[20]"The dignity of a king had been no better observed by Saul when he lay down naked in the company of the prophets. But this she chose to forget" (H. P. Smith, *A Critical and Exegetical Commentary on the Books of Samuel*, Edinburgh, 1912, p. 296).

And one interesting piece of information preserved about King Rehoboam is that he loved one of his wives, a lady called Maacah (II Chron. 11:21). Not much that is good is recorded about this king. Because of his folly Israel was divided into two kingdoms. He then tried to wage a war against the northerners and was dissuaded only by the intervention of the prophet Shemaiah (II Chron. 11:1ff.). We are also told that he had a harem of eighteen wives and sixty concubines by which he sired twenty-eight sons and sixty daughters (II Chron. 11:21). Thus we get the impression that he was a haughty oriental despot, living only to satisfy his own desires. But there is this one redeeming feature: his real love for Maacah. She was not his first wife, but he loved her above all of the others and made her son his heir (contrary to the provisions of Deut. 21:15–17). Another royal love is that of King Ahasuerus for Esther (Esther 2:17). The story shows that the monarch genuinely loved her (a fact that was strategic in God's working out of his divine purpose). He was ready to listen to her and to agree to her wishes, which points to something more than the lust that builds a harem.

The passages we have considered mostly point to that love between the sexes that is at the basis of stable married life. But occasionally problems developed, as they did in Michal's marriage. Another and perhaps more striking example is provided by Samson's marriage. His wife made her contribution to their wedding feast by weeping before him for seven days and complaining that he did not love her. How could he when he had not told her his riddle (Judg. 14:16f.)? When he finally relented, she, of course, passed on the information to his adversaries. Delilah, her spiritual cousin, complained, "How can you say, 'I love you,' when your heart is not with me? You have mocked me these three times, and you have not told me wherein your great strength lies" (Judg. 16:15). But despite all that, Samson did love her (Judg. 16:4), and that love proved his undoing. Clearly, the fault in Samson's love life was that he persisted in lavishing his affection on unworthy objects.[21]

Worse was Amnon's love for Tamar. The lady behaved honorably throughout their relationship, but Amnon's love (like his subsequent hatred) was consistently disgraceful (II

---

[21]Cf. A. E. Cundall: "Samson had not the same opportunities as Solomon, but his unbridled passions were akin to those of the great king and brought about his downfall" (*Judges*, London, 1968, p. 175).

Sam. 13). Perhaps Solomon's love for "many foreign women" (I Kings 11:1f.) was not as evil a thing in itself, for as far as we know he did not sin against any of them; he simply added them to his large harem. But his actions had worse consequences, because Solomon was king, and when his wives turned his heart from Yahweh and led him to worship other gods (I Kings 11:4ff.), all of Israel was affected.

We should notice one further reference to "the love of women" in these books, a reference which is sometimes taken to indicate that this love is of no great importance. When David lamented over Jonathan, he said, "Your love to me was wonderful, passing the love of women" (II Sam. 1:26). But this comment is complimentary, not disparaging: David is saying in effect, "The love of women is wonderful (everyone knows that). People will understand that your love was something very special when I say that it was more wonderful even than that love."[22] The love of women is the standard by which this other love may be tested. The term that David uses to indicate this special love (used of Jonathan and Saul) is *beloved* (II Sam. 1:23; his word is *hanne'^{e}hābhiym*).[23]

Clearly, David was capable of deeply loving others. He was also loved: we have already noticed that Michal and Jonathan both loved him. In fact, this particular word group is used often in passages about David: the verb is used six times to refer to people who loved David; the corresponding noun is used four times. Obviously, he must have been an attractive and lovable person. His friendship with Jonathan is a classic example of the love of friends, marked by mutually strong devotion. More than once we are told that Jonathan loved David "as he loved his own soul" (I Sam. 18:1, 3; 20:17; cf. II Sam. 1:26).[24] But it was not only David's most intimate

---

[22]Cf. C. F. Keil and F. Delitzsch: "Comparison to the love of woman is expressive of the deepest earnestness of devoted love" (*Biblical Commentary on the Books of Samuel,* Grand Rapids, 1950, p. 292). H. P. Smith thinks that the expression "may be supposed to include both the love of the bride for her husband and the love of the mother for her son" (*A Critical and Exegetical Commentary on the Books of Samuel,* Edinburgh, 1961, p. 264).

[23]This participle (the only occurrence in the Old Testament of the niphal of this verb) means "worthy to be loved, loveable," according to KB.

[24]H. W. Hertzberg speaks of the friendship of David and Jonathan as "the most beautiful description of a friendship which the

friends who loved him. King Saul loved him when he first met him (I Sam. 16:21), though that love did not last—it faded in the light of the monarch's jealousy. At a later time another king, Huram of Tyre, is said to have loved David (I Kings 5:1). In fact, whole groups of people loved him, such as Saul's servants (I Sam. 18:22) and even "all Israel" (I Sam. 18:28), "all Israel and Judah" (I Sam. 18:16).[25] Even when Joab was complaining about David's conduct he could recognize that the people loved him (II Sam. 19:6). Sometimes we have indications of the devotion David could inspire in others even when the words for love are not used. An outstanding example is the occasion when, hard pressed by the enemy, David expressed a desire for a drink from the well by the gate of Bethlehem. Three mighty men brought him that water, even though they had to break through the Philistine lines to do it. And it says something about David that he recognized that this brave action had made the water too precious to drink. He therefore made it a drink offering to the Lord (II Sam. 23:13–17; I Chron. 11:15–19).[26]

David was not the only one who had friends, but there were few who could arouse the affection and devotion that David could. In the book of Esther we read of some friends of Haman (literally those who "love" him; Esther 5:10, 14; 6:13).[27] But clearly their affection was not very deep, because as soon as his importance waned they abandoned him. Saul's love for David was also ephemeral. He is said to have loved the young man (I Sam. 16:21), and we have no reason to think that this love was not real—but it was not lasting. It was speedily replaced by anger and envy so great that Saul became David's

---

Bible offers us." He later says, "David is evidently a man with particularly attractive features.... He takes hearts by storm, and everyone falls for him" (*I and II Samuel,* p. 154).

[25]J. A. Thompson argues that there are political overtones in such passages (*VT,* XXIV, 1974, 334–38; XXVII, 1977, 475–81).

[26]G. Ganse Little comments, "This whole story of David's plaintive longing for water from the well of Bethlehem is a gem"; "One can understand why David was beloved alike of God and of his own comrades-in-arms. He knew the secret of true greatness—the accurate appreciation and evaluation of the mercies in his life, what they cost others, and what they were meant to be used for in his own experience" (*IB,* II, 1169f., 1171).

[27]The participle of the verb "to love"—i.e., "he who loves"—is frequently translated as "friend."

enemy (I Sam. 18:29) and tried to kill him (I Sam. 18:17, 25; 19:9f.).

Sometimes a man's conduct may hurt his friends. In fact, Joab once complained to David, "You love those who hate you and hate those who love you" (II Sam. 19:6). Again David's appeal to others is obvious, though on this occasion Joab could see that the way he was acting brought them no help; rather, it aided his enemies. Similar to Joab's reproof are the words of Hanani the seer to Jehoshaphat when he accused the king of loving those who hate the Lord (Il Chron. 19:2).

Although these books do not emphasize love for God in the same way they stress love among people, love for God is nonetheless apparent. For example, Joshua exhorted the people from the two-and-a-half tribes to take good care that they love the Lord their God (Josh. 22:5), an exhortation that was repeated to all Israel (Josh. 23:11). Sometimes we hear of those who love God and who have accordingly received the blessing of the God who loves them. Similar to these passages is the prayer "Thy friends [i.e., those who love thee] be like the sun as he rises in his might" (Judg. 5:31), a piece of expansive imagery that suggests the warmth of God's blessing.[28] And Nehemiah knows that God, besides being "the great and terrible God," is one "who keeps covenant and steadfast love with those who love him and keep his commandments" (Neh. 1:5). Though not many passages in the Old Testament declare an individual's love for God, one passage about Solomon's early reign says simply, "Solomon loved the Lord" (I Kings 3:3). The rarity of such references may be due to the awe with which the people regarded God.

Usage in the Pentateuch differs from that in the historical books. In both, the words from this root are most frequently used to refer to sexual love, but in the historical books the next most frequent usage refers to the love of friends, a usage that does not occur in the Pentateuch. On the other hand, the Pentateuch uses the word quite often to refer to familial love, a use which is practically absent from the historical books (the one

---

[28]G. F. Moore says that this image suggests that God's love is "splendid, invincible; vanquishing, annihilating the darkness of the night, the mists of dawn. No more fitting or impressive figure could be conceived" (*A Critical and Exegetical Commentary on Judges,* Edinburgh, 1958, p. 169).

exception is Ruth 4:15, in which Ruth's love[29] for Naomi is
mentioned). In both there are references to love for God, but
there is nothing in the historical books to parallel the concentration on this subject in Deuteronomy.

LOVE AMONG THE POETS

When we turn to the poetical books (we notice Psalms,
Song of Songs, and Lamentations), we find a greater use of the
noun. The poets sing of love among people on twenty-four
occasions, the noun being used thirteen times and the verb,
eleven. Frequently they are occupied with love for things (seventeen references are made, all of them using the verb).
Sometimes these are very ordinary things. For example, the
psalmist refers to the man who loves (RSV, "covets") many
days "that he may enjoy good" (Ps. 34:12), a verse expressing
the common enough desire for long life and prosperity. But
frequently men are said to love or are exhorted to love things
associated with God or with qualities God desires in man. Outstanding is Psalm 119, with its exultant joy in God's revelation and its frequent references to love for God's word, his
law, his commands, his testimonies, and the like (see verses
47, 48, 97, 113, 119, 127, 140, 159, 163, 165, and 167 for specific
references to love for these things). Christians today often
think of the law as a burdensome restriction, but that was not
the way the psalmist responded to it. To him the law was God's
loving gift meant to guide his people in the right way, and the
psalmist welcomed it, exulted in it, and loved it.

Then there is love for worship. Those who truly love God
have in all ages delighted in worshipping him, and the Psalms
show that from very early days worshippers loved everything
associated with the activity of honoring God. So we find references to love for God's house (Ps. 26:8); for Jerusalem, where
that house was (Ps. 122:6); for God's name (Ps. 5:11; 69:36;
119:132); and for his salvation (Ps. 40:16; 70:4).

True believers also love the qualities that God loves. If

---

[29]Edward F. Campbell, Jr., brings out something of the significance of this single use of the word in the whole book: "Perhaps we
can say that to make Ruth the subject of the sole use of the verb 'to
love,' in a story whose words mean so much, belongs also to the
ultimate in approbation" (*Ruth*, New York, 1975, p. 168).

they genuinely experience God's love and respond with a true love for him, they cannot live self-centered lives. They love righteousness (Ps. 45:7) as God loves judgment (Ps. 99:4),[30] qualities that God looks for in his people, as the Old Testament points out frequently. Since this means commending what is in itself admirable and is associated with God, we are not surprised to find reference to it in Scripture. It is perhaps worth noting that this idea emphasizes the individual. Some aspects of Old Testament teaching emphasize the body of believers, but developing a love for righteousness and the like is an individual activity.

Sometimes, however, the psalmist notices that people love evil—in fact, they may love evil more than good. His complaint goes on, "[You love] lying more than speaking the truth. You love all words that devour, O deceitful tongue" (Ps. 52:3f.). Or men may love "vain words" (Ps. 4:2), specifically cursing (Ps. 109:17). And then there is the man who "loves violence," who is warned that the Lord's "soul" hates him (Ps. 11:5).

When we examine the references to love among people, we notice several that talk about love for friends. But in the poetical books these are invariably false friends; none of these writers seems to sing about the love of a true friend. Two references in Lamentations illustrate this. In one verse the poet says, "Among all her lovers she has none to comfort her; all her friends have dealt treacherously with her, they have become her enemies"; in another verse in the lament of the city the poet mourns, "I called to my lovers but they deceived me" (Lam. 1:2, 19). In each case the meaning appears to be that the city's so-called "friends"[31] deserted her in her time of need. They are not unlike those of whom the psalmist complained, "My friends and companions stand aloof from my plague, and my kinsmen stand afar off" (Ps. 38:11); "Thou hast caused

---

[30]This verse may possibly refer to Israel's king; see above, p. 32 and n.51.

[31]The imagery may, of course, be sexual, but on the whole it seems that the term denotes something less passionate than that. A. W. Streane sees a reference to "the neighboring states, with whom in the sunshine of prosperity she was on friendly terms" (*The Book of the Prophet Jeremiah together with the Lamentations,* Cambridge, 1926, p. 330). Delbert R. Hillers thinks of "the faithless allies of Israel" and goes on to refer to her "alliance with other nations and gods" (*Lamentations,* New York, 1972, p. 19).

lover and friend to shun me; my companions are in darkness"
(Ps. 88:18). Another psalm paints a similarly sad picture: "In
return for my love they accuse me, even as I make prayer for
them. So they reward me evil for good, and hatred for my
love" (Ps. 109:4f.).

In these books the majority of references to love among
people refer to sexual love. But in fact these references are
confined to the Song of Songs. This does not, of course, make
them any less important; it simply means that this significant
aspect of life is not dwelt on in the other poetic literature. But
this Song is full of the idea of romantic love. There are many
examples of the use both of the verb (Song of Sol. 1:3, 4, 7; 3:1,
2, 3, 4) and of the noun (Song of Sol. 2:4, 5, 7; 3:5, 10; 5:8; 7:6;
8:4, 6, 7). The physical aspects of this love are stressed in a
way that Christians have sometimes found embarrassing—but
the Song is about a lofty and pure passion. And because sexual
love is part of God's creation,[32] there is nothing demeaning or
degrading about it.[33] At its best "love is strong as death"
(Song of Sol. 8:6), and as invincible: "Many waters cannot
quench love, neither can floods drown it. If a man offered for
love all the wealth of his house, it would be utterly scorned"
(Song of Sol. 8:7). Love between the sexes can be a beautiful,
stabilizing force. When it is debased, society suffers; when it is
honored and practiced rightly, society builds on its solid base.

These books do not say much about love for God, but what
they do say is important. In Psalm 31 is a command to love, as

---

[32]Raymond F. Collins quotes the well-known words of Rabbi
Akiba: "All the world is not as worthy as the day on which the Song
of Songs was given to Israel, for all the writings are holy, but the Song
of Songs is the Holy of Holies." Collins adds that this collection of
poems "simply celebrates the apex of God's very good creation. male
and female in the reality of their sexual attraction for one another"
(*Biblical Theology Bulletin,* VII, 1977, 158).

[33]Cf. W. Zimmerli: "There is expressed in the Song of Songs,
and in what it says of love and sexuality, something which is quite in
the spirit of the Old Testament. This whole aspect of life is 'the
world,' in the sense in which the world appears in the creation stories:
something created, shaped by the creator, living and called into life by
his word of blessing, never idealized in the name of religion nor misunderstood as part of the life of God" (*The Old Testament and the
World,* p. 34). Later he draws attention to the importance of the fact
that, while the Old Testament knows of many sexual sins, it never
advocates asceticism (pp. 38f.).

forthright an imperative as we find anywhere: "Love the Lord, all you his saints" (Ps. 31:23). In another psalm we come across one of the rare affirmations in the Old Testament of a personal love for God: "I love the Lord" (Ps. 116:1).[34] Here love for God is more than an academic possibility—it is a reality. In this psalm the singer counts the blessings he had received when the Lord heard his prayer, which is the theme of the declaration "The Lord preserves all who love him" (Ps. 145:20). This promise must have been extremely comforting to people confronted with the many enemies that beset the men of the Old Testament. Whatever trials and misfortunes they might encounter along the way, in the end those who love God can know that nothing less than the Lord's rich blessing awaits them, the blessing the psalmist sings about. I do not think that the Old Testament teaches, either here or elsewhere, that we ought to love God for what we can get out of him. We should love God because he first loved us, because our love is the appropriate response to his love. What the psalmist is saying is that when we do love God we will be included in the sphere of his blessing.

---

[34]This is the rendering of the RSV. The Hebrew reads simply, "I love because Yahweh will hear ... ," but most agree with the RSV. A. A. Anderson says, "It is clear from the context that the Psalmist refers to Yahweh; in the cultic setting of the Psalm this must have been even more obvious." He also says, "In essence this verse anticipates 1 Jn 4:19: 'We love, because he first loved us' " (*The Book of Psalms*, II, London, 1972, 791). C. A. Briggs and E. G. Briggs think that originally the verb had an object—"Yahweh, my strength"—but that this "has been omitted by copyist's error" (*A Critical and Exegetical Commentary on the Book of Psalms*, II, Edinburgh, 1960, 398). Mitchell Dahood is a dissenter; he takes the text to mean, "Out of love for me Yahweh did hear," repointing the verb to give a substantive which he then explains as "an accusative of cause followed by the objective genitive ending of the first-person singular." Or, he says, one "may analyze the ending as the third-person singular" (*Psalms III*, New York, 1970, 145). But the RSV rendering is simpler. W. E. Barnes thinks the construction is due in the first instance to conciseness. He also thinks the psalmist feels a "reverence or awe which prevents him from saying outright, 'I love Jehovah.' " He paraphrases, "I am in a glow of love, because Jehovah heareth" (*The Psalms*, II, London, 1931, 552). H. G. Wood takes up the suggestion of J. Jeremias that *agapaō* may have the meaning "feel gratitude" or the like, and understands the LXX as "I feel the deepest thankfulness ..." (*ET*, LXVI, 1954–55, 319f.). But this is scarcely justified.

Those who love God also develop a fierce hatred of what is wrong: "You who love the Lord hate evil" (Ps. 97:10, RSV mg.).[35] There is no room for half-measures in loving God. Because God is totally opposed to everything evil, the man who loves him must likewise be implacably opposed to evil. Love for God cannot co-exist with a love for evil. The very fact of the believer's love for God means that he is dedicated to stamping out evil.

Sometimes love for God is expressed by speaking of love for his "name." In antiquity a name stood for the whole person; thus in such passages God's name is not to be distinguished from God himself. Those who love God's name "exult" in him (Ps. 5:11) and rejoice in his blessing. Indeed, one can pray, "Turn to me and be gracious to me, as is thy wont toward those who love thy name" (Ps. 119:132). The lover of God can rely on God's graciousness. In a time of trouble, the psalmist looks forward to the time when God "will save Zion and rebuild the cities of Judah." He expresses the conviction that "those who love his name shall dwell in it" (Ps. 69:35f.). In none of these passages is there any tendency to dwell on God's greatness. Rather, in each case the psalmist is concerned with the fact that love for God has important consequences for the lover: it brings him emotional and spiritual peace, and it brings him within the sphere of God's blessing.

THE WISDOM LITERATURE

Under this heading we consider three books: Proverbs, Job, and Ecclesiastes. (Job might have been included with the poetical books, but it fits in well with the wisdom books, too.

---

[35]The RSV reads, "The Lord loves those who hate evil," but notes that this is conjecture; the margin gives the sense of the Hebrew. This is accepted, for example, by J. H. Eaton: "They are admonished that to love this Lord means also to set oneself resolutely against 'evil' (we may keep the received text, RSV note k)" (*Psalms,* London, 1967, p. 236). D. Kidner, C. A. Briggs and E. G. Briggs, and others support this view. A. A. Anderson notes that the text of the RSV presupposes "a slight emendation" but holds that this "provides a better agreement with the following two lines" (*The Book of Psalms,* II, 690). But this scarcely seems adequate; the traditional way of interpreting the words fits the context. There is no reason to reject the Hebrew text. Cf. the NIV: "Let those who love the Lord hate evil."

In any case, it is not crucial here, because it has so few examples of our word group). The poetical books differ from the earlier groupings because they contain more references to the love of things. The wisdom books repeat this tendency, but with a difference: the poets talked of love for good things much more than love for evil things, whereas the writers of the wisdom books tip the balance slightly in the other direction (love for evil things is mentioned ten times; love for good things, nine times). Love among people is mentioned seventeen times, mostly to indicate the love of friends (the noun is used seven times; the verb, ten times). In this literature there are no examples of the use of our word group for God's love.[36] This love is implied almost everywhere, but it is not stated in specific terms.

We begin with the love of good things. Four times a love for wisdom is extolled (Prov. 4:6; 8:17, 21; 29:3), and once wisdom is said to love those who love her (Prov. 8:17). Those who diligently seek her out will find her. Wisdom brings "wealth" to those who love her (Prov. 8:21); she will "guard" them (Prov. 4:6). Akin to the love of wisdom are the loves of discipline and knowledge (Prov. 12:1). Indeed, there is no real love for wisdom without them. Similar things are said about the love for "purity of heart" (Prov. 22:11, RSV).[37] True wisdom is not self-seeking, and purity of heart is a necessary part

---

[36]Unless we read with LXX, "The Lord loves holy hearts" in Proverbs 22:11. R. B. Y. Scott translates this verse to read, "The Lord loves a man of pure mind." He comments, "The subject of *loves* is supplied from LXX. Without it the verse reads literally, 'One who loves pureness of mind, grace of speech, his friend is a king.' The verse has been damaged in transmission; LXX inserts, after *mind*, 'all who are blameless are acceptable to him,' and another line is missing altogether" (*Proverbs. Ecclesiastes,* New York, 1965, p. 128). Cf. W. O. E. Oesterley: "On the basis of the Versions, the first line may be rendered: 'The Lord loveth the pure in heart' " (*The Book of Proverbs,* London, 1929, p. 186). C. H. Toy comments on the defectiveness of the text and notices the readings of the Latin and LXX. He thinks "the most probable sense" to be "the king loves the pure in heart" (*A Critical and Exegetical Commentary on the Book of Proverbs,* Edinburgh, 1959, p. 418). C. T. Fritsch thinks the sense of the RSV is best (*IB,* IV, 908). In short, opinions vary, and we cannot safely accept the view that the text refers to God's love.

[37]See previous note. If Scott's view is accepted, the verse reinforces the demand for uprightness in the pursuit of wisdom.

of it. Throughout the whole of this literature the pursuit of wisdom is steadfastly kept in mind. It is basic to one's self-esteem: "He who gets wisdom loves himself" (Prov. 19:8).[38] It is foolish to think that there is a better way than that of loving wisdom, and it is equally foolish to think that one can genuinely love wisdom and yet act in ways that are harmful to oneself or to others. The love of wisdom leads to love for oneself and for one's fellowman.

Of the loves of things not good, some are more serious than others. Thus a warning against pleasure simply emphasizes that pursuing pleasure is not the way to succeed in life: "He who loves pleasure will be a poor man; he who loves wine and oil will not be rich" (Prov. 21:17). It is like the warning against too great a concern for sleep: "Love not sleep, lest you come to poverty" (Prov. 20:13). Similarly, the man who loves money or wealth will never be satisfied (Eccles. 5:10). That appetite is never sated, because the urge to obtain more is only fueled by acquiring. Also relevant here is the serious assertion that the man who "loves transgression loves strife" (Prov. 17:19), a line which Scott paraphrases as, "One who is fond of crime must be fond of trouble."[39] Other maxims stress the importance of pursuing wisdom. Consider, for example, Proverbs 18:21: "Death and life are in the power of the tongue, and those who love it will eat its fruits." According to this verse, speech is a serious matter.[40] So is a turning against wisdom, for

---

[38]The Hebrew does not use the word for wisdom but uses *lēbh*, which means "heart" or "mind." R. B. Y. Scott translates, "He who develops his mind is his own best friend" and comments, "Or, 'obtains wisdom'; literally 'obtains mind'" (*Proverbs. Ecclesiastes*, p. 117). For our present purpose it does not matter greatly which way we prefer to understand the word. Any reasonable interpretation shows that the way of wisdom is being commended.

[39]*Proverbs. Ecclesiastes*, p. 109.

[40]W. O. E. Oesterley holds that the meaning is "hasty and inconsiderate words make enemies, and the result might easily, in those days, be fatal. On the other hand, judicious and well-spoken words, by making a favorable impression, would gain friends through whom prosperity ('life') would be achieved." Of the words about love he says, "As the reference here is obviously to the tongue, 'they that love it' must be understood in the sense of those who love to use it, though, it must be allowed, this is stretching the meaning of the Hebr. word" (*The Book of Proverbs*, p. 151). C. H. Toy agrees that the reference must be to using the tongue, "but the verb is not natural,

those who hate it "love death" (Prov. 8:36). Today we appreciate simplicity, which in many ways is good—but it is possible to love being "simple" in a way that refuses the way of wisdom. (Prov. 1:22).[41]

These books refer a number of times to the love of friendship. Sometimes this is a false friendship, a love lightly given that vanishes in the day of difficulty. It was this kind of love that Job had received when he complained, "All my intimate friends abhor me, and those whom I loved have turned against me" (Job 19:19). These false friends are the subject of the worldly-wise observation that "the rich has many friends" (Prov. 14:20). In an obscure passage Qoheleth says, "The righteous and the wise and their deeds are in the hand of God; whether it is love or hate man does not know" (Eccles. 9:1).[42] In the same book we are reminded of the finality of death: the love, the hatred, and the envy of the dead have all perished (Eccles. 9:6).

But the Bible knows a love that is better than all this, and it has a good deal to say about it. Real love may exist in utter poverty, but it is superior to unhappy wealth, for "better is a

---

and the text is perhaps wrong" (*A Critical and Exegetical Commentary on the Book of Proverbs,* p. 365).

[41]C. H. Toy sees a reference to "those who positively love ignorance, and deliberately refuse to listen to instruction in right living" (*A Critical and Exegetical Commentary on the Book of Proverbs,* p. 23).

[42]G. Quell holds that the author, "having pointed to the hand of God which ordains the action of the righteous and the wise... , reverently maintains that man's most elemental feelings of love and hate remain mysterious to himself" (*TDNT,* I, 25, n.24). Derek Kidner, however, thinks that it is divine and not human love that is in mind: "Whether we take the words *love or hate* here to be a biblical way of saying 'acceptance or rejection,' or to have their simple, primary sense, we shall have, either way, only an uncertain answer about the Creator's character from the world we live in, with its mixture of delight and terror, beauty and repulsiveness." In a footnote he observes that the words might conceivably refer to human love and hate, which would suggest that "man is not sufficiently master of himself to know whether he will feel love or hate in a given situation." Kidner feels that "the emphasis on God's inscrutability in 8:17, immediately before this verse, makes it more likely (and more relevant to the argument) that His attitude rather than man's is the issue here" (*A Time to Mourn, and a Time to Dance,* 1976, p. 80 and n.).

dinner of herbs where love is than a fatted ox and hatred with
it" (Prov. 15:17). Similarly, the friend "who sticks closer than
a brother" is preferable to "friends who pretend to be friends"
(Prov. 18:24). The Bible extols the true friend's virtues, saying,
"Faithful are the wounds of a friend" (Prov. 27:6),[43] and "A
friend loves at all times, and a brother is born for adversity"
(Prov. 17:17). This kind of love will inevitably find an outlet,
because love that does not express itself is useless: "Better is
open rebuke than hidden love" (Prov. 27:5). At least open
rebuke is honest and fruitful; secret love is not. Above all, love
is forgiving: "He who forgives an offense seeks love, but he
who repeats a matter alienates a friend" (Prov. 17:9). So
"hatred stirs up strife, but love covers all offenses" (Prov.
10:12).

The wise man in these books is concerned to do what is
best and to turn away from what is inferior. Accordingly, he
will love one who rebukes him (Prov. 9:8). On the other hand,
a "scoffer"[44] will hate anyone who corrects him; he will not
love anyone who reproves him (Prov. 9:8; 15:12). Uprightness
commends a man in the highest circles: a king is sure to love
him "who speaks what is right" (Prov. 16:13).

Love within the family is not often mentioned in specific
terms in this literature. But fathers are told that "he who
spares the rod hates his son, but he who loves him is diligent to
discipline him" (Prov. 13:24). Married love is not often mentioned in this literature, either, but it is everywhere assumed to
be a normal, healthy state. Sometimes this is expressed in an
exhortation like Ecclesiastes 9:9—"Enjoy life with the wife
whom you love, all the days of your vain life."[45] A very similar

---

[43]Derek Kidner couples this with the words "A man that flat-
tereth his friend spreadeth a net for his feet" (Prov. 29:5) and comments, "David shirked his duty to Adonijah his son ('he had not
displeased him at any time in saying, Why hast thou done so?' 1 Ki.
1:6), and it cost that son his life" (*The Proverbs*, London, 1964, p. 45).
Complaisance is not the way of love. Kidner also makes the point that
"the neighbourly qualities which Proverbs urges on the reader add up
to nothing less than love, though the word itself is not prominent" (p.
44).

[44]R. B. Y. Scott explains this term as "the arrogant, cynical,
worldly, opposite and opponent of the religious wise man" (*Proverbs.
Ecclesiastes*, p. 77).

[45]There is no article with the word rendered "wife," and some
understand the passage accordingly in this sense: "Enjoy life with a

passage is this one: "Rejoice in the wife of your youth, a lovely hind, a graceful doe. Let her affection fill you at all times with delight, be infatuated always with her love" (Prov. 5:18f.).[46] This love is to be preferred above being "infatuated . . . with a loose woman" and embracing "the bosom of an adventuress" (Prov. 5:20). Similarly, the temptress of Proverbs 7:6ff. is described as a woman to be shunned, and there are warnings against "the evil woman," "the strange woman," and others. Clearly, these writers are concerned with orderly family life, and picture love within the family circle as both natural and desirable. There is "a time to love" (Eccles. 3:8), and within the family they see that time as always with us.

We should not conclude this section without noticing that these writers have a good deal to say about fearing God. If it is true that God loves men and that they should return that love, it is also true that God is one who is rightly to be feared.[47] Believers have an obligation to walk in his ways. Modern men usually regard fear and love as opposites, and these days there is a marked reluctance to see obedience to God's commands as a response of love. We tend to assume that obedience to a code has little to do with love. But the men of the Old Testament did not see things this way. They understood that love for God is not presumptuous, but has a proper regard for God's greatness, righteousness, and holiness. This does not mean that a believer's love will be a cringing, cowardly love—certainly rejoicing in the Lord is a very real part of Old Testament religion. But this joy and this love are the companions of a proper

---

woman you love" (so the NEB has it). G. A. Barton cites C. D. Ginsburg for the view that the writer is giving "a command to embrace whatever woman pleased one," and he is inclined to accept this view himself (*A Critical and Exegetical Commentary on the Book of Ecclesiastes*, Edinburgh, 1947, pp. 163, 166). But it is not easy to see how "all the days of your vain life" can be squared with a casual alliance. Thus the RSV is to be preferred.

[46]Cf. Derek Kidner: "The language is frankly erotic. . . . Such an emphasis is rather rare in Scripture, simply because nature already provides it, and therefore the complementary aspects of marriage need to be stressed. But it is highly important to see sexual delight in marriage as God-given" (*The Proverbs*, p. 71).

[47]W. Eichrodt sees a link between the love of God and the fear of God: "Fear and love can be used in the same breath, as descriptions of right conduct toward God" (*Theology of the Old Testament*, II, 299).

fear of God.[48] The wisdom writers assure us that "the fear of
the Lord, that is wisdom; and to depart from evil is understanding" (Job 28:28; cf. Prov. 1:7; 9:10; 14:26f.; Eccles. 12:13;
etc.). And, as H. H. Rowley reminds us, "When the Wisdom
writers speak of the fear of the Lord, they are not thinking of
something quite other than that love of God. They recognize
that God is the source of the good life, and that his will is the
foundation of human well-being."[49] We should not miss the
point of what these writers are saying. They are not suggesting
that men cringe in terror before a cruel and implacable deity;
they are urging a proper reverence for a God who is the constant source of blessing.

THE PROPHETS AND THE LOVE OF MAN

When we turn to the prophetic writings, we are struck by
the fact that the largest single category in the passages speaking of men's love is that referring to the love of evil things. As
we have seen, such a love is mentioned in other writings, but it
is not nearly as strongly emphasized as it is in the writings of
the prophets. Here it is found no less than thirty-two times (the
verb is used thirty-one times; the noun, once). This is more
than half the total number of such references—sixty-one—in
this section of Scripture (the verb is used fifty-two times; the
noun, nine times). Next most frequent in occurrence are the
seventeen references to the love of God at which we looked in
Chapter One (the verb is used eleven times; the noun, six
times). But the two kinds of love are related: as the prophets
constantly point out, God loves the people but, instead of returning his love, the people lavish their love on idols. There are
a few references to love among people (three to love of friends
and two to sexual love) and to the love of things (three in all,

---

[48]Adam C. Welch emphasizes the importance of love in
Deuteronomy. This book teaches in Deuteronomy 6:4–9 "that the
right religious attitude of every true Israelite is reverent love"; the
people are "to cherish a reverent love to their God and to bring this
right temper into association with all their life." He also says, "It is
natural that he, who has been requiring love to God, should continue
in v. 13 by speaking in the same breath of the fear of God" (ET, XLI,
1929–30, 549). The two belong together.

[49]The Faith of Israel, London, 1956, p. 136.

with one using the noun), and two to love for God (with one using the noun).

We begin with love for God, for although there are only two explicit references to this love, it is implicitly stressed in much of the prophets' teaching. For example, Daniel speaks in his prayer about those "who love him and keep his commandments" (Dan. 9:4). And Isaiah refers to the "foreigners who join themselves to the Lord" as people who "love the name of the Lord" (Isa. 56:6). This passage is particularly interesting, because it shows that people outside the commonwealth of Israel might love God. How much greater is the opportunity for those within it!

Love for God is implied in the many passages we looked at in Chapter One in which bridal imagery is used to describe the relationship between God and his people. In a marriage a partner should return the other's love, and, the prophets point out, God seeks love from his people. The very use of this imagery contains an implied demand for love, a demand which is for the most part not met. Love for God may also be indicated by terms besides the usual ones for *love*. Thus Hosea is really talking about loving God when he says, "The spirit of harlotry is within them, and they know not the Lord" (Hos. 5:4). This may well be behind his complaint that there is "no knowledge of God in the land" (Hos. 4:1) and his further lament, "My people are destroyed for lack of knowledge" (Hos. 4:6; cf. 6:6, etc.). As Walther Eichrodt says, this knowledge is "no merely theoretical knowledge of God's nature and will but the practical application of a relationship of love and trust, as this is seen at its loveliest in the association of a true wife and her husband."[50] The verb "to know" is of course used in the Old Testament to refer to the sex act,[51] which reminds us that it is not to be understood in merely intellectual terms. To know God is more than a cerebral activity—it is genuine love translated into acts of devotion and service.

But, unfortunately, the response God looked for was not the response that the men of the Old Testament invariably made. They had good intentions, but sometimes little more than that (similar to people of other ages). We have already

---

[50] *Theology of the Old Testament,* II, 291.

[51] E.g., Gen. 4:1; I Sam. 1:19. It may be used in this sense to describe heterosexual relationships (Num. 31:17, 18). It is used also to indicate homosexuality (Gen. 19:5).

noticed the passage in which Yahweh says, "I remember the devotion of your youth, your love as a bride" (Jer. 2:2), a passage that leads on to a denunciation of the nation for its wrongdoing. There was nothing wrong with Israel's professions of love to God in those early days. Indeed, the prophet sees Israel during the wilderness period as behaving like a bride with her husband, lost in the wonder of love. Hosea is probably referring to the same thing when he describes Ephraim with different imagery: she was "a trained heifer that loved to thresh" (Hos. 10:11). Unlike the "stubborn heifer" (Hos. 4:16), she did her work well and loved it. Yahweh saw that she was fitted for the more significant (and demanding) work of ploughing. But she did not continue in the right way: "You have plowed iniquity, you have reaped injustice, you have eaten the fruit of lies" (Hos. 10:13).[52] There was nothing lasting or deep about Israel's early love—in fact, even in the wilderness Israel's love was found wanting several times.

And throughout the centuries the people were all too ready to abandon the Lord and serve idols, a weakness that Jeremiah describes as playing the harlot (Jer. 3:1). "How well you direct your course to seek lovers!" he says of Israel's continual pursuit of idols in his day (Jer. 2:33); and again, "But you said, 'It is hopeless, for I have loved strangers . . .'" (Jer. 2:25; cf. 8:2). Other prophets use this imagery as well. Isaiah employs the metaphor of adultery when he says, "You have loved their bed" (Isa. 57:8). In a vivid passage Ezekiel pictures God as saying, "I will gather all your lovers, with whom you took pleasure, all those you loved and all those you loathed; I will gather them against you from every side . . . and I will judge you as women who break wedlock and shed blood are judged" (Ezek. 16:37f.).[53] Hosea complains, "You have loved a harlot's hire," and goes on to comment that the people "became detestable like the thing they loved" (Hos. 9:1, 10). Amos sees

---

[52]Cf. H. W. Wolff: "With these metaphors, Hosea pictures Israel's election as an election to service. The concept of election means to commission someone with a greater task. . . . The wilderness should be considered the place of the election, as in 9:10" (*Hosea,* Philadelphia, 1974, p. 185).

[53]John B. Taylor points out that in chapter 25 the Ammonites, Moabites, Edomites, and Philistines take part in the overthrow of the nation, "so the words *all your lovers* (37) are truer than would at first appear" (*Ezekiel,* London, 1969, p. 140).

the nation as loving the kind of worship that went on at Bethel and Gilgal (Amos 4:5), which, while it may or may not have been idolatry in the strict sense, was nonetheless idolatrous in its denial of all that Yahweh wanted from his people. Not infrequently the prophets use the participle of the verb to mean "lovers" as a way of referring to the idols that were the objects of Israel's infatuation (Jer. 22:20, 22; 30:14; Ezek. 16:33, 36, 37; 23:5, 9, 22; Hos. 2:5, 7, 10, 12, 13). There is a special poignancy in this usage, because it reveals idolatry as the horrible thing it is: a sin against God's love.[54]

But idolatry is far from being the only evil the people loved. At one time or another they lavished their love on a variety of wrong objects. Sometimes the prophets describe this misdirected love in general terms: they say that the people love to wander (Jer. 14:10), or that they love evil (Mic. 3:2) or shame (Hos. 4:18). Or the accusation may be specific: Jeremiah, for example, laments that the prophets prophesy falsely, the priests rule accordingly, and "my people love to have it so" (Jer. 5:31). Hosea complains about those who love oppression (Hos. 12:7), Isaiah about those who love bribes (Isa. 1:23) and about the watchmen who love to sleep (Isa. 56:10). The love for "cakes of raisins" (Hos. 3:1) may describe a passion for this food,[55] or it may refer to some kind of idolatry.[56] And Zechariah passes on Yahweh's command to "love no false oath" (Zech. 8:17), implying that the people loved to take advantage of one another, even when this involved perjury.

---

[54]Cf. W. G. Cole: "The whole Old Testament, from Genesis to Malachi, was preoccupied with the problem of idolatry, which is not essentially a bowing before images of wood or stone, but the investment of one's love in the wrong place" (*Sex and Love in the Bible*, New York, 1959, p. 55).

[55]It appears to be a delicacy (Song of Sol. 2:5; Isa. 16:7) and could be used in times of celebration in Israel (II Sam. 6:19; I Chron. 16:3).

[56]W. R. Harper speaks of the Israelites as "becoming lovers of *raisin-cakes*, and adopting the customs of the Canaanitish cult in their worship of Yahweh" (*A Critical and Exegetical Commentary on Amos and Hosea*, New York, 1905, p. 218). Some link with idolatry seems indicated by its connection here with "they turn to other gods." J. L. Mays thinks that the link is that "they mistakenly thought that the good things of the fertile land were the gifts of the Baals" (*Hosea*, Philadelphia, 1969, p. 57).

On the other hand, sometimes the prophets use the terminology of love to describe the positive conduct for which they look. Amos calls on the men of his day to "hate evil, and love good, and establish justice in the gate" (Amos 5:15), an urging in which "good" is quite general but very meaningful, especially in conjunction with the reference to justice. Zechariah looks for a love of "truth and peace" (Zech. 8:19). Isaiah sees joy as the lot of all who love Jerusalem (Isa. 66:10), love that will surely grow because the city is so firmly associated with the worship of Yahweh; it is a love for all that the holy city stands for. And in one of those passages that everyone quotes, Micah holds that God requires three things of his servant—"to do justice, and to love kindness, and to walk humbly with your God" (Mic. 6:8). In the next chapter we will be concerned with the meaning of the term translated "kindness" (ḥesedh). Here it is sufficient to notice that Micah calls for men not only to regard this virtue highly but to love it. He wants them to be committed to all that it stands for.

There are a few examples of love between people. Hosea speaks of his love for his errant wife, a lady who was also loved by her paramour (Hos. 3:1). Occasionally the prophets refer to the love of friends, though none of the references appears to indicate a deep, genuine love. There are the friends of the priest Pashhur, friends to whom that ecclesiastic has prophesied falsely and who will share in the punishment that will in due course overtake him (Jer. 20:4, 6). And Zechariah speaks of a prophet who refers to "the wounds I received in the house of my friends" (Zech. 13:6). Clearly, this particular kind of love was of minor importance to the prophets. For them the great thing was God's love for man and the grateful answering love that men should give. Their attention was focused on God's love and on the love the people so frequently diverted toward unworthy objects.

*   *   *   *   *

Men's love may thus be various. It may be for persons or things; it may be a profound and gripping emotion or something not much more than a casual preference. But at best it is a response to God's love, a response that leads to action as God's beloved ones seek to live out the implications of their love for him. They may take special care to love their neighbor, or to nurture a special love for their friends or the members of their household. Such love can be uplifting and ennobling. But the terminology of love points to danger: men may love the evil (idols) or the trivial (talking, sleep). Love will not automatically be positive, and certainly a wrong love is a disaster. But true love is the highest of blessings.

CHAPTER THREE

Love and Loyalty

O_{NE} of the most important words for love in the Old Testament is *hesedh*, a term extraordinarily difficult to translate into English. Our language has no obvious equivalent.[1] But serious attention must be given to it because, as E. W. Heaton points out, the word expresses "one of the most profound ideas in Hebrew religion." He goes on to stress its links with terms like "devotion," "fidelity," "loyalty," and even "the knowledge of God."[2] Clearly, the word is important, but equally clear is that its precise significance is not easy to convey in English.

All of the English versions known to me translate the word in a great variety of ways. The term occurs 245 times in the Old Testament,[3] and no translation comes close to using a single equivalent. The most consistent version I have found is the RSV, in which "steadfast love" is the rendering 178 times. But, all told, the translators working on that version had to use fifteen different translations, and in this respect they were more conservative than most. The old AV made "mercy" its favorite equivalent, and it employed eleven different renderings. With some of the more recent translations it is not easy to give exact figures, because they tend to render the word less

---

[1] A. Lods complains that there is no French equivalent, either, and he notes translations like *piété, bonté, amour* and *grâce*. He thinks that the word corresponds somewhat to the Latin *pietas,* and sees some of its meaning in the attitude of a believer towards God or that of a son to his father, but also in that of God or of a leader to his subordinates. He also finds relevant the affection of members of a family or of a tribe for one another, and he draws attention further to Hosea's linking of it with "the knowledge of God" (*Les Prophètes D'Israël,* Paris, 1935, p. 100). Clearly, the idea conveyed by the term is complex.

[2] *The Old Testament Prophets,* Harmondsworth, 1961, p. 64.

[3] According to *TDNT,* IX, 384, the word is used 237 times; a footnote adds that the word occurs two more times in Lamentations.

precisely. Because it is an increasingly accepted idea that the
unit translated must be the sentence rather than the word, the
sense of a whole sentence is often given in a "dynamic equivalent," and thus it is not always easy to discern the exact contribution of any particular word. This is especially true of a
word like *ḥesedh*, which has no accepted English equivalent.
But we can say that the NEB seems to translate the term
thirty-three different ways (and perhaps more, because in eight
passages I am unable to discern an equivalent). Its most frequent translation is "love" (used eighty-five times), to which
we should add a number of renderings which include the word
love, like "true love," "love unfailing" or "unfailing love,"
"constant love," "strong love," "faithful love," and the like.
The GNB is similar: it uses "love" eighty-seven times and
"constant love" seventy-one times. All told it uses at least
thirty-one different renderings (and has five passages in which
I cannot discern an equivalent). The NIV uses "love" 128
times, to which it adds a number of variants like "unfailing
love," "great love," "wonderful love," and the like. Once it
revives the AV's "lovingkindness." All told, it uses twenty-
five different renderings.

Because there are so many fine modern translations, it is
impossible to go through them all. Nonetheless, this representative sampling shows that the translators have difficulty when
they come to this word. But we should not then conclude that
all is confusion: if we compare similar renderings, like the
variants of "love," some important groupings emerge. We
might set out the result in tabular form as follows:

	AV	RSV	NEB	GNB	NIV
Love words		182	149	162	171
Lovingkindness	30				1
Kindness words	43	29	4	19	49
Mercy words	155	2			7
Loyalty words		21	61	20	3
Promise				9	
Devotion words		2			5
Favor	3	3		6	4
Goodness words	14	3			
Miscellaneous		3	31	29	5

The table shows plainly that modern translators find "love," either by itself or in some combination, to be the most suitable rendering. It shows also that when this word is not used the tendency is to employ one of the "kindness" words[4] or one of the "loyalty" words. We could simplify the classification still more if we were to combine the "kindness" words with those denoting "favor" and perhaps "goodness." Similarly, the "promise" and "devotion" words might be linked with the "loyalty" words. Whether this be done or not, the efforts of modern translators seem to show that love, kindness, and loyalty are the three principal meanings suggested by *ḥesedh*, with the emphasis markedly on love.[5]

Perhaps the most important study of the word is that made by Nelson Glueck.[6] He first surveys the people to whom it refers and finds that it always indicates some kind of relationship. This may be a family relationship (by blood or marriage) or a kinship among clans. It may be the relationship of host to guest, of allies to one another, of friends, or of ruler and subject. It may arise when one stranger helps another, and the helped man must then respond when he has the opportunity.[7] Initially at least, *ḥesedh* is not used to express the feeling between man and his fellowmen but "between people who are in some close relationship to one another."[8] It is a strong and

---

[4]James A. Montgomery holds that "for expression of *ḥesed* in English, 'kindness' might be the best representative" (*HTR*, XXXII, 1939, 101).

[5]The difficulty of rendering the word in English may be illustrated by its use in Job. In this book it occurs three times, and all of the versions we have studied use three different translations. Moreover, none of them agrees with any of the others with one exception: the RSV and the NIV both use "love" in Job 37:13. In the fifteen renderings of our word, eleven different equivalents are used.

[6]*Ḥesed in the Bible*, Cincinnati, 1967. This is the one study of the word referred to in KB, I, 318. But it is curiously ignored in several treatments of the word in English.

[7]An example is the time when the spies promised *ḥesedh* to a man they met if he would show them the way into the city of Bethel (Judg. 1:24). When he did this he put the spies under obligation to him, and they saw to it that his life was spared in the general destruction of the city. Another example arose from the help Barzillai gave to David when that king fled from Absalom. David charged his son Solomon to show *ḥesedh* to the sons of Barzillai (I Kings 2:7).

[8]Glueck, *Ḥesed in the Bible*, p. 37.

persistent attitude and is not dissolved by death. Thus Naomi exclaims, "Blessed be he by the Lord, whose kindness [hesedh] has not forsaken the living or the dead" (Ruth 2:20).[9] Similarly, David commended the men of Jabesh-gilead for showing hesedh to Saul when they buried him after he was killed in battle (II Sam. 2:5).

Hesedh, then, implies relationship and indicates a deep, lasting affection. Some have gone on from there to maintain that it points to a particular type of relationship—that of covenant, which is so important in the Old Testament.[10] This is, of course, a relationship in which the exercise of hesedh is of the utmost importance. It is also the case that hesedh is linked with covenant in quite a few passages.[11] But we must also bear in mind that our word is used quite often when there is no mention of covenant and when, as far as we can see, covenant is not in mind. Thus we have no reason for thinking that there was a covenant between Abraham and Laban, although the former's servant, at the conclusion of his successful mission to obtain a bride for Isaac, said, "Now then, if you will deal loyally [i.e., do hesedh] and truly with my master, tell me"

---

[9]Glueck takes exception to the view that the passage refers to God's hesedh, for the dead "in the Hebrew Bible generally are described as having absolutely no relationship with God." He understands the passage to refer to Boaz (Hesed in the Bible, p. 41). But Naomi is giving thanks for what God has done (her words are not unlike those of Abraham's servant, Gen. 24:27). Edward F. Campbell, Jr. notices that there is a "genuine ambiguity" here, but he is not convinced by Glueck; he thinks that "the much more likely antecedent is Yahweh" (Ruth, New York, 1975, p. 106). See also L. Morris, Ruth, London, 1968, p. 280.

[10]For example, Daniel Day Williams says forthrightly, "Chesed . . . always implies a covenant" (The Spirit and the Forms of Love, Welwyn, 1968, p. 19). N. Snaith holds that hesedh "in all its varied shades of meaning, is conditional upon there being a covenant. Without the prior existence of a covenant, there could never be any chesed at all" (The Distinctive Ideas of the Old Testament, London, 1953, pp. 94f.). He further speaks of the word's "close and inalienable connection with the idea of covenant" and maintains that its "true meaning" can never be understood unless this is realized (p. 98).

[11]I have noticed the following: Deut. 7:9, 12; I Sam. 20:8; I Kings 8:23; II Chron. 6:14; Neh. 1:5; 9:32; Ps. 25:10; 89:28, 33f.; 103:17f.; 106:45; Isa. 54:10; 55:3; Dan. 9:4; Hos. 2:18f.; 6:6f.; cf. also Ps. 50:5.

(Gen. 24:49). Here we do not need the idea of covenant to make sense of his words—and similar examples abound.

Most scholars agree with Glueck that the term makes a more general reference to relationship,[12] whether the tie be a covenant bond or some other kind. Walther Zimmerli, for example, thinks that "the nature of *ḥesedh* is conduct in relation, and in demonstration of this relation. It is grace shown, or ready to show itself, in relation."[13] It is too much to say that the word originates in the usages of covenant. We can say, however, that it is the right word to designate the attitude that the partners of a covenant ought to have toward one another.[14] It is possible to have *ḥesedh* without a covenant, but it is not possible to have a covenant without *ḥesedh*.

Ḥesedh, then, arises out of relationship. But what does the word tell us about that relationship? What is the attitude it denotes? Very plainly it is an attitude of goodwill. But it is more than that—it is love strengthened by loyalty. Glueck puts some emphasis on the importance of mutual loyalty in the relationship: *Ḥesed* was not merely love dependent solely on the subject but was, at the same time, loyalty and duty."[15]

---

[12]Cf. L. Koehler: "Nelson Glueck has shown that *ḥesedh* means 'fellowship' or 'solidarity' " (*Old Testament Theology*, London, 1957, p. 240, n.25).

[13]*TDNT*, IX, 382. Zimmerli also says that, in contrast to *ḥnn*, our noun "has in view right conduct in free kindness within a given relation" (p. 386). R. Bultmann also stresses relation: "In the OT *ḥsd* denotes an attitude of man or God which arises out of a mutual relationship. It is the attitude which the one expects of the other in this relationship, and to which he is pledged in relation to him" (*TDNT*, II, 479; he goes on to note the relationships "between relatives and friends, hosts and guests, masters and subjects, or others in covenant relation"). He thinks that the meaning of the term "fluctuates between (covenant) faithfulness, obligation, and love or grace" (p. 479).

[14]Nelson Glueck says, "The obligations and rights acquired through a covenant are translated into corresponding actions through *ḥesed*. *Ḥesed* is the real essence of *bᵉrith*, and it can almost be said that it is its very content" (*Ḥesed in the Bible*, p. 47). Bultmann makes a similar comment: "The thought of *ḥesedh* and the thought of covenant belong together" (*TDNT*, II, 480).

[15]*Ḥesed in the Bible*, p. 40. Glueck stresses the importance of loyalty. He holds that even when *'emeth* ("truth") is not explicitly linked with *ḥesedh* (as it often is), "one may still picture mentally *'mth* next to *ḥsd*" (p. 40). Again, "Love, friendship, brotherliness, loyalty

Accordingly, he lists what he calls "the component parts of the general concept" as follows: "reciprocity, mutual assistance, sincerity, friendliness, brotherliness, duty, loyalty, and love."[16] He obviously sees it as a very complex term, and it is noteworthy that he brings out both the love and the loyalty it connotes.

It is thus clear that we cannot do justice to the use of this term without understanding it to denote both love and loyalty. While we may well hold that love is basic to the term's definition, we should not fail to give due weight to the loyalty the term suggests. Norman Snaith stresses both the "love, mercy" and the "loyalty, steadfastness, faithfulness" he finds in the word. He holds that it means " 'faithfulness' rather than 'kindness,' for we find the word to involve, in almost every case, a substratum of fixed, determined, almost stubborn steadfastness."[17] C. H. Dodd combines the two concepts in his definition of the term—"loyal affection."[18]

COVENANT

We saw that there is not sufficient reason to claim that *ḥesedh* necessarily involves covenant, but that the two ideas go naturally together, and that *ḥesedh* is the attitude the parties of a covenant should display. It will be helpful to consider covenant more fully, because then we will learn the nature of the *ḥesedh* that is a necessary component of it. We immediately see that a covenant develops out of a warm reciprocal relation like love,[19] because one does not make a covenant

---

are all inherent in the concept of *ḥesed*. It is possible to do justice to the different shades of meaning only when *ḥesed* is understood as conduct in accordance with a mutual relationship of rights and duties" (p. 50; cf. p. 102). E. M. Good also emphasizes the importance of faithfulness in this word and holds that it is "most clearly shown by the associations between *ḥsd* and the root *'mn*" (*IDB*, III, 167). The two roots are frequently linked in the Old Testament.

[16] *Ḥesed in the Bible*, p. 55. He further comments, "In the older sources, the common usage of *ḥesed* never means an arbitrary demonstration of grace, kindliness, favor, or love" (p. 55).

[17] *The Distinctive Ideas of the Old Testament*, p. 99.

[18] *The Bible and the Greeks*, London, 1964, p. 60. He compares the various senses of the Latin, *pius, pietas*.

[19] Cf. Edward F. Campbell, Jr.: *Ḥesedh* "is more than the loyalty which one expects if he stands in covenant with another person—it is

with someone one detests or opposes. But it is not love simply that is in mind; it is a love that is strengthened by loyalty to the promises made and the people involved. It is saying much the same thing to affirm that the partners of a covenant ought to be true to one another. Perhaps we could take the attitude of David and Jonathan toward one another as an example (I Sam. 20:8, 14).

In the Old Testament God sometimes makes covenants with individuals and shows them love; an example is his covenant with David (II Sam. 23:5). But the really fundamental covenant is that which God makes with his people Israel (Ex. 24:1–8).[20] This covenant governs all subsequent relations between God and the nation;[21] it is a vehicle God uses to express his love for his people. Although "covenant" is a legal word, it must not be understood to apply to relationships that are no more than legal. There would be no covenant at all between God and the nation were it not that God loved the people. In his love he freely entered into a covenantal relationship with them. A word that suggests loyalty and constancy as well as indicating love is obviously a good word for the attitude of partners in such a covenant. Specifically, it indicates the importance and value of God's love for Israel.

---

that extra which both establishes and sustains covenant. It is more than ordinary human loyalty; it imitates the divine initiative which comes without being deserved" (*Ruth*, p. 81).

[20]W. Eichrodt sees covenant as so significant for an understanding of the Old Testament that, after his introductory chapter, he brings it into the title of every chapter in the first volume of his *Theology*—"The Covenant Relationship," "The Covenant Statutes," "The Nature of the Covenant God," and so on. He says, "The concept in which Israelite thought gave definitive expression to the binding of the people of God and by means of which they established firmly from the start the particularity of their knowledge of him was the covenant" (*Theology of the Old Testament*, I, London, 1961, 36). In the Preface to the fifth edition he points out that it is not the presence or absence of the term $b^e riyth$ that matters, "but the fact that every expression of the OT which is determinative for its faith rests on the explicit or implicit assumption that a free act of God, consummated in history, has raised Israel to the rank of the People of God" (p. 14).

[21]T. H. Robinson refers to "the formula of adoption, the principle of 'Covenant,' which persisted all through the history of Israel. It was the foundation on which the whole of the later edifice was erected" (*Prophecy and the Prophets in Ancient Israel*, London, 1941, p. 14).

But in a covenant a proper attitude is demanded on the part of both parties.[22] Israel should be faithful to that covenant that made her the people of God in a way that no other people was (Ex. 19:4–6; 24:1–8; etc.). But over and over we read that the people fell short of this standard. As we might perhaps expect, it is Hosea who documents this most poignantly. "There is no faithfulness," he writes, "or kindness [ḥesedh], and no knowledge of God in the land" (Hos. 4:1). But there should have been, because God told the people plainly what he expected of them: "I desire steadfast love [ḥesedh], and not sacrifice, the knowledge of God, rather than burnt offerings" (Hos. 6:6). The people thought that their pitiful sacrifices were all that God required—the sacrifice of animals that they possessed only because God gave them the animals! It did not particularly matter how they spent the rest of their time, or whether they loved God or not. They were ready to lavish their love on the Baalim and thus compound their shortcomings. But Hosea makes it clear that the one thing God expected from them was ḥesedh or "steadfast love," that attitude that should have developed out of their loyalty to the covenant, which demanded of them upright living and a concern for justice.

It is interesting that Hosea speaks of ḥesedh so often as a quality that should be shown to man. One might have expected that he would concentrate on man's proper attitude toward God. But God's love does not mean that the Israelite should simply love God in return and neglect his neighbor.[23] "Sow for yourselves righteousness," the prophet says, "Reap the fruit of

---

[22]Cf. Johannes Pedersen: "Love and justice are mutually necessary. Solidarity with those in the covenant only he can have whose soul is healthy, so that it submits harmoniously to the common will. But if one has love, then one must also act according to the law of the covenant. ... Righteousness manifests itself in love, because it consists in maintaining the covenant" (*Israel: Its Life and Culture*, I–II, London and Copenhagen, 1954, 341). We should not see love and right as quite different or as opposed to one another. They belong together, as the concept of covenant so well shows.

[23]Martin Buber comments, "*Hesed* is not demanded as something to be done to God, but as a general goodwill manifested to all"; "the text speaks of a following in God's footsteps and so serving His work in the world: His lovingkindness to Israel must continue and operate in Israel's lovingkindness to all. And so here, too, there is no concept of *reciprocity* between God and the people, but rather one of *conjunction* between God and the people" (*The Prophetic Faith*, New

steadfast love"; "hold fast to love and justice" (Hos. 10:12; 12:6). But the nation did not respond. Yahweh once said about Israel, "I will betroth you to me in righteousness and in justice, in steadfast love, and in mercy" (Hos. 2:19), but sometime later made this lament: "Your love is like a morning cloud, like the dew that goes early away" (Hos. 6:4). The people were well-intentioned, but they were inconstant. We have already noticed that Hosea saw clearly that Israel's sin would inevitably bring punishment. As Johannes Pedersen says, "Love and righteousness are the prerequisite for the maintenance of a normal community,"[24] and Israel's waywardness invited trouble. But the passages we have listed also show that Hosea saw clearly that the nation's unfaithfulness could not destroy God's faithful love. God's ḥesedh will never cease.

A BRIDE PRICE

Hosea makes use of the bride price to bring out the greatness of God's faithfulness. The bride price was a price paid by a husband-to-be to the bride's relatives, originally as a compensation for their loss of a member of the family. Abraham's servant gave costly presents to Rebecca's family (Gen. 24:53), Jacob gave seven years' labor for each of his wives (Gen. 29:18, 27), Shechem announced his readiness to pay a large sum for Dinah (Gen. 34:12), and David's bride price was the slaughter of a hundred Philistines (II Sam. 3:14). Clearly the price might be varied, a fact that prepares us for the unusual form it takes when God offers it: "I will betroth you to me for ever; I will betroth you to me in righteousness and in justice, in steadfast love, and in mercy. I will betroth you to me in faithfulness" (Hos. 2:19f.). Norman Snaith comments, "If Israel had possessed these originally, there would never have been any breakdown of the first covenant, nor any necessity for her to be exiled from the land which Jehovah had given her. These four qualities are the conditions under which the new marriage covenant can be established and maintained."[25] This is, of

---

York, 1949, p. 114; Buber's italics). I think that Buber goes a little too far. Hosea does look for the people to return God's love. But Buber's emphasis on their joining God in loving others is timely.

[24]*Israel: Its Life and Culture*, III–IV, London and Copenhagen, 1953, 540.

[25]*Mercy and Sacrifice*, London, 1953, p. 70.

course, quite true. But Hosea is not saying that these are qualities that Israel must bring to the marriage; he is saying that God is so faithful and loving that he will bring all of these attributes to the new relationship.[26] It is true that Israel, too, ought to bring such qualities to the marriage, and it is also true that Israel did not. She did not display the righteousness or the justice or the steadfast love or the mercy or the faithfulness that her relationship to God required. But that is not what the prophet is saying at this point. He is saying that, despite Israel's shortcomings, God still manifests these qualities.

Prophets other than Hosea document Israel's failure. They all make it clear that evil cannot go unpunished in a world ruled by a righteous God. God is faithful, but he is faithful to what is right as well as faithful to his people. In Isaiah we read that God said, "In overflowing wrath for a moment I hid my face from you, but with everlasting love [hesedh] I will have compassion on you, says the Lord, your Redeemer" (Isa. 54:8).[27] The sin was real and so, accordingly, was God's wrath. "The Lord will rise up as on Mount Perazim, he will be wroth as in the valley of Gibeon; to do his deed—strange is his deed! and to work his work—alien is his work!" (Isa. 28:21).[28] In such a way the prophets repeatedly emphasize the seriousness with which God views sin and the certainty that in the end he will punish it.

---

[26]Cf. H. W. Wolff: "The five nouns prefixed with b denote the 'bridal price' Yahweh 'pays' for Israel.... Taken together, the five concepts serve to guarantee the indissolubility of the community." Specifically, ḥsd "denotes kindhearted actions that, by spontaneous love and the faithful meeting of responsibilities, create or establish a sense of community" (Hosea, Philadelphia, 1974, p. 52). J. L. Mays and G. A. F. Knight are other commentators who think this passage refers to a bride price.

[27]On this passage A. B. Davidson comments, "This love of Jehovah to Israel is entirely inexplicable. It was certainly not due to any loveliness on Israel's part, for Israel has been a 'transgressor from the womb' (xlviii.8), and her 'first father sinned against the Lord' (xliii.27)" (The Theology of the Old Testament, Edinburgh, 1904, pp. 170f.).

[28]It is common to the prophets (and other Old Testament writers) to see the wrath of God as a grim reality but also to see the love of God as constant and enduring. This is not the teaching of this prophet or that but the thrust of Old Testament teaching as a whole. Modern men often find it difficult to balance the wrath of God and the love of God. But the biblical writers do not seem to have found this a problem.

THE FAITHFULNESS OF GOD

The last word, however, is not a wrathful one, but a loving one:[29] "The mountains may depart, and the hills be removed, but my steadfast love shall not depart from you, and my covenant of peace shall not be removed, says the Lord, who has compassion on you" (Isa. 54:10); "I will make with you an everlasting covenant, my steadfast, sure love for David" (Isa. 55:3). Again, God "keeps covenant and steadfast love with those that love him and keep his commandments, to a thousand generations" (Deut. 7:9; see also Neh. 1:5; Dan. 9:4). In the second commandment we find that God shows steadfast love to "thousands," which appears to mean "thousands of generations" (Ex. 20:6; Deut. 5:10, GNB).[30] There are many passages in which it is made clear that God's *ḥesedh* lasts forever. Indeed, this idea is worked up into a refrain which occurs twenty-six times in Psalm 136[31] and quite often in other Psalms (e.g., Ps. 100:5; 106:1; 107:1; 118:1, 2, 3, 4, 29)—and, for that matter, outside the Psalms (e.g., I Chron. 16:34, 41; II Chron. 7:3, 6; 20:21; Jer. 33:11). God's *ḥesedh* "is better than life" (Ps. 63:3).

Such passages as these, taken in conjunction with the Old Testament's consistent presentation of Israel as failing to measure up to the standard set before them, lead many to think that "mercy" is the appropriate rendering of *ḥesedh* (we noticed earlier that this is the AV's favorite translation of the term). The term comes close to indicating this meaning in some passages, but it is more than doubtful that we should see this as

---

[29]This is an idea expressed frequently in the Old Testament. H. Wheeler Robinson examines the attitude of Job in his sufferings and concludes, "He has won through man's theories about God to God himself. Like Hosea, he sees God's love to be deeper than God's wrath" (*The Cross in the Old Testament,* London, 1955, p. 31).

[30]Brevard S. Childs notes that there is a division of opinion about whether we should understand the Hebrew as the "thousandth generation" or "with unrestricted sense." He himself favors the former (*Exodus,* London, 1974, p. 388). Martin Noth has this interpretation: "the steadfast love of God is generally promised to 'thousands'—i.e., an inconceivable number" (*Exodus,* London, 1962, p. 163).

[31]About *ḥesedh* George S. Gunn says, "Its fulness of meaning can be seen only in God; and the refrain of Psalm 136 presents it as the essential and unalterable constituent in His nature" (*God in the Psalms,* Edinburgh, 1956, p. 126).

typical. As Glueck points out, *hesedh*, "though related to *rahamim*, is not quite synonymous with it and ought not to be understood as mercy."[32] It is rather love and loyalty that the term primarily indicates. Of course, love and loyalty may produce actions that could be characterized as "merciful," but this should not mislead us about the essential meaning of *hesedh*.

MICAH

We should not think that because God is persistently loving he will not punish sinful men. There are some wonderful passages expressing the certainty of God's faithfulness, his longsuffering, and the like. But there are also some forthright declarations of the suffering that is inevitable when people continue to sin. For example, Micah sees Samaria becoming "a heap in the open country" (Mic. 1:6). He pictures the people saying, "We are utterly ruined. . . . Among our captors he divides our fields" (Mic. 2:4). He points out that Zion is built "with blood and Jerusalem with wrong" (Mic. 3:10), and that therefore "Zion shall be plowed as a field; Jerusalem shall become a heap of ruins" (Mic. 3:12).

In a very celebrated passage he calls people away from all this. He asks, "What does the Lord require of you but to do justice, and to love kindness [*hesedh*], and to walk humbly with your God?" (Mic. 6:8).[33] God looks to the people to live

---

[32] *Hesed in the Bible*, p. 99. Some words of S. R. Driver are also worth pondering: "*hsd* is a wider and more comprehensive term than 'mercy'; 'mercy' is properly the quality by which a person renounces, out of motives of benevolence or compassion, his legitimate rights against one, for instance, who has offended or injured him; but *hsd* is a quality exercised mutually among equals; it is the kindliness of feeling, consideration, and courtesy, which adds a grace and softness to the relations subsisting between members of the same society" (*A Critical and Exegetical Commentary on Deuteronomy*, Edinburgh, 1973, p. 102).

[33] Commenting on this passage, J. H. Gailey maintains that the term *hesedh* "suggests sweet and gentle behaviour, the *noblesse oblige* of the nineteenth-century code of the gentleman." He continues, "The Hebrew word involves all these qualities and more. It means the fulfilment of the obligations which are inherent in a relationship, even when no laws cover that relationship. Husbands owe certain duties to wives, not because they are defined in a marriage contract, but because they are inherent in the common understanding and practice of

up to their part in the relationship, but they do not. They lack many qualities, specifically the love for God and men that *hesedh* denotes.[34]

The people do not respond as they should to God's great love. We might anticipate that the prophet would see only disaster as a result, but as he ends his prophecy Micah asks, "Who is a God like thee, pardoning iniquity and passing over transgression for the remnant of his inheritance? He does not retain his anger for ever because he delights in steadfast love [*hesedh*]" (Mic. 7:18). And his very last words are "Thou wilt show faithfulness to Jacob and steadfast love [*hesedh*] to Abraham, as thou hast sworn to our fathers from the days of old" (Mic. 7:20). Micah cannot imagine God ceasing to love. His attitude is not unlike that expressed in Solomon's prayer: "There is no God like thee, in heaven above or on earth beneath, keeping covenant and showing steadfast love to thy servants who walk before thee with all their heart; who hast kept with David my father what thou didst declare to him" (I Kings 8:23). Because God is God he will never cease to love.

GOD AND *Hesedh*

"To thee, O Lord, belongs steadfast love," sings the psalmist (Ps. 62:12), words that seem to root *hesedh* in the divine nature. It is not a human achievement but a quality we know from God (a quality men are expected to emulate).[35] Some passages relate *hesedh* to God's essential nature by using an expression like "for thy name's sake." For example, the psalmist says, "But thou, O God my Lord, deal on my

---

the relationship. So also . . . between man and God, many obligations are inherent without being defined by legal codes or negotiated agreement" (*Micah to Malachi*, London, 1963, p. 32).

[34]Leslie C. Allen sees the term as used "to describe not only the response of man to God but also the manifestation toward one another of this same loyal spirit" (*The Books of Joel, Obadiah, Jonah and Micah*, Grand Rapids, 1976, p. 373).

[35]A. E. Goodman holds that the expression quoted "indicates *hsd* in its fullest sense as being an integral part of the divine character" (Peter R. Ackroyd and Barnabas Lindars, eds., *Words and Meanings*, Cambridge, 1968, p. 106). He also says that in the Psalms *hesedh* "is above all the divine prerogative, exhibited by God in his dealings with man" (p. 107).

behalf for thy name's sake; because thy steadfast love is good, deliver me" (Ps. 109:21). In antiquity, of course, a name was more than a label: in some way that was not defined it summed up all that a person was. So there is much more than a mere appellation in mind when we read, "All the paths of the Lord are steadfast love and faithfulness.... For thy name's sake, O Lord, pardon my guilt, for it is great" (Ps. 25:10f.). Similar expressions are found in Psalms 23:3–6;[36] 106:7f.; 143:11f.

Such links between God's love and his name's sake are significant, because they indicate that love is at the center of God's being. We are probably right in thinking that when God is said to act in a way favorable to his people "for his name's sake" (or when similar words are used), the thought of his constant love is implied, even though no such word as *hesedh* is specifically employed.[37] Norman Snaith says of such passages, "Often these writers say 'for His Name's sake' because they scarce know what else to say. They meant that Jehovah loved them, because that was what He was like. 'He hath loved, He hath loved us, because He would love.'"[38] Certainly his love for the people was not due to some special attractiveness in them—in fact, the entire Old Testament makes it clear that this was not the case. Thus Snaith is surely right in seeing the source of that love within God himself and not within the people.

There are many passages that speak of God's acting compassionately toward a sinful and unworthy people. Even though such passages may not use any of the words for love, they are all relevant to our inquiry because God's love is implied in them all—they do not make sense without it. In short: the idea of God's love is much more pervasive than the specific use of the terminology of love.

---

[36]Cf. Cyril S. Rodd: "The psalmist sees that Yahweh watches over him like a Shepherd, not as any reward for his faithfulness, but simply because 'Thy nature and Thy name is Love'.... In other psalms the phrase *'for his name's sake'* recurs, and each time Yahweh's nature is revealed in forgiving and cleansing sin, delivering from danger, and giving new life" (*Psalms 1–72*, London, 1963, p. 51).

[37]Such passages include I Sam. 12:22; II Sam. 7:21 (cf. v.15); II Kings 19:34; 20:6; Ps. 25:7; 31:3 (cf. v. 7); 79:9; Isa. 37:35; 43:25; 48:9, 11; Jer. 14:7, 21; Ezek. 20:9, 22, 44; 36:22; Dan. 9:17, 19.

[38]*The Distinctive Ideas of the Old Testament*, p. 136.

GOD'S LOVE FOR ALL

Certainly God loves more than just Israel. It is true that the Old Testament mainly concentrates on this nation, but this fact should not surprise us. Because God first revealed himself to them and worked out his purpose through them, it is only natural that the Scriptures recording this should largely concentrate on that one people. But it is not confined to that one people. The little book of Ruth, for example, shows that a Moabite might know the mercy of the Lord. And it is very revealing that Naomi anticipated that the Lord might show his *hesedh* to two Moabite girls in their own country. As she bids Ruth and Orpah return, she prays, "May the Lord deal kindly with you" (Ruth 1:8; her prayer shows that she meant that the Lord should give each of them a husband back in Moab). Similarly, David prays for a foreigner when he asks God to show *hesedh* to Ittai the Gittite (II Sam. 15:20).

The book of Jonah makes the same point from a different angle. The prophet tells us that his reason for fleeing in the first instance and refusing to take the message to Nineveh was that he knew that God is gracious and merciful and that he abounds "in steadfast love" (Jon. 4:2). He feared that God would spare Nineveh because of his love for that pagan city. This book emphatically makes the point that God's love is not limited. As J. N. Schofield puts it, the book "contrasts the greatness of God's love with the narrowness of man's forgiveness."[39]

Amos is another prophet who recognizes that God loves more than Israel. He likens God's treatment of the Ethiopians to the way he treated Israel. He speaks of God's bringing up the Philistines from Caphtor and the Syrians from Kir in the same breath that he refers to God's bringing up Israel from Egypt (Amos 9:7). There are similar passages in Isaiah. That prophet looked for a day when there would be an altar to God in Egypt, when the Egyptians would cry to the Lord and he would send them a savior, when he would make himself known to the Egyptians, when the Egyptians would worship him and the Lord would hear their prayers. He links Assyria with Egypt in this grand vision, and sees all three nations coming within the scope of the divine blessing (Isa. 19:19–24; cf. also Isa. 42:1–6;[40] 49:6).

---

[39] *Introducing Old Testament Theology*, London, 1964, p. 70.

[40] Reuben Levy translates verse 6 as "I have guarded thee and given thee for a universal covenant"; or, he comments, the last phrase

Sometimes this far-reaching vision appears in the Psalms. For instance, immediately after a reference to God's *hesedh* we read, "The Lord is good to all, and his compassion is over all that he has made" (Ps. 145:9f.; the psalmist has just said in verse 6, "Men shall proclaim the might of thy terrible acts," a statement in which the general term points to men at large rather than the Israelites specifically). Similarly, it is God who "gives food to all flesh, for his steadfast love endures for ever" (Ps. 136:25). It is hard to limit to Israel—or, for that matter, to any restricted group—the words "The earth is full of the stead-fast love of the Lord" (Ps. 33:5; similar is Ps. 119:64). And in the shortest of all the Psalms there is the call: "Praise the Lord, all nations! Extol him, all peoples!" Why this exhortation? Because "great is his steadfast love toward us" (Ps. 117:1f.). In these places it seems quite clear that God's *hesedh* reaches far beyond the nation Israel. God being the God that he is, his love is for all he has made.

Since God's love is for all men, it is to be expected that God's people will have a similar love for their fellowmen. This does not appear to be stated explicitly, but it is difficult to think that a believer could read Ruth or Jonah without realizing that he is expected to emulate God's attitude toward the nations. Nelson Glueck finds this the thrust of the teaching of other prophets. Indeed, he points out, "In the prophetic literature the concept of *hesed* was greatly expanded. From the mode of conduct of certain groups standing in a mutual relationship of rights and duties to one another, *hesed* becomes the conduct of all men toward one another." In Hosea, *hesedh* "is no longer conduct corresponding to a reciprocal relationship within a narrow circle, but the proper conduct of all men toward one another."[41] In Micah, "Every man becomes every other man's brother, [and] *hesed* becomes the mutual or reciprocal relationship of all men toward each other and toward God."[42]

Throughout the wisdom literature *hesedh* seems to be used in this way. The word itself is rarely used explicitly, but it

---

could be read as *a covenant to mankind*. Some such rendering as this is necessitated by the parallel with 'a light to the nations'" (*Deutero-Isaiah*, London, 1925, p. 147).

[41] *Ḥesed in the Bible*, pp. 56, 57.

[42] *Ḥesed in the Bible*, p. 61. When he begins his summary of this chapter, Glueck says, "*Ḥesed* is practiced mutually by all men, as co-equal members of human society" (p. 69).

seems implicit everywhere. For example, we read, "Let not loyalty [*hesedh*] and faithfulness forsake you; bind them about your neck, write them on the tablet of your heart. So you will find favor and good repute in the sight of God and man" (Prov. 3:3f.). Certainly this points to much more than a formal, shallow admiration. And obviously *hesedh* is very important—in fact, *hesedh* is to guide all conduct. When such a term is related to "God and man," it is not easy to think that the writer means no more than "God and your fellow Israelite."

In the Old Testament as a whole, *hesedh* is characteristic of God rather than of men. In men it is the ideal; in God it is the actual. Moreover, the writers seem more interested in the great truth that God displays *hesedh* than in the way men do or do not display it. Of the 245 occurrences of the word, no less than 186 refer to God; only 59 refer to men. The term thus relates to God more than three times as often as it does to men.[43] It must also be kept in mind that, when the word is used to refer to men, in many instances *hesedh* is simply looked for or even held to be fleeting or non-existent. Thus *hesedh* actually indicates a quality found in men even less often than the previous figure might suggest.[44]

The term is used different ways in different parts of Scripture. In the Pentateuch, for example, it is used fourteen times to refer to God (plus once to refer to God's angels), and five times to refer to men. The historical books apply the term to God twenty-six times and to men twenty-eight times. In the poetical books the usage is markedly different: the word is used to refer to God's love 126 times and to men only three times (this is largely due to the Psalms, in which the figures are

---

[43]References to *hesedh* overwhelmingly indicate that *hesedh* is characteristic of God. We read 117 times that he is a God who shows *hesedh* (this and similar expressions are used), and 13 times that he will show *hesedh*. It is prayed for 16 times, and it is described as the ground of prayer 15 times; of hope, 4 times; and of trust, once. It is said 19 times that God has displayed *hesedh,* and once he is said to have withdrawn his *hesedh* from some persistent sinners.

[44]Generalizations are made about *hesedh* seven times. Twenty-four times it is looked for from men (or asked of them or promised to them); it is described as "performed" seventeen times. It is described twice as done, six times as not done, and twice as being fleeting. And once a prayer is offered that men will not show *hesedh* to a heinous sinner.

124 and three respectively). In the wisdom literature eleven occurrences refer to men and two to God. Finally, the prophets use the term twenty-nine times, seventeen times referring to God and twelve times referring to men.

LOVE AND WRATH

Two points keep recurring. The first is that men do not display the love they should; they sin constantly and draw down on themselves the inevitable consequences of their wrongdoing. The other is that the love of God is just as constant. There is an interesting connection of these ideas in the sayings that speak of God as "slow to anger" and go on to refer to his unfailing love.[45] "Slow to anger" does not mean "never angry"; it means that God is not irascible, that his wrath is not easily aroused. But God's wrath is real, and it is taken seriously throughout the Old Testament. But his love is also real, and it receives the emphasis. The wrath is but the other side of the love.[46] As H. H. Rowley puts it, "The wrath of God and his love are not to be set over against one another. His wrath was the expression of his love, no less than his justice was. For love is not soft indulgence; nor is the wrath of God a display of temper."[47]

There is an interesting combination of these two ideas in Lamentations, a book written in the shadow of the fall of Jerusalem and filled with the poet's sorrow at what has befallen his nation, particularly its capital city. But he shows no bitterness against God. He does not say that God ought to have

---

[45]Ex. 34:6; Num. 14:18; Neh. 9:17; Ps. 86:15; 103:8; 145:8; Joel 2:13; Jon. 4:2.

[46]Cf. J. N. Schofield: "The love of God that ceaselessly works to save sinners is ruthlessly active to destroy evil from the world he loves. If we identify ourself with evil, his love must become for us the wrath of God and destroy us. There is nothing capricious about his destructive wrath. It is so terrible because it is the other side of his love, and it is as great as his love" (*Introducing Old Testament Theology*, pp. 53f.). Schofield also speaks of the wrath of God as "the necessary corollary to the love of God"; this wrath "flashes out for a moment against all that would send a streak of evil through his creation or destroy it, or against anyone who persistently identifies himself with that evil" (p. 44).

[47]*The Faith of Israel*, London, 1956, p. 65.

saved the city in some way, nor does he ask the question so frequently on the lips of modern man when disaster strikes: "Why should this happen to me?" On the contrary, he recognizes that what has happened is just: "The Lord has made her suffer for the multitude of her transgressions" (Lam. 1:5); "Jerusalem sinned grievously" (Lam. 1:8). He pictures the city saying, "My transgressions were bound into a yoke; by his hand they were fastened together; they were set upon my neck" (Lam. 1:14). The Lord's hand is in it all, but it is because of the people's sin that the calamity has fallen. Jerusalem comes to recognize this: "The Lord is in the right, for I have rebelled against his word" (Lam. 1:18).

The poet is saying that the nation deserved what it got. Because God is just, it must be expected that sin will be punished. But we should not miss the further point that sin must be punished because God is loving. As Rowley points out, in the Old Testament "the justice and the love of God are not attributes to be set over against one another, between which there was a tension." God's discipline of Israel "was as much the expression of his love as of his justice"; "His justice visits man's iniquity upon him, because that iniquity is man's own worst foe."[48]

The paradox is crystal clear to the author of Lamentations. He portrays vividly the bitter grief and the painful suffering of the city. The depth of this sensitive writer's compassion for his people comes through in every line. But there is no suggestion that God has abandoned his people, that he has stopped loving his wayward and suffering children. In fact, the writer proclaims, "The steadfast love of the Lord never ceases, his mercies never come to an end" (Lam. 3:22); "The Lord will not cast off for ever, but, though he cause grief, he will have compassion according to the abundance of his steadfast love" (Lam. 3:31f.).

The writer makes it clear that God views sin in the most serious manner. The sinner must never think that he can get away with his wrongdoing, that God's mercy will "let him off." God has made this a moral universe, an ordered universe in which sin in due time reaps an inevitable harvest. But this does not mean that God is a vindictive God, waiting until a man sins so that he can pounce and punish him. God loves men

---

[48] *The Faith of Israel*, pp. 64f.

with a love that is constant, and there is nothing that men can do to destroy it. As Norman Snaith points out, "The most important of all the distinctive ideas of the Old Testament is God's steady and extraordinary persistence in continuing to love wayward Israel in spite of Israel's insistent waywardness."[49] He further explains, "The word *chesed* stands for God's steady, persistent love for the Israel of His choice. It is the love that will not let us go, the love that not all man's weakness and sinfulness and stubbornness can destroy."[50]

This is the love with which we are loved eternally.

---

[49] *The Distinctive Ideas of the Old Testament*, p. 102.
[50] *Mercy and Sacrifice*, p. 80.

CHAPTER FOUR

Compassion and Delight

*T*HE two principal roots for love in the Old Testament are those we have examined in the previous chapters—*'hb* and *ḥsd*. But they are not the only ones; there is a cluster of words closely related to *love*. Some convey compassion, some convey mercy or pity, qualities easily associated with love. Then there are words that primarily signify delight, those that refer to sexual desires and others. Quite a number of words whose primary significance is something different will in certain contexts suggest love. Because there are many such words, it would not be easy to deal with all of them. But we should notice some of them at least if we are to get a balanced view of the concept of love as the Old Testament writers knew it. I will not attempt a detailed treatment of any of these terms; it will be sufficient to indicate in a general way their contribution to our subject. Some of these words are used mostly to refer to God, others mostly to men—and some are used freely to refer to both. Such complex usages reflect the complexity of love.

We start with *raḥᵃmiym*. This is the plural of *reḥem*, meaning "womb." The singular is most often used literally and does not indicate "love" or "compassion." But the plural never seems to be used to mean "wombs." Like other physiological terms, the term is used in a metaphorical sense to refer to aspects of man's emotions, thoughts, will, and the like. In this case the plural is invariably used in this way, often conveying a meaning very much like love. We read, for example, that Joseph's "heart yearned for his brother" (Gen. 43:30; cf. the similar usage in I Kings 3:26). The term can indicate simply affection or an emotion like it. Characteristically, it means something like "compassion" or "mercy."[1] It may be

---

[1] J. W. L. Hoad says that the word "expresses the affective aspect of love: its compassion and pity," and he quotes Barth, who says, "The personal God has a heart" (*NBD*, p. 809).

used in this sense to refer to men (Zech. 7:9) or, more often, to refer to God (II Sam. 24:14; Neh. 9:19; Isa. 54:7; etc.). A number of times it is linked with *hesedh* in such a way that it indicates that the two words are not markedly different (e.g., Ps. 25:6; 51:1; Hos. 2:19). But there is always this difference: when *rah^amiym* is used there is no implication of loyalty to an obligation,[2] as is the case with *hesedh*, which seems normally to imply a relationship with corresponding duties (perhaps a covenant). Accordingly, Walther Eichrodt claims that the word indicates "a quite spontaneous expression of love, evoked by no kind of obligation."[3]

When this term is used, the meaning "love" is never far from the surface, though characteristically it is love for those in distress or in need. But this is not the whole story, because the word can also be used to describe God's love for all men—in fact, for all creation: "The Lord is good to all, and his compassion is over all that he has made" (Ps. 145:9). There is no limit to this love; God's compassion touches every part of his creation.[4] In a more restricted sense the term is the final part of the "bride price" in Yahweh's marriage to Israel: "I will betroth you to me in... steadfast love and in mercy" (Hos. 2:19). Nelson Glueck comments that *rah^amiym* "exceeds the bounds of *hesed*," making the contrast more succinct when he says, "*Hesed* is covenantal loyalty; *rah^amim* is forgiving love."[5] In all, the noun is used thirty-nine times, twenty-seven times to refer to God and only twelve times to refer to men. Love of this kind is especially characteristic of the Lord; the term is a way of emphasizing the abundance of his grace.

---

[2] Cf. Nelson Glueck: "*Hesed*, however, embodies the idea of obligation, which is not at all the case with *rahamim*" (*Hesed in the Bible*, Cincinnati, 1967, p. 62).

[3] *Theology of the Old Testament*, I, London, 1961, 237f.

[4] "Though the mighty wondrous deeds of God and the 'terrible acts' of his judgment (v. 6) manifest the sovereignty of his power, the true greatness of God lies in the tenderness and intimacy of the compassion with which the divine father loves his creatures" (A. Weiser, *The Psalms*, London, 1962, p. 827).

[5] *Hesed in the Bible*, p. 84. J. L. Mays sees *rah^amiym* as "active sympathy toward one who stands in a relation of dependence or need" (*Hosea*, Philadelphia, 1969, p. 51). H. W. Wolff holds that it "emphasizes a loving sensitivity founded on an indissoluble togetherness, which is sympathetically moved to pity, especially for those in need of help" (*Hosea*, Philadelphia, 1974, pp. 52f.).

The corresponding verb *rāḥam* is used in much the same way. Its characteristic translation is "to have mercy" (Ex. 33:19, etc.), and its connection with Yahweh is even more marked than is the case with the noun. Of its forty-nine occurrences, no less than forty refer to the Lord's showing of mercy or compassion or love. There is an adjective, *rāḥûm*, which is not used as frequently as the other words from the root (thirteen times in all). It is invariably used to refer to God. Usually it is linked with the thought of grace (eleven times), as it is when we read, "Thou, O Lord, art a God merciful and gracious" (Ps. 86:15; the verse goes on to speak of God's *ḥesedh*, a phenomenon we find in other places where this adjective is used). God's gracious love for the afflicted is an important part of the Old Testament idea.

There are some words that are used entirely, or almost entirely, to refer to human love. Thus the noun *dôdh* is used many times in the Song of Songs by the maiden as she talks about her beloved.[6] Of course, if we are to understand this book as an allegory of divine love, we will interpret this to refer to God's love. But as the book stands the term is constantly used to refer to human love.[7] It seems always to refer to a beloved man. If one wishes to speak of a beloved woman, the term is *rā'yāh* (Song of Sol. 1:9, 15, etc.), which is the feminine of *rē(a)'*, meaning "friend, companion."[8] Quite a number of times *dôdh* refers to a kinsman, generally an uncle. In the plural it means "love" (Prov. 7:18; Song of Sol. 1:2; Ezek. 16:8; etc.).

The adjective *yādhiydh*, meaning "beloved," is generally

---

[6]Commenting on Song 1:12–14, J. C. Rylaarsdam says, "As before, physical comparisons serve to get at an invisible dimension in the relationship: his influence upon her is irrepressible, strong, inescapable—and as delightful as perfume" (*Proverbs to Song of Solomon*, London, 1965, p. 144). It is this kind of love which has led many to interpret the book as an allegory of divine love. It is certainly a wonderful illustration of the way God's love transforms and blesses.

[7]"What inspires the writer is the power, the everlastingness, the freedom of love between the sexes, and its exclusiveness when it is real. . . . The praise of such love cannot but become a satire upon what usually passes for love in a world in which polygamy is practised" (Andrew Harper, *The Song of Solomon*, Cambridge, 1902, p. xxxi).

[8]In Song of Solomon 1:9, Harper translates, "O my friend" and adds, "cp. the use of *ami* in French between lovers" (*The Song of Solomon*, p. 5).

used to refer to God's love. For instance, the tribe of Benjamin
is called his "beloved" (Deut. 33:12)[9] and Israel as a whole is
his beloved whom he delivers (Ps. 60:5; 108:6) and to whom he
gives sleep (or "in sleep," as the RSV has it, Ps. 127:2).
Jeremiah pictures God asking, "What right has my beloved in
my house, when she has done vile deeds? Can vows and sacrificial flesh avert your doom?" (Jer. 11:15). The questions show
that Jeremiah doesn't doubt Israel's unworthiness and superfi-
ciality. But he has no doubt, either, that Israel is still "beloved." God's love is enduring. We see something of the same
tension in that prophet's use of the cognate $y^e dhiydh\hat{u}th$ (here
only in the Old Testament): " I have given the beloved of my
soul into the hands of her enemies. My heritage has become to
me like a lion in the forest..." (Jer. 12:7f.).[10] The nation's sin
cannot go unpunished, and Yahweh detests it. But he still sees
the people as "the beloved of my soul."

Sometimes $y\bar{a}dhiydh$ is used to refer to the love of man, as
it does in the heading of Psalm 45, "a love song."[11] It is used
also to refer to the temple in the verse "How lovely is thy

---

[9]S. R. Driver sees the word as "a poetical word, choicer than
'hwb." He thinks that "perhaps the smallness of the tribe, and the
recollection of the affection with which, as tradition told, its ancestor,
the child of Jacob's old age, had been regarded by his father... may
have contributed towards its being so described" (A Critical and
Exegetical Commentary on Deuteronomy, Edinburgh, 1973, p. 403).
There is nothing in the text to indicate that merit or attractiveness
elicited God's love.

[10]Yahweh's revulsion against the evil in the nation is emphasized
by his bitter conclusion: "Therefore I hate her." This is to be understood not as God's permanent attitude toward the nation, but as his
attitude toward the sin just mentioned.

[11]C. S. Lewis has a helpful comment on the interpretation of
Psalm 45 and the Song of Songs which sees the Bridegroom as Christ
and the bride as the church: "As we read the frank erotic poetry of the
latter and contrast it with the edifying headlines in our Bibles, it is
easy to be moved to a smile, even a cynically knowing smile, as if the
pious interpreters were feigning an absurd innocence. I should still
find it very hard to believe that anything like the 'spiritual' sense was
remotely intended by the original writers. But no one now (I fancy)
who accepts that spiritual or second sense is denying, or saying anything against, the very plain sense which the writers did intend. The
Psalm remains a rich, festive Epithalamium, the *Song* remains fine,
sometimes exquisite, love poetry, and this is not in the least obliter-

dwelling place" (Ps. 84:1); what is in mind is the worshipper's attitude toward the holy place, not that of God. Then there is the very beautiful and touching passage in which the prophet sings a song to Yahweh, whom he calls "my beloved" (Isa. 5:1).[12] He goes on to use the metaphor of the vigneron as he makes it clear that Yahweh has done all that could be done for his vineyard. But he is faced in the end with this question: "Why did it yield wild grapes?" Despite all the love lavished on it, the nation constantly failed to produce.[13]

The verb ḥāshaq ("be attached to, love," BDB) may be used to refer to human love, such as Shechem's passion for Dinah (Gen. 34:8), or the love an Israelite warrior might feel for a beautiful woman captive (Deut. 21:11). But it is the word used also to refer to Solomon's love for building (I Kings 9:19; II Chron. 8:6), so there is nothing essentially sexual about it. In addition, it may be used to refer to man's love for God, as it is in the Lord's promise to the devout worshipper: "Because he cleaves to me in love, I will deliver him" (Ps. 91:14).

But the most significant passages containing this word are two in Deuteronomy which emphasize the truth that God's love is not motivated by human excellence. The first reads, "It was not because you were more in number than any other people that the Lord set his love upon you and chose you, for you were the fewest of all peoples; but it is because the Lord

---

ated by the burden of the new meaning" (*Reflections on the Psalms*, London, 1958, pp. 128f.). These rich statements about human love are telling us something important about divine love.

[12]John T. Willis has an extensive examination of the passage ("The Genre of Isaiah 5:1–7," *JBL*, 96, 1977, 337–62). He reviews a dozen ways of interpreting the passage and opts for seeing it as a parable. He rejects the view that it is a love song, but agrees that "my beloved" refers to Yahweh and accepts the prophet's use of "friend" in a sense similar to that in which Abraham can be called Yahweh's friend, 'ōhēbh (Isa. 41:8 and II Chron. 20:7; p. 362).

[13]A number of commentators are impressed with the conjunction of love and concern over the sad sin of the people. For example, G. Ernest Wright thinks that the opening of the poem "calls to mind the love poetry in the Song of Solomon." But "what the prophet has to say in the song is a very bitter word" (*Isaiah*, London, 1965, p. 31). George Adam Smith sees the song as "a noble piece of patriotism." But, he says, "Other patriots have wept to sing their country's woes; Isaiah's burden is his people's guilt" (*The Book of Isaiah*, I, New York, 1901, 37).

loves you, and is keeping the oath which he swore to your fathers" (Deut. 7:7f.).[14] Here the nation's weakness is stressed, but so is the fact that God still loves the people. The reference to the fathers does not indicate merit, for no reason is given for his choice of the men of old. Both they and their descendants should receive God's love with gratitude and awe. It is surprising that God should love them in this way, but he does. Later we read, "Behold, to the Lord your God belong heaven and the heaven of heavens, the earth with all that is in it; yet the Lord set his heart in love upon your fathers and chose their descendants after them, you above all peoples, as at this day" (Deut. 10:14f.). Once again God's unmotivated love is stressed;[15] his love of the fathers is mentioned once more. We might reason that God loved the fathers because they were upright and honorable men, but that would be our reasoning—Deuteronomy does not say this. No reason is given for God's love; apparently it is regarded as simply the way God behaves. He loves because he is the kind of God he is.[16]

There is a dispute about the correct reading in Isaiah 38:17, but it seems that our verb should be read. The message is not clear beyond a doubt, but it seems that we should understand the passage to mean, "You have loved my soul out of the pit" (cf. the NEB: "Thou by thy love has brought me back from the pit of destruction").[17] One of the reasons for the

---

[14]"Here in the Old Covenant we have the assertion of that principle of justification by faith so determinative of Christian perspective. Israel has been chosen, not because of its greatness or goodness, but because of the love and faithfulness of Israel's God" (H. Cunliffe-Jones, *Deuteronomy*, London, 1951, p. 64).

[15]Cf. J. A. Thompson: "Israel was to love God because God first loved her. Here is a magnificent picture of the grandeur of God to whom belong the heavens and the earth. The contrast with insignificant Israel is striking. Yet Yahweh loved her" (*Deuteronomy*, London, 1974, p. 148).

[16]Cf. Lawrence E. Toombs: "The question 'Why does God love?' cannot be answered except with silent awe in the presence of an unfathomable mystery or by the paradoxical repetition of the question: 'He loves because he loves'" (*Interpretation*, XIX, 1965, 404).

[17]Cf. E. J. Young: "He had been in the very pit of destruction and yet God had so loved him as to bring him out of it" (*The Book of Isaiah*, II, Grand Rapids, 1969, 525). G. G. D. Kilpatrick remarks, "The KJV does not do justice to the pregnant construction of the Hebrew, which reads, lit., 'Thou hast loved my soul out of the pit of

textual problem may be that this is an uncommon expression, one that the scribes found confusing. But the writer seems to be combining the thoughts of the power of God's love and the helplessness of his loved one.

There is one occurrence of the verb *hābhabh* in a passage that the RSV translates, "He [i.e., Yahweh] loved his people" (Deut. 33:3). But this is an emendation, for the Hebrew has the plural "peoples." Considering this noun makes us wonder if God's love is extended to all nations. The context favors a reference to Israel; this is probably the reason why many students accept the emendation. But as it stands, the text favors a reference to a love which is given to more than Israel alone. Perhaps we should add this passage to those in Ruth and Jonah and the others we noted earlier[18] that show that God's love is not limited to any one nation.[19]

The verb *'āghabh* has the meaning "have inordinate affection, lust" (BDB), and it is used figuratively to refer to the nation's harlotries as she went after the gods of other peoples (Ezek. 23:7, 9, 12, etc.; Jer. 4:30). The corresponding nouns *'āghābh* and *'aghābhāh* are used to refer to "[sensuous] love" and "lustfulness" (BDB) respectively (Ezek. 33:31; 23:11). Of the words that are developed from this root, the only usage suggesting "respectable" love is the reference to "love songs" (Ezek. 33:32).[20] Clearly, the Hebrews did not see this root as suitable for conveying anything about divine love. But equally clear is the fact that they found it appropriate to describe Israel's affection for idols as the evil thing it was. The people maintained that they loved the gods; the prophets saw this as nothing but cheap harlotry.

---

destruction.' It means, 'Thou hast loved, and by thy love lifted me.' That Hezekiah is not thinking only of deliverance from physical death is clear from the words he adds: 'Thou hast cast all my sins behind thy back.'" Kilpatrick adds the penetrating comment, "For every man who is persuaded of the love of God by the beneficence of life, by beauty, by experience of joy and peace, there are a thousand who have found their certainty in forgiveness" (*IB*, V, 377).

[18]See above, pp. 79ff., for a discussion of those passages.

[19]P. Bonnard cites this verse as indicating that "if Yahweh loves this people first He also loves 'other peoples'" (though he adds that this is "an obscure text"; J.-J. von Allmen, ed., *Vocabulary of the Bible*, London, 1958, p. 243).

[20]Cf. John B. Taylor, who defines this as "lit. 'a song of love,' especially of a highly sensuous kind" (*Ezekiel*, London, 1969, p. 218).

Other words with meanings like "delight in," "favor," or "exercise goodwill" should be considered here. Because they express, at the very least, benevolence, and sometimes more, they are part of the way the Old Testament conveys the idea of love. There is, for example, the verb *ḥāphēṣ* (which occurs seventy-five times), and its cognate noun (used forty times) and adjective (used eleven times). The basic idea the word suggests is "delight in" (BDB).[21] Altogether the root is used to refer to human delight seventy-eight times and to that of God forty-eight times. "To delight in" a person and to love him are not far apart, as we see from the passages in which sexual attraction is described. Thus it is used to describe Shechem's love for Jacob's daughter (Gen. 34:19) and other sexual loves (Deut. 21:14; 25:8). But most often it is used to refer to other attractions, especially men's delight in things good and bad. Thus the Psalmist says, "I delight to do thy will, O my God; thy law is within my heart" (Ps. 40:8); and, again, "There is nothing upon earth that I desire besides thee. My flesh and my heart may fail, but God is the strength of my heart and my portion for ever" (Ps. 73:25f.). Such passages give emphatic expression to heartfelt love for God, and passionate devotion to him. Unfortunately, the root is used more often to refer to lesser loves, such as that for "abominations" (Isa. 66:3), or for pleasure when there ought to be fasting (Isa. 58:3). The most frequent use, however, is for blameless delight in things or people, such as Saul's delight in David (I Sam. 18:22).

A significant number of passages use these words to describe Yahweh's attitudes. Sometimes the meaning "delight in" is proper, as when the prophet refers to the things that please God (Isa. 56:4) and the psalmist talks about God doing what he pleases (Ps. 115:3). But in other places the words clearly refer to an attitude of love,[22] as when Joshua and Caleb said to the people, "If the Lord delights in us, he will bring us

---

[21]W. L. Walker sees the original meaning as "to bend," hence "incline to" and so "take pleasure in." He notes that it is used to refer to both God and man. Of the latter he says, "The element of joy, of delight in God and His law and will in the Heb religion is noteworthy as being something which we are apt to fall beneath even in the clearer light of Christianity" (*ISBE*, II, 820).

[22]Mitchell Dahood translates the second line in Psalm 18:19 as Yahweh "liberated me because he loved me" (*Psalms 1–50*, New York, 1966, p. 102).

into this land" (Num. 14:8), and when David sang in praise, "He delivered me, because he delighted in me" (II Sam. 22:20).[23]

No more than the other words for love do these words indicate a reason for God's affection. It might be argued that God loves the people because there is something in them that delights him, but there is never an indication of what brings about this delight. It seems that God delights in this people simply because he chooses to do so. Thus we are faced once more with his love for people who have done nothing to merit that love. This is clear in the psalm in which the author says of himself, "I am a worm, and no man; scorned by men, and despised by the people. All who see me mock at me, they make mouths at me, they wag their heads." Part of their mockery is their suggestion that God deliver him: "Let him rescue him, for he delights in him" (Ps. 22:6–8).[24] The words make it quite clear that there is nothing attractive in the psalmist, yet he is confident that God will deliver him (cf. v. 24). God does delight in him despite his unattractiveness. The same should probably be said about Hephzibah, the new name for Jerusalem with the meaning "My delight is in her," because this follows the explicit statement "You shall no more be termed Forsaken, and your land shall no more be termed Desolate" (Isa. 62:4).[25] There is nothing attractive about being forsaken and desolate, yet the Lord delights in these people.

The verb *rāṣāh* means "be pleased with, accept favor-

---

[23]H. W. Hertzberg comments, "It would be a misunderstanding of the text to think that man in effect holds his fate in his own hands as a result of his righteous actions. In the end, the operation of God's righteousness is determined by his power and his grace. He need not consider the actions of men, but he does so" (*I & II Samuel*, London, 1964, p. 396).

[24]J. H. Eaton thinks that the words "He delights in him" seem "to echo the formula from the royal initiation ceremonies where God declares to all the world that his choice and favour rest upon this king" (*Psalms*, London, 1967, p. 73). Not all are persuaded that we have a reference to royal initiation ceremonies, but the words do express publicly the favor God has for his own.

[25]F. Delitzsch comments, "She is now the object of true affection on the part of Jehovah. With the rejoicing of a bridegroom in his bride . . . will her God rejoice in her, turning to her again with a love as strong and deep as the first love of a bridal pair" (*Biblical Commentary on the Prophecies of Isaiah*, Grand Rapids, 1954, p. 436).

ably'' (BDB), and the related noun, *rāṣôn*, means "good-will, favour, acceptance, will" (BDB). The verb is used to refer to Yahweh more often than it is used to refer to men (thirty-five and twenty-two occurrences respectively), but the noun is used much more often to refer to God (thirty-eight times compared with eighteen times). The word group basically indicates "being pleased," and when this means being pleased with people the meaning often suggests something like love. It may be used in parallel with *'āhēbh*—for example, "The Lord reproves him whom he loves, as a father the son in whom he delights" (Prov. 3:12). It is thus clear that the word can convey the idea of love. It is surely this that is in mind when Yahweh speaks of "my chosen, in whom my soul delights" (Isa. 42:1). The fact that the Lord has "chosen" the servant indicates the divine initiative and shows us yet once more that it is not human merit that elicits his favor. This fact is obvious again when we read, "The Lord takes pleasure in his people; he adorns the humble with victory" (Ps. 149:4; note the reference to "the humble," those without the resources to obtain the victory for themselves).[26] In another psalm we read of Israel's victory as due not to the people's own sword or their own arm, "but thy right hand, and thy arm, and the light of thy countenance; for thou didst delight in them" (Ps. 44:3).[27] The noun is used when the psalmist prays to God, "Remember me, O Lord, when thou showest favor to thy people" (Ps. 106:4). But it is obvious that no merit elicited this favor, because the writer says plainly, "Both we and our fathers have sinned; we have committed iniquity, we have done wickedly" (v. 6; the psalmist goes on to catalog a number of evils perpetrated by the nation).

By referring to a number of passages in Proverbs, one could make a case for the Lord's favor being the reward of meritorious action—for example, "He who finds me [i.e., wisdom] finds life and obtains favor from the Lord" (Prov. 8:35). But while such passages indicate that the Lord is ready to reward those who do right, it is going too far to suggest that

---

[26]C. A. and E. G. Briggs explain the meaning of the verb: The people "are the special objects of His good pleasure and His favour" (*A Critical and Exegetical Commentary on the Book of Psalms,* II, Edinburgh, 1909, 542).

[27]"Israel's history is a story of grace" (William R. Taylor, *IB,* IV, 229).

these passages teach that the righteous are so meritorious that they win the love of an otherwise unloving God. J. C. Rylaarsdam explains the passage just quoted in these terms: "To 'find' Wisdom is to find 'life' (vs. 35). Not something about God, but God himself is the real gift: to know God is to participate in his life and to live in fellowship with him."[28] It is surely something like this that the text is saying: the writer is referring to a gift of God, not an achievement of man. It is the same with the other passages that are sometimes cited. God loves righteousness and he responds to righteousness in his people, but the passages in question do not demonstrate that God's favor is aroused by human action rather than his own prior love.

We should also take notice of the verb *ḥānan* ("shew favour, be gracious," BDB), together with its cognate noun *ḥēn* ("favour, grace," BDB). The verb is found seventy-six times, seventeen times in the hithpaʻel with the meaning "make supplication" or the like. But our concern is with the Qal, in which the RSV characteristically translates the word with expressions such as "deal graciously with" or "be gracious to." This suggests a loving disposition, but there is more—the verb usually indicates performance of a benevolent action born of that loving disposition.[29] Where the term is used to refer to God (which happens thirty-nine times), it may be suggested that this graciousness proceeds from God's own nature. Thus we read the word of the Lord: "I will be gracious to whom I will be gracious" (Ex. 33:19).[30] It is not a matter of men winning God's favor; his graciousness proceeds from what he is, not from what we are. This conviction that God is essentially loving lies behind the psalmist's incredulous question, "Has God forgotten to be gracious?" (Ps. 77:9; the previous verse

---

[28] *Proverbs to Song of Solomon,* p. 46.

[29] Cf. W. Zimmerli: The verb "denotes the kind turning of one person to another as expressed in an act of assistance"; it "means the attitude of a person in its direction to another in a specific gracious action" (*TDNT,* IX, 377).

[30] Brevard S. Childs comments, "The name of God, which like his glory and his face [is a vehicle] of his essential nature, is defined in terms of his compassionate acts of mercy" (*Exodus,* London, 1974, p. 596). A. H. McNeile says, "Yahweh is one who can of His own sovereign will be gracious and merciful even to those who have sinned against Him" (*The Book of Exodus,* London, 1917, p. 215).

contains a similar question: "Has his steadfast love forever ceased?"). In the same spirit the psalmist prays, "Have mercy on me, O God," and adds, "according to thy steadfast love" (Ps. 51:1). The prophet's words of reassurance are similarly confident: "The Lord waits to be gracious to you.... Yea, O people in Zion who dwell at Jerusalem; you shall weep no more. He will surely be gracious to you" (Isa. 30:18f.). Over and over we come across the prayer "Be gracious to me" (Ps. 4:1; 6:2; 9:13; Isa. 33:2; etc.). And this idea is behind the great words of blessing: "The Lord bless you and keep you: the Lord make his face to shine upon you and be gracious to you..." (Num. 6:24f.).[31] The usage of this verb shows plainly that the writers who employed it thought of God as habitually ready to show his love for his people. Things might not be going well for them, but they unhesitatingly appealed to God's graciousness.

The noun *ḥēn* is found sixty-eight times, but it does not help our inquiry greatly. It is mostly used in the sense "so-and-so found favor in the sight of so-and-so," a formula that occurs often (e.g., in Gen. 30:27; 32:5). Sometimes it is said that God gave someone favor in someone's eyes (Gen. 39:21; Ex. 3:21; 11:3; 12:36).[32] Such passages show us that God may be active in helping his people, but they scarcely show more. In seventeen passages people are said to have found favor in God's eyes—people like Noah (Gen. 6:8) and Moses (Ex. 33:12f.). It is not said why most of these people were favored, so we may put such passages alongside those we have already noticed that show us that God's love is not drawn from him by human attractiveness. But on the whole this noun adds little to our store of information on this subject.[33]

---

[31]W. Zimmerli hold that this "refers to the gracious will of Yahweh, who has pledged Himself to His people in His special covenant. But this graciousness is always God's free gift" (*TDNT*, IX, 378).

[32]The noun "is generally translated as 'favour' (and sometimes 'grace'), and... means characteristically favour shown without obligation, especially by a superior to an inferior" (Philip S. Watson, *The Concept of Grace*, London, 1959, pp. 11f.).

[33]Henry Townsend maintains that the word "denotes a kindly disposition manifested in kindly acts; it is favour bestowed when it is unearned and might be withheld." But he also holds that it "has no evangelical significance; it is not used of redemption from sin; and it fails to deepen in meaning as the redemptive purpose of God in the

More important for our purposes is the adjective *ḥannûn*, meaning "gracious," which occurs thirteen times, always in a reference to Yahweh. Eleven times the term is linked with *rāḥûm*; apparently it came naturally to the Hebrew to speak of God as "merciful and gracious." As the psalmist says, "The Lord is merciful and gracious, slow to anger and abounding in steadfast love" (Ps. 103:8). Clearly, this term stresses God's grace as he gives his love freely to men. Other words from this root include *teḥinnāh*. The word usually means "supplication," but it refers to the Lord's grace in Ezra 9:8 (and to the Canaanites receiving none at the hands of Israel in Joshua 11:20). *taḥanûn* is invariably plural and always means "supplications." *ḥaniynāh* is found only in Jeremiah 16:13.[34] We should also notice the Aramaic verb *ḥanan*, which is used to refer to showing mercy to the oppressed (Dan. 4:27) and to making supplication to God (Dan. 6:11).

Another verb of some interest is *dābhaq*, meaning "cling, cleave, keep close" (BDB). It is used to refer to physical clinging, as when Eleazar the son of Dodo smote the Philistines "until his hand was weary, and his hand clove to the sword" (II Sam. 23:10). Similarly, a man's loincloth clings to his loins (Jer. 13:11). Several times the tongue is said to cleave to the roof of the mouth (Job 29:10; Ps. 137:6; Lam. 4:4; Ezek. 3:26). The term may be used metaphorically—for example, it may refer to famine that cannot be shaken off (Jer. 42:16) or the inheritance of one's fathers, to which everyone should cleave (Num. 36:7, 9). More important is the use of the verb for cleaving to people. This may denote no more than physical proximity, as when Boaz told Ruth to remain close to his maidens (Ruth 2:8, 21, 23). But the word may also denote affection, as it does when Ruth 1:14 says that Ruth clung to Naomi. This is especially true of sexual love: this is the way it is to be with

---

Old Testament is unveiled" (*The Doctrine of Grace in the Synoptic Gospels,* London, 1919, pp. 8, 10f.). William L. Reed, however, finds the word is related to *ḥesedh* and holds that "it is clear that the Hebrew word *ḥen* has important implications for Old Testament religion as a word which shows that God was considered capable of good will and mercy" (*JBL,* LXXIII, 1954, 41).

[34] J. A. Thompson is uncertain who it is that will "show no favor," Yahweh or "the deities in the land to which they were sent" (*The Book of Jeremiah,* Grand Rapids, 1980, p. 408). But the meaning of *ḥaniynāh* is not in doubt.

man and wife, even at the expense of the man's leaving his parents (Gen. 2:24).[35] Our verb is used to refer to Shechem's love for Dinah (Gen. 34:3)[36] and that of Solomon, who "clung in love" to his foreign wives (I Kings 11:2).

There are some important passages in which this idea of "cleaving in love" is used to describe the attitude God's people should have for him. They should be found "loving the Lord [their] God, walking in all his ways, and cleaving to him" (Deut. 11:22; cf. 30:20; Josh. 22:5). This attitude of love is compatible with serving God, fearing him, and the like (Deut. 10:20;[37] 13:4). There is an interesting passage in which the Lord says to the people, "For as the waistcloth clings to the loins of a man, so I made the whole house of Israel and the whole house of Judah cling to me, says the Lord, that they might be for me a people, a name, a praise, and a glory, but they would not listen" (Jer. 13:11). Here we see the divine initiative at work. The Lord was making Israel and Judah cling to him; it was not an act of their own volition. But it was not something automatic, either, because the last words are very sad ones—"they would not listen." God's love is real and constant and active, but the human response is lacking.

From all this it is plain to see that there are many words that bring out the truth that God loves his people and is active on their behalf. We should further bear in mind that God's love is the necessary presupposition of much Old Testament teaching that lacks any of the words for love. For example, election is meaningless apart from the divine love that accomplishes it. The image of father and son is sometimes used (e.g., Ex. 4:22), and, though the father in ancient times was something of a dictator in his family circle, love is a response never absent

---

[35] John Calvin comments, "It is less lawful to desert a wife than parents" (*Genesis*, London, 1965, p. 136). Gerhard von Rad speaks of "this love 'strong as death' (S. of Sol. 8.6) and stronger than the tie to one's own parents," and of "this inner clinging to each other, this drive toward each other which does not rest until it again becomes one flesh in the child" (*Genesis*, Philadelphia, 1972, p. 85).

[36] G. von Rad speaks of "the emphasis on the great love for the girl, which brooks no hindrance" (*Genesis*, p. 331).

[37] P. C. Craigie comments, "The language indicates a very close and intimate relationship" (*The Book of Deuteronomy*, Grand Rapids, 1976, p. 207). He illustrates the closeness by reminding us that the verb is used to refer to the relationship of man and wife (Gen. 2:24) and the "'clinging' of human bones to skin" (Job 19:20).

from the divine fatherhood. Or we might think of the shepherd
and his flock (Ps. 78:52 and elsewhere), or of the vinedresser
and his vineyard (Isa. 5:1ff.). All such imagery is unintelligible
apart from the knowledge that God's loving care is basic. Even
such images as those of the potter and the clay (Jer. 18) bear on
our theme. At first sight this is simply a splendid way of bringing out the complete mastery of the potter over his material
and, accordingly, of God over Israel. But no potter makes a
vessel with the idea of discarding it; he brings pride and purpose to his work. Similarly, God did not create man and the
world with the idea of destroying it. There is a purpose behind
God's activity in creation, a purpose of love.[38] This is splen-
didly brought out in Psalm 136:4ff., with the refrain "for his
steadfast love endures for ever" appended to chosen items in
God's creating activity.[39] This is found in other psalms also
(e.g., Ps. 33:5; 36:7; 119:64). Creation in the biblical sense
cannot be understood apart from divine love.[40]

* * * * *

It is clear, then, that love is one of the fundamental ideas of
the Old Testament.[41] It is conveyed by a variety of words,
each of which has its own contribution to make to our under-

---

[38]H. Cunliffe-Jones says of this passage, "God is not only sovereign Lord free to do what he wills, but he is patient and loving, and
will not let them defeat his intention to make them a people for his
own possession" (*The Book of Jeremiah,* London, 1960, p. 137).

[39]Derek Kidner has a helpful comment. The creation theme,
"wherever it comes in the Psalter... , invites the Christian not to
wrangle over cosmological theories but to delight in his environment,
known to him as no mere mechanism but a work of 'steadfast love.'
No unbeliever has grounds for any such quality of joy" (*Psalms 73–
150,* London, 1975, p. 458).

[40]"If, however, we look at creation through the eyes of love, then
we shall understand it" (Hans Urs Von Balthasar, *Love Alone,* New
York, 1969, p. 115). Earlier he has said, "Love is built into the foundations of living beings" (p. 51).

[41]Viktor Warnach finds many characteristics of love in the Old
Testament that are often thought to be found for the first time in the
New Testament. The extent of the Old Testament's teaching on love
is not always realized. Warnach goes so far as to say that in the Old
Testament "the idea of love exercises a controlling influence which is
not the less strong for being hidden" (Johannes B. Bauer, ed., *Encyclopedia of Biblical Theology,* II, London and Sydney, 1970, 526).

standing of the whole. Together they show that love has many facets—particularly God's love. Two things about God's love are repeatedly emphasized: it is constant, and it is exercised despite the fact that the people God loves are so unworthy. This is a great comfort to God's people. Of course, they must be constantly vigilant in their efforts to avoid evil and to do things that please God. But they need not fear that when they slip into sin God will cease to love them. He will not. His love never wavers, never ceases. This is an Old Testament truth of permanent force and validity, one that we cannot do without.

CHAPTER FIVE

Love in the Septuagint

*I*T seems the early Christians read their Bibles mainly in the Septuagint, the translation of the Old Testament into Greek. Doubtless some of them knew and used the Hebrew Bible. But because Greek was widely spoken, the Septuagint version was for most people the most accessible form of Scripture. We must accordingly give attention to the usage of this version, all the more so because here we find the actual words for love used in the New Testament, not merely their equivalents in another language. This will not lead us to any earthshaking discoveries; in a translation it is not to be expected that there will be radical advances beyond the original. But a few variations are both interesting and fairly important.

In the Septuagint the two important New Testament verbs *agapaō* and *phileō* occur (together with their cognates). Of the two, *agapaō* is far and away the more common.[1] The words of this family are the usual translation of the Hebrew root *'hb*.[2]

---

[1] *agapaō* occurs 270 times in the LXX; 216 references are in passages in Hebrew books and 54 are in the apocryphal books (where there is usually no underlying Hebrew). The noun *agapē* occurs 20 times (16 + 4); *agapēsis*, 11 times (9 + 2); and the adjective *agapētos*, 23 times (18 + 5). According to these figures, all of the words in this word group are used a total of 324 times (259 + 65). I have taken the numbers from Hatch and Redpath's *Concordance*. G. Stählin gives the total for *agapaō* as 266, with a footnote citing E. Buonaiuti for the number 268 (*TDNT*, IX, p. 124 and n.115). The differences are probably due to different ways of evaluating variant readings.

[2] Of the 259 passages in which there is a Hebrew original, 196 times it is *'hb*. The next most common root, *ydd*, occurs ten times; *yhd* occurs eight times; *rhm*, six times; *yshrn*, four times, *hps*, two times; and *bw'*, two times. Fourteen roots are represented only once; eight times there is no Hebrew; and nine times the Hebrew cannot be identified with certainty.

Because this root is so translated 196 times and no other root is represented more than 10 times, it is plain that the translators regarded *agapaō* and its cognates as the best equivalent. But there are a few differences in the ways the two word groups are used. The most important is that the *agapaō* words are used more often than the *'hb* words to refer to God's love. This is, of course, partly accounted for by the fact that the Septuagint includes the apocryphal books, which are not in the Hebrew Old Testament. But there are also fourteen places where the Septuagint translates another root than *'hb* by an *agapaō* word, and seven places where it presupposes a different text. Putting it all together, the *'hb* words are used to refer to God's love thirty-nine times, but the *agapaō* words are used seventy-eight times.[3] This is quite a significant increase. Practically a quarter of all the occurrences of the *agapaō* words refer to divine love. This does not mean that the Septuagint teaches a different doctrine of divine love, but it does mean that it has a different emphasis. The translators were sure that God loves men and that God loves good, and they made their certainty ring throughout their translation. We are in no doubt about the importance of God's love as we read the Septuagint.

In view of the importance of *agapē* in the New Testament, it is worth pointing out that there is no place in the Septuagint where it certainly refers to God's love. It is most commonly used to refer to sexual love (used fourteen times altogether, eleven times in the Song of Songs). In addition, it is used twice to refer to love for wisdom and twice in a general sense. In the remaining two passages it is unclear if it refers to God's love or man's love. In Wisdom 3:9 we read, "The faithful will abide with him in love." "In love" might mean "in their love for him" or "in his love for them." Perhaps it is a little more likely to be the former.[4] The other passage is Sirach 48:11: "those who have been adorned in love" (RSV). This could well mean

---

[3] *agapaō* is used 71 times; *agapēsis*, 3 times; *agapētos*, 4 times. There is no passage in which *agapē* is certainly used to refer to God's love, but this may be the meaning in either of two passages (Wisdom 3:9; Sirach 48:11; see below, and n.4).

[4] JB opts for this, with its note, "Knowledge and love together constitute the happiness of the faithful"; cf. the NEB: "The faithful shall attend upon him in love." Joseph Reider, however, thinks this means "they shall be loved by God" (*The Book of Wisdom,* New York, 1957, p. 74). Similarly, J. A. F. Gregg says the line means

that human love beautifies those who possess it. The NEB, however, renders the line "were honoured with your love," and this may be right. There seems no way of deciding the point. This evidence suggests that the term usually denotes a sensual love, though it has other usages. Many suggest that these translators used the term primarily to avoid words like *erōs*, not because the word had a particularly positive connotation. Clearly, the use of the term in the Septuagint is a far cry from that in the New Testament.[5]

It may be profitable to look at some of the passages in which the Septuagint uses one of the *agapaō* words whereas the Hebrew text does not. Take, for example, the way the translators handle the term that we know in our transliteration as "Jeshurun" (Deut. 32:15; 33:5, 26; Isa. 44:2). In each case they use as their equivalent the passive participle of *agapaō* with the meaning "beloved." It is not easy to see why. Most scholars connect *Jeshurun* with the root *yshr*, which suggests uprightness. They understand it to mean the "upright one." Thus BDB say the word is the "poetic name of Israel, designating it under its *ideal* character." They note the conjecture that it should be understood as a diminutive,[6] but see "no evidence that *-ûn* has a dimin. force"; most recent scholars define it as a denominative with a meaning like *Rechtvolk*. Another opinion is that of T. K. Cheyne, who rejects the view that the term is connected with *yshr* and sees it as "nothing

---

"shall be loved by God. . . . The faithful shall attain to fuller perception, and shall be conscious of the Divine love embracing them" (*The Wisdom of Solomon*, Cambridge, 1909. p. 28).

[5]Cf. H. B. Swete: "*Agapē* in the LXX. rarely rises above the lower sense of the sexual passion, or at best the affection of human friendship; the exceptions are limited to the Greek Book of Wisdom (Sap. iii.9, vi.18). But in the N.T., where the word is more frequent, it is used only of the love of God for men, or of men for God or Christ, or for the children of God as such" (*An Introduction to the Old Testament in Greek*, Cambridge, 1902, p. 456). This is one of the examples he uses to demonstrate his point that "on the whole it is clear that caution must be used in employing the practice of the LXX. to determine the connotation of N.T. words" (p. 457).

[6]Cf. Douglas R. Jones, who says that the term is "probably a diminutive from a word meaning 'upright' . . . i.e., a poetic name for Israel under her ideal character" (M. Black and H. H. Rowley, eds., *Peake's Commentary on the Bible*, London, 1975, p. 521).

more than a synonym for Israel."[7] G. E. Mendenhall remarks
that the term is "conceivably intended to emphasize the root
meaning 'upright' " and that the Septuagint translates it "very
curiously."[8] In none of these discussions is there any serious
suggestion that the word is in any way connected with the idea
of love, which makes the Septuagint's usage in all four passages an interesting one. If we could be sure that the word was
a diminutive, we could then assume that it was used as a pet
name and thus indicative of someone loved. But no one seems
to have produced solid evidence that the word is a diminutive. It
is obvious that the Septuagint translators thought the term
pointed to Israel as the special object of God's love; why they
did so is not.[9] It is significant that where we see no reason for
connecting the word with love they found one: because they
were so sure of God's love, they found evidence of it in a
variety of places.

We should notice some passages in which the Greek obviously refers to a Hebrew text different from that which we now
have. The first is in a prayer of King David: "Who am I, O
Lord God," he asks, "and what is my house, that thou hast
brought me thus far?" (II Sam. 7:18 = I Chron. 17:16). It is not
easy to see why in both places the Septuagint replaces
"brought" with "loved" unless the translators had a different
text before them. There are three passages in the Psalms. In
the first the singer thinks that God makes Lebanon skip like a

---

[7] *EB*, 2434. Cheyne also holds that the term is "probably not a
diminutive." S. R. Driver sees it as a derivative of "upright" and
as used reproachfully in Deuteronomy 32:15, but elsewhere as a title
of honor (*A Critical and Exegetical Commentary on Deuteronomy*,
Edinburgh, 1973, p. 361). R. R. Ottley accepts the connection with
yshr and sees *Jeshurun* as "used of the nation apparently in an ideal
aspect, going beyond the name *Israel* as that itself transcended
Jacob" (*The Book of Isaiah according to the Septuagint*, II, Cambridge, 1906, 313). But he offers no suggestion about why the Septuagint translators four times chose "beloved" as their rendering.

[8] *IDB*, II, 868.

[9] Markus Barth notes that the participle *ēgapēmenos* translates
Jeshurun or *yadhiydh*, and adds that these are "titles or attributes
that almost mean 'darling' " (*Ephesians*, I, New York, 1974, 82). But
he gives no reason for seeing this meaning in *Jeshurun*. The same
meaning, "darling," is given in the *Jerome Bible Commentary* for
Deuteronomy 32:15; 33:26; and Isaiah 44:2, but, again, no reason is
given for this.

calf, "and Siryon like the son of a wild ox" (Ps. 29:6). In the second line, the Greek has "the beloved one is like a young unicorn," but it is not apparent how the translators arrived at "beloved" or "unicorn." In Psalm 84:11 "the Lord God is a sun and shield" becomes in the Septuagint "the Lord loves mercy and truth," while in Psalm 94:19 "your [i.e., God's] consolations cheer my soul" appears as the very difficult "your consolations loved my soul." Then there is the passage in Proverbs where "he who loves purity of heart" (referring to a human activity) becomes, in the Greek, "the Lord loves holy hearts" (Prov. 22:11).[10] Finally, there is God's description of Abraham: "When he was but one I called him, and I blessed him and I multiplied him." Here the Septuagint inserts "I loved him" after "I blessed him" (Isa. 51:2).[11]

Some of these renderings make curious reading in the Greek, and it is all the more significant that the translators have chosen the renderings in question. Taken together, they indicate a readiness to include a reference to God's love where that could conveniently be done (and sometimes where it could not). The translators evidently were quite sure of divine love and found it natural to include references to it.

The other passages scarcely need commentary. Those in which the Septuagint uses another of the words for love ("delight in" or the like) simply represent alternative views of the best way to render the Hebrew. It is perhaps significant that in so many places these translators chose *agapaō*, etc., but more

---

[10]See above, p. 54, n.36.

[11]R. R. Ottley thinks '*hbtw*, "I loved him," has probably been read for '*rbhw*, "I multiplied him." But LXX adds, "I multiplied him"; it does not substitute "I loved him" for it. If Ottley is right, the word would have had to be misread and translated and then read correctly and translated once more. This scarcely seems probable. Ottley notes that this line is "apparently a duplicate," and proceeds, "Otherwise the insertion of *kai ēgapēsa auton* has to be accounted for" (*The Book of Isaiah according to the Septuagint,* II, 337). It is not easy to account for it. However, there is certainly textual disorder here (Ottley notes that some MSS omit the words and others the preceding words), and the true explanation may be related to the textual history of the passage. It is impossible for us to say whether the Septuagint translators had MSS which included the words about love or whether they inserted them. For our present purpose it is sufficient to notice that the addition, however it was made, gives further emphasis to God's love, an emphasis that the translators find agreeable.

than that we cannot say. And of the passages in the Apocrypha it is simply to be noted that these books make interesting additions to our list. Thus to the man who is kind to orphans and their mother it is said, "You will then be like a son of the Most High, and he will love you more than does your mother" (Sirach 4:10). Clearly, God-like conduct is that which prompts one to care for the defenseless; further, God's love is greater than the best earthly love.

THE LOVE OF MEN

When we turn to love among people, the words most frequently indicate love between the sexes.[12] In most places it is used to refer to love for one's spouse—for example, to Isaac's love for Rebecca (Gen. 24:67), or to married love in general (e.g., Eccles. 9:9).[13] But it is also used to refer to less noble loves, such as that of Shechem for Dinah (Gen. 34:3) or that of Amnon for Tamar (II Sam. 13:1, 4, 15). In addition, the term is used to refer to familial love (Gen. 22:2; Prov. 4:3). Very important is man's love for God (mentioned forty-three times). This love is commonly attributed to groups, as it is when we read of the thousands who love God and keep his commandments (Ex. 20:6). But this term may also be used to refer to an individual's love for God, such as that of Solomon (I Kings 3:3) and David (Sirach 47:8).

When we consider the passages referring to men's love for God with the greater number which tell of God's love, we see that in the Septuagint love takes on a markedly religious color-

---

[12]In this way *agapaō* is used 34 times; *agapē*, 14 times; *agapēsis*, 2 times; and *agapētos*, once—a total of 51 times. In particular this is the most frequent use of *agapē* (used 14 out of 20 times), which is also used twice where the object is uncertain (Eccles. 9:1, 6), twice to refer to the love of wisdom, and twice where it is uncertain whether it is man's love or God's love that is meant.

[13]F. C. Conybeare and St. George Stock, discussing the Septuagint story of Joseph, say, "Among the Greek moralists the tendency was to regard love as a disease from which the sage would not suffer. In the early Greek drama the delineation of this feeling was thought to be below the dignity of tragedy, and Euripides was regarded by the older school as having degraded the stage by depicting the passion of Phaedra for Hippolytus" (*Selections from the Septuagint*, Boston, 1905, p. 102). There is nothing of this attitude in the Septuagint; love there is natural and right.

ing. This is apparent in many of the places where the love of things is brought up, because the love of good things (mentioned fifty-one times) means the love of what God approves. Indeed, the things in question are often connected explicitly with God. For example, we read of loving righteousness (Ps. 45:7) or God's commandments (Ps. 119:47, 48) or simply the good (Amos 5:15). A link with God may be implied in some of the more neutral things a man may love (mentioned eight times), such as Jerusalem (Tobit 13:12, 14), for in part at least this city is beloved because it is the site of God's temple, the center of worship. The love of good days (Ps. 34:12) will be a love for those days in which God's blessing is manifest; it is not a purely secular love. We may discern the same religious emphasis in passages (twenty-five in all) where the love of evil things is mentioned, because in each case the evil thing is condemned as contrary to the will of God. This is so, for example, when the people who love vanity (Ps. 4:2) or unrighteousness (Ps. 11:5) are blamed.

This word group is also used (forty-one times) to refer to the love a man should have for his friends or his neighbors or the like. God commands his people to love those of their own race (Lev. 19:18), but not only those—they are also to love the resident alien (Lev. 19:34). That such love is part of the religion of Israel is obvious partly because it is the object of a divine command, and partly because God himself practices such love (Deut. 10:18). Then there is the love of those whom God accepts, a love that is valued highly (Sirach 3:17).

FRIENDSHIP

We have noticed that *agapaō* and its cognates are used to refer to the love of friendship, but in Greek this love is most often indicated by the *phileō* words. These words are not found in the Septuagint as often as the *agapaō* words are, but they are not without importance. The verb *phileō* occurs thirty-three times;[14] the noun *philia*, thirty-eight times, with *philēma* occurring twice; and the verb *philiazō* occurs six

---

[14]G. Stählin gives the number as fifteen (*TDNT*, IX, p. 124 and n. 115). But this must be a mistake. The word is found in the following passages: Gen. 27:4, 9, 14, 26; 27:27; 29:11, 13; 33:4; 37:4; 48:10; 50:1; Ex. 18:7; I Kings 10:1; Tobit 5:16; 6:14, 17; 10:13; Esther 4:17; 10:3; Job 31:27; Prov. 7:13; 8:17; 21:17; 24:26; 29:3; Eccles. 3:8; Song of

times. The most frequently used member of this group is *philos*, which is found 188 times. The large number is accounted for by the fact that the term *friend* (which it represents) occurs 123 times in the Apocrypha and the apocryphal additions to the canonical books. It is not so strongly represented in the translation of the canonical Scriptures.

The words of this group are used in ways markedly different from the ways in which the *agapaō* words are used. *phileō* is predominantly used (seventeen times) to refer to kissing, usually chaste salutes within the family—e.g., Jacob kissing Isaac (Gen. 27:26) and Moses kissing Jethro (Ex. 18:7). The compound *kataphileō* is found twenty times, always meaning "to kiss." We should also include here, of course, the two occurrences of *philēma*, "kiss" (which is used once to refer to the false kisses of an enemy, Prov. 27:6, and once to the passionate kisses of a lover, Song of Sol. 1:2). This particular expression of love seems strongly linked to the *phileō* words.

The verb *phileō* is used to refer to the love of specific people only three times (Gen. 37:4; Tobit 6:17; Esther 10:3), though "a time to love" (Eccles. 3:8) is similar, because who is to be loved at the appropriate time other than people? We may possibly interpret in a similar way the love of Jerusalem (Jer. 22:22; Lam. 1:2) if we take the love of the city to mean the love of the people who live in it. There is one example of the love of a demon for a woman (Tobit 6:14). Of the references to love of things (which occur nine times), five are concerned with love of food and drink and one with love of sleep. There are three references to love for wisdom.

All in all, then, this verb does not add greatly to our information about the Old Testament idea of love. It is never used to refer to God's love for man or man's love for God. The loves it denotes are strangely varied: it points to an admirable love like that of Tobias for Sarah, but also to a detestable love—namely, that of the demon for the same Sarah. The love of food or sleep

---

Sol. 1:2; 8:1; Wisdom 8:2; Hos. 3:1; Isa. 56:10; Jer. 22:22; Lam. 1:2. B. B. Warfield comments, "This word, the common word for love in the classics, is used in the Septuagint in only a little more than five per cent of the instances where love falls to be mentioned: in nearly ninety-five percent *agapan* is used. Here is a complete reversal of the relative positions of the two words" (*PTR*, XVI, 1918, 153).

scarcely deserves the name of love. And, while kissing may be a fine expression of love, when the words are used to refer to this admirable activity they generally appear to indicate little more than a greeting of goodwill.

We should pay some attention to *philia*. This word denotes friendship rather than love, though we can, of course, speak of the love of friendship. But quite often this term is used to refer to friendship between nations, sometimes in connection with treaties (used in this way seventeen times). Such a treaty may link nations—for example, Israel and Rome. But a treaty of friendship is largely a formal affair, and its existence tells us little about love,[15] admirable though the state of affairs it indicates may be. A couple of times it is used to refer to friendship with those in high places—i.e., in a position to help or to harm. But is this love or simply political astuteness? The term is sometimes used to refer to friendship with one's neighbor, a relationship that may be indicated in as many as ten passages. The uncertainty about the number arises because some passages are rather general, as this one is: "Better is open reproof than hidden love" (Prov. 27:5; hidden love for whom?). Once the word is used to refer to love for children. Sometimes it refers to sexual love—four times to love for a wife and twice to lust after another woman. There is one reference to the love of wisdom and another to the truth that those who get wisdom obtain friendship with God. It appears, then, that, while the term can denote the warmth of love, most of the time it is concerned with nothing more than friendship, and often a cool friendship at that, such as the friendship between nations, one that is primarily formal.

The verb *philiazō*—meaning "be a friend, act in a friendly manner"—occurs six times. But the most common word from this root, as we have noticed, is *philos*. This word is almost invariably used to denote a friend, though it is often used to refer to the formal friendship established with those in high places. It is used fifty-nine times to refer to friends of people

---

[15]Cf. Jonathan A. Goldstein: " 'Friendship' (*amicitia*) was an official status in Roman international relations, approximately the equivalent of modern diplomatic recognition. It could exist with or without a formal treaty. The precise content of the term is difficult to establish, probably because the Romans themselves did not use it consistently" (*I Maccabees*, New York, 1976; p. 350).

like kings. Often the word seems to indicate an official status rather than any real affection.[16] For example, we read concerning Alexander's treatment of Jonathan, "The king honored him and enrolled him among his chief friends..." (I Maccabees 10:65); similar is "We have appointed you today to be the high priest of your nation; you are to be called the king's friend" (v. 20). And in another passage we read, "Ptolemy promptly appointed Nicanor the son of Patroclus, one of the king's chief friends..." (II Maccabees 8:9). In some such places the meaning may be that the king had friends just like anyone else. But in quite a few instances it seems that the word refers to an official relationship with the king, one that tells us nothing about love.

The word is used 123 times to refer to an ordinary friend, the kind that anyone—king or commoner—might have. This is clearly the normal use of the term. But there are also a few usages that do not fall into this category. Three times men are called friends of God, once the term is applied to a wife, once death is greeted as a friend, and once self-control is called "friend." It is noteworthy that the word occurs often (123 times) in the apocryphal books. There is normally no Hebrew root in such places with which we can link the term. In the canonical books where there is such a root, the terms used most frequently are *r'* (used 38 times) and *'hb* (used 10 times).

We should also notice that there are forty-six compounds created with *phil-*. To go through them all would be a wearisome process, and one probably unnecessary for our purpose. Suffice to say that the prefix conveys the idea of "love for _____." This may point to a virtue such as "love for the good," "brotherly love," or "love of mankind." Or a vice may be indicated, such as "love of money" or "love of strife." The constant force of the prefix is love for the quality or thing that follows. Curiously, *agapaō* does not form compounds in this way. Whenever it is desired to express love for a quality

---

[16]Cf. Jonathan Goldstein: "The Friends of the King had the privileges of members of the royal court. They were entitled to wear purple broad-brimmed Macedonian hats and purple robes" (*I Maccabees,* p. 232); and again, "The order of the King's Friends had several ranks: simple 'Friends,' 'Honored Friends,' 'Friends of the First Rank,' and probably also, at the top, 'Highly Honored Friends of the First Rank'" (p. 416; he is, of course, referring to the Seleucids).

or thing by means of a compound word, it is thus necessary to use *phil-*.

CONCLUSION

This examination shows that *agapaō* is much more significant for an understanding of love in the Old Testament than is *phileō*. This is true first of all because the term occurs so much more often, and secondly because it is found in contexts that better bring out the characteristic idea. C. H. Dodd finds in this usage the beginning of a process in which *agapaō* is filled with a new and distinctive content. This verb, he says, "is a comparatively cool and colourless word." He goes on to say, "It is this word, with its noun, that the translators of the Old Testament used by preference for the love of God to man and man's response, and by doing so they began to fill it with a distinctive content for which paganism, even in its highest forms, had no proper expression."[17] This development is important, but it is only beginning in the Septuagint. It would be hazardous to reason that the translators saw some important difference in meaning between the two words—in fact, a number of passages seem to show that they discerned no significant difference.[18] For instance, we read that Jacob loved Joseph more than his other sons (Gen. 37:3) and, in the verse immediately following, that the brothers saw that their father loved him more than them (Gen. 37:4). In both verses the Hebrew verb is *'hb*, but the Septuagint uses *agapaō* in verse three and *phileō* in verse four. The variation appears to be purely stylistic.[19] No reason appears for rendering the identical Hebrew two different ways in such a brief passage. Again, in Lamentations 1:2

---

[17]*The Johannine Epistles*, London, 1961, p. 111. He proceeds, "In the New Testament this fresh content is enlarged and intensified through meditation upon the meaning of the death of Christ."

[18]Conybeare and Stock have the concise note on Judges 16:4: "*ēgapēsen = ephilēsen*" (*Selections from the Septuagint*, p. 240).

[19]H. Highfield argues that the passage "seems to establish a practical equality for *agapan* and *philein* as used in Hellenistic Greek" (*ET*, XXXVIII, 1926–27, 44). In the face of an objection by C. F. Hogg (pp. 379f.), he reiterates his position: he maintains that "changes in the translation, where the original used both the same verb (*āhēv*) and the same preposition (*min*) in both clauses, should be regarded as ornamental rather than real" (p. 525).

the participles of both verbs are used for "those who love her [i.e., Jerusalem]"; no difference in meaning is apparent. In another interesting passage wisdom says, "I love [agapō] those who love [tous philountes] me" (Prov. 8:17). It might be possible to work out an edifying difference in meaning, but none is obvious. The two verbs seem to denote the same kind of love. This is also the case when we read, "A poor man loves [agapai] festivity, loving [philōn] wine and oil in abundance" (Prov. 21:17).[20]

The Septuagint makes use of some words for love not found in the New Testament. One is erastēs, meaning "lover." This word is used nineteen times in all, with no less than seventeen uses referring to the idols, seen as lovers of faithless Israel (e.g., Hos. 2:5, 7, 10, 12, 13; Jer. 4:30; 22:20; Ezek. 16:33). Once the word is used to refer to a passionate love for the beauty of wisdom (Wisdom 8:2) and once to a lust after evil things (Wisdom 15:6).[21] The cognate verb erasthai is used twice to refer to love for women (I Esdras 4:24; Esther 2:17) and once to the love of instruction (Prov. 4:6). Mostly these words translate the Hebrew 'hb (the noun, fourteen times; the verb, twice), the only other Hebrew root represented being 'gb (used once). We cannot say that these words add much to our knowledge of love in the Old Testament. They show that the translators envisaged the people's lust for idols in a very sensuous way, and that very occasionally the words might be used in a good sense (e.g., to indicate love for wisdom). But that is all.

The Sepuagint is important because it shows us the way that the words for love were used in the Bible of the early Christians.[22] It is important to see that the teaching we found in the Old Testament is here unchanged, with perhaps some

---

[20]We should also notice the textual problem in Tobit 6:17, where AB read ephilēsen and S reads ēgapēsen. It seems probable that the scribes saw little difference. A similar situation might be posited for Ecclesiastes 9:1: Hatch and Redpath tell us that Symmachus has philia while the Septuagint reads agapē.

[21]A. T. S. Goodrick holds that erastēs "is capable of the most sensuous meaning, which it actually seems to have in 15:6" (The Book of Wisdom, London, 1913, p. 203).

[22]It is possible, as some scholars suggest, that the Septuagint simply reflects current usage at the time of translation. They hold that the phileō words were in the process of being replaced by the agapaō

intensification in the emphasis on God's love. The version is important also because it brings us the first use of the noun agapē. In the Septuagint itself the term is of marginal importance, used mostly to refer to sexual love. But it gave the early Christians a word that was recognizable (from its obvious kinship with agapaō) yet lacked the associations of the words generally used for love throughout the Greek-speaking world. This was to have important consequences when the New Testament came to be written.

---

words, a process they find complete in modern Greek, where they tell us that the use of the phileō words is confined to references to kissing. From this viewpoint the use of agapē in the New Testament is not significant; it had simply become the normal word for love. This is possible, but it rests heavily on presuppositions. No solid evidence is cited for it.

CHAPTER SIX

Greek Words for Love

*T*HE Greek language is rich in words for love. Whereas English makes one word refer to a variety of loves, Greek preferred to use different words. This gave the Greek a precision that the English term lacks,[1] though it might be countered that there is a corresponding disadvantage—namely, that the Greek does not indicate the kinship that links various kinds of love. Be that as it may, Greek usage is interesting, and it will benefit us to consider briefly some of the Greek terms used for love.[2]

NATURAL AFFECTION

We begin with *storgē.* This term means something like "natural love" or "family love." It is the love that binds people in some natural group—the love of the family, for example.[3] Parents love children and children love parents and

---

[1]The English word can be used in a very broad sense. Cf. Jules A. Delanghe: "If you take the word *love* in the broad sense, meaning everything we want and everything we try to achieve, then love stands for all our conscious activities, for everything we plan and everything we do" (*The Philosophy of Jesus: Real Love,* Philadelphia, 1973, p. 6).

[2]In what follows I try to give the characteristic emphases of each of the terms. But it must be borne in mind that there is considerable overlap, as B. B. Warfield showed long ago (*PTR,* XVI, 1918, 1–45, 153–203). It would be a mistake to think that any of these terms is used in a narrow sense.

[3]Cf. W. Barclay: "The Greek word *storgē* is the word which is used especially of *family love,* the love of child for parent and parent for child. If there is no human affection, then the family cannot exist" (*The Letters to Timothy, Titus and Philemon,* Edinburgh, 1975, p. 216). Kenneth S. Wuest helps us see something of the meaning of the term when he comments on the negative *astorgos,* meaning "without natural affection." This, he holds, points to the lack of love of "parents

114

children love one another. Of course, the modern nuclear family was not the norm in ancient times, so *storgē* probably had a much wider reference than we would at first think. Presumably it embraced uncles, aunts, grandparents, and many more relatives. The term was also extended to include kinds of love for those beyond the family: it can be used, for example, to indicate love of one's country. But the familial reference was the basic and characteristic one. Membership in a family meant a great deal to most people in antiquity, and *storgē* accordingly was both a valuable and valued element in one's life. Without it, what was possible was nothing more than a miserable and deprived existence, something that could scarcely be called life.

C. S. Lewis finds this form of love very important. He calls it "Affection," and says of it, "The image we must start with is that of a mother nursing a baby, a bitch or a cat with a basketful of puppies or kittens; all in a squeaking, nuzzling heap together; purrings, lickings, baby-talk, milk, warmth, the smell of young life."[4] But if we start with this image we by no means stop there. Lewis finds this kind of love in all sorts of places. His "Affection" is an undiscriminating love, according to his explanation:

> Almost anyone can become an object of Affection; the ugly, the stupid, even the exasperating. There need be no apparent fitness between those whom it unites. I have seen it felt for an imbecile not only by his parents but by his brothers. It ignores the barriers of age, sex, class and education. It can exist between a clever young man from the university and an old nurse, though their minds inhabit different worlds. It ignores even the barriers of species. We see it not only between dog and man but, more surprisingly, between dog and cat. Gilbert White claims to have discovered it between a horse and a hen.[5]

The objects of this kind of love must be familiar (cf. the use of "old" as a term of affection). This love often combines with other loves that "would not perhaps wear very well without it."[6] Thus in an old friend all sorts of things that at first had nothing to do

---

for children, children for parents, husband for wife and wife for husband" (*Romans in the Greek New Testament,* London, n.d., p. 38).

[4]*The Four Loves,* London, 1960, p. 42.

[5]*The Four Loves,* p. 43.

[6]*The Four Loves,* p. 45.

with the friendship become dear with familiarity. This is important in erotic love, which by itself might well become very unpleasant. It needs "this homespun clothing of affection."[7] Affection does not arise from appreciation, but it can lead to it. Interestingly, it can even lead to an appreciation of qualities not at first perceived, even ones that we would not admire originally. Affection enlarges our horizons.

But there are dangers in this form of love. One danger arises from the fact that it is not automatic, and we may expect others to love us in this way when they do not. We can become very bitter when instead of attracting them we repel them and they show us no love, as Lewis points out: "For the very same conditions of intimacy which make Affection possible also—and no less naturally—make possible a peculiarly incurable distaste; a hatred as immemorial, constant, unemphatic, almost at times unconscious, as the corresponding form of love."[8] In addition, the sacrifices we exact from those near and dear to us can be terrible to behold. We often justify our behavior by pointing out that with these intimates we can relax—we need not put on a front. Lewis agrees, but at the same time reminds us of the danger of becoming *too* comfortable: "Affection is an affair of old clothes, and ease, of the unguarded moment, of liberties which would be ill-bred if we took them with strangers. But old clothes are one thing; to wear the same shirt till it stank would be another."[9]

Such a discussion leaves us in no doubt but that *storgē* is a wonderful part of life. Even if Lewis extends the term a trifle farther than first-century men would naturally have done, it is clear that natural affection is important. Life could scarcely go on without it—certainly civilized life could not.

It is all the more interesting that the term is never used in the New Testament. Coming closest to it is the negative form of the corresponding adjective, which indicates disapproval. Twice people "without natural affection" are condemned (Rom. 1:31; II Tim. 3:3). There can be no doubt from the general thrust of New Testament teaching, and specifically from what it has to say about the family, that the early Christians saw *storgē* as natural and right. But their failure to use the word in the New Testament documents shows that it was

---

[7] *The Four Loves*, p. 46.
[8] *The Four Loves*, p. 52.
[9] *The Four Loves*, p. 54.

not *storgē* that they had in mind when they spoke of love. We must realize at the beginning that Christian love is not simply a family tie, an emotion that might be expected to occur in any natural grouping. It is probably significant that when they spoke of the Father's love for the Son they did not use *storgē* nor any word from this root. Rather, the Son is "Beloved," *agapētos*, of the Father (Matt. 3:17; 17:5; Mark 9:7; etc.).[10] Christians may thus assume that *storgē* is important and indeed necessary, but not the distinctive Christian idea of love.

FRIENDSHIP

A second word for love is *philia*, which means the love of friendship.[11] It is the love of a man for his fellow, of a woman for her friend. This, too, points us to something of great value in life. It would be possible to live without friends, but it would be a very impoverished existence. Lewis points out

---

[10]C. Spicq thinks that the use of this term for God's love is significant: "God loves his son, not like a father bending down to his little one with a rush of warm feeling, but in strict equality and with the intention of honoring him" (*Agape in the New Testament*, I, St. Louis and London, 1963, 39). He also notices that the first mention of love in the New Testament (Matt. 3:17) coincides with the proclaiming of the divinity of Jesus (p. 49).

[11]Robert Flacelière sees considerable variety in *philia*: "The word *philia* designates any feeling of attachment and affection between two persons, but the philosophers distinguished four kinds: the natural or parental *philia* (*physikè*), uniting those of the same blood; the *philia* between host and guests (*xenikè*), which indicates the importance of the virtues of hospitality; the *philia* between friends (*hetairikè*), which alone corresponds to friendship, strictly speaking; lastly, the amorous *philia* (*erotikè*), between persons of the same sex or of different sex. Further, to distinguish the various nuances of love, the Greeks possessed many words, aside from *philia* and *eros*: *eunoia*, designating dedicated devotion; *agapè*, disinterested affected; *storgè*, tenderness; *pothos*, desire; *charis*, gratitude and kindness; *mania*, unleashed passion. This enumeration, moreover, is far from complete" (cited in Denis de Rougemont, *Love Declared*, New York, 1963, p. 6, n.3). De Rougemont adds more words of his own. I do not wish to endorse this list, for I think some things in it might have been expressed differently. One would not gather, for example, that *agapē* is found rarely before the New Testament. What is valuable is the demonstration that there were many Greek words for love.

that we do not seem to make as much of friendship these days as did the ancients, when Aristotle could classify it as one of the virtues and when Cicero could write a book about it. Lewis finds it "the least *natural* of loves; the least instinctive, organic, biological, gregarious and necessary." He explains by saying, "Without Eros none of us would have been begotten and without Affection none of us would have been reared; but we can live and breed without Friendship. The species, biologically considered, has no need of it." In the same spirit he says, "Friendship is unnecessary, like philosophy, like art, like the universe itself (for God did not need to create). It has no survival value; rather it is one of those things which give value to survival."[12]

Friendship, as Lewis understands it, is built on common insight or interest or taste, something that the friends have in common but that other people do not share.[13] Eros is a private love between two people, whereas friendship is a "public" love that may exist between any number of people. There is no jealousy in friendship.[14] It begins with a shared interest but leads to an appreciation so deep that often "each member of the circle feels, in his secret heart, humbled before all the rest. Sometimes he wonders what he is doing there among his betters."[15]

Friendship is a stimulating affair, bringing out the best in each of the friends. But, even though each is strengthened by the contribution of the others, this very strength can be a danger, as Lewis notes: "Friendship (as the ancients saw) can be a school of virtue; but also (as they did not see) a school of vice. It is ambivalent. It makes good men better and bad men worse."[16] Just as the group strengthens the friends' good points, so it serves as a justification for their weaknesses. The

---

[12]*The Four Loves*, p. 70; p. 84.

[13]Paul Tillich says, "*Agapē* cuts through the separation of equals and unequals, of sympathy and antipathy, of friendship and indifference, of desire and disgust. It needs no sympathy in order to love; it loves what it has to reject in terms of *philia*" (*Love, Power, and Justice*, New York, 1960, p. 119). He is, of course, concerned here with *agapē*, but his idea is interesting because it recognizes Lewis' point that *philia* of necessity excludes some.

[14]Lewis, *The Four Loves*, p. 80.

[15]Lewis, *The Four Loves*, p. 85.

[16]*The Four Loves*, pp. 94f.

friends refuse to be controlled by outside opinion, because this is part of what friendship means. This means that when outsiders are wrong, friends strengthen one another in the right. But it also means that when those outside are right, the friends may well encourage one another to continue in a wrong way. Their very friendship hinders them from seeing what is right in the contentions of outsiders. Further, their bond may lead to pride, which despises those not admitted to the intimacy of the circle. Thus this love, just like *storgē*, has limitations as well as tremendous value.

And we must dismiss this term—as we dismiss *storgē*—if we are looking for the essential New Testament idea of love. The term is found only once in the New Testament writings—namely, when James tells us that "the friendship of the world is enmity against God" (James 4:4).[17] The term is not used to refer to God's attitude toward men, or to Christians' attitudes toward God, other Christians, or outsiders. In short, it does not indicate Christian love.[18]

PASSION

We should possibly take notice of a third word, *epithymia*. This term denotes strong desire, and in Greek writings generally it is often used to refer to sexual desire and thus may denote a passionate love.[19] Sometimes in the New Testament it has a positive meaning, as when Jesus spoke of his strong

---

[17]R. V. G. Tasker comments, "Selfishness in any form, whether it be the love of pleasure, self-gratification, or arrogant self-seeking, is all 'friendship with the world'; and for the time being it causes the Christian to be at war with God" (*The General Epistle of James,* London, 1956, p. 89).

[18]This has sometimes been overlooked. John Burnaby cites Abelard as "the first of the mediaevals to claim that men should love God as a friend loves a friend" (*Amor Dei,* London, 1960, p. 257; he also cites Thomas Aquinas as arguing for this kind of love, p. 267). We may agree that we should love God without looking for reward. But on biblical principles *philia* is not the way to express this truth (though it is certainly characteristic of *philia* as well).

[19]Gene Outka thinks of a "vital energy" which "might be called sexual eros or epithymia." He thinks that "no love-relation is ever devoid of epithymia: love would be impoverished without it" (*Agape,* New Haven and London, 1972, pp. 287, 288).

desire to eat the Passover with his disciples (Luke 22:15). It is also used to refer to the prophets' desire to see what the disciples saw (Matt. 13:17) and to Paul's longing to depart this life and be with the Lord (Phil. 1:23). But it is more often used to mean "lust" or "coveting."[20] In this negative sense it is used to refer to "the lust of the flesh" (1 John 2:16) or "evil passion" (Col. 3:5). In the New Testament the noun is used thirty-eight times; the cognate noun *epithymētēs*, once; and the verb *epithymeō*, sixteen times. But none of them is ever translated as "love" in the AV or the RSV. Thus we cannot regard this word group as significant to the New Testament idea of love (though D. D. Williams puts it first in his four words in "the vocabulary of love"[21]).

Erōs

A fourth word, *erōs*, is not found in the New Testament at all. But it is an important word in Greek literature. We must take it seriously both for this reason and also because something like *erōs* is what most people today have in mind when they think of love. Basically, *erōs* is romantic love, sexual love. It is the name of the little Greek god with the bow and arrows. The word is used to refer to affections other than romantic love, but this is its typical meaning, the one that gives it its particular character.

We should note at the outset that *erōs* is more than sexual experience. It is possible for the sex act to take place without love, as it does when a woman is raped or when a man "uses" a prostitute. And it is possible for a person to feel *erōs* without intercourse occurring. But the sex act is the fitting expression of *erōs*. It is not itself *erōs*, because affection is a primary element in this kind of love.

Two things are especially characteristic of *erōs*: it is the love of the worthy, and it is a love that desires to possess. By "the love of the worthy" I do not mean, of course, that the beloved is necessarily as worthy of being loved as the lover

---

[20]Paul Tillich comments that traditionally this "is considered the lowest quality of love. It is identified with the desire to sensual self-fulfilment" (*Love, Power, and Justice*, p. 28). He thinks of "love as one" (p. 28), but distinguishes among the qualities of love—namely, "the *libido*, the *philia*, the *erōs*, the *agapē* qualities of love" (p. 5).

[21]*The Spirit and the Forms of Love*, Welwyn, 1968, p. 2.

thinks. Life teaches us that all too often this is not so. But "beauty is in the eye of the beholder," and *erōs* is the kind of love that is directed at someone the beholder sees as beautiful.[22] When a young man or a young woman falls in love, it is always because the beloved is seen as attractive. This may not be obvious to others. Friends may say, "I can't imagine what he [she] sees in her [him]!" But if he (she) is in love, then it is axiomatic that he (she) sees something attractive in the beloved. If the lover thought that the other was just the worst possible type, a bundle of the things of which the lover disapproves, then love would be bestowed elsewhere.

Erōs also longs for possession.[23] We never meet a young man who says, "I'm head over heels in love with Mary, but I really don't care who marries the girl!" If he really loves her, then he is determined to make her his own. Life without her is unbearable and unthinkable. She *must* be his.[24]

In all of the manifold uses of *erōs* it seems that these two things remain characteristic. And we should understand that the word *does* have a wide variety of uses: it may denote a crude lust,[25] a pure and lofty passion,[26] or almost any response

---

[22]Plato has Socrates ask, "Must not love [*Erōs*] be only love of beauty, and not of ugliness?" (*Symposium,* 201A; all quotations from Plato are taken from the Loeb edition).

[23]*Erōs* "ever dwells with want" (Plato, *Symposium,* 203D; cf. also 200A–B).

[24]Philip S. Watson thinks that for *erōs* response is unimportant; it is possession that matters: "For Eros does not seek to be accepted by its object, but to gain possession of it." *Agapē,* by contrast, "seeks to be accepted by those to whom it is offered. Why else should it be offered?" (Preface to A. Nygren, *Agape and Eros,* London, 1953, pp. ix–x). C. S. Lewis speaks of *erōs* as "ready for every sacrifice except renunciation" (*The Four Loves,* p. 124).

[25]James Moffatt thinks this makes the word unattractive to New Testament writers: "In spite of its devotional possibilities, the term had been compromised by its lower associations of sensuous desire and lust" (*Love in the New Testament,* London, 1932, p. 38).

[26]Plato emphasizes this in the speech of Pausanius. He stresses the point that there are two loves, the popular and the heavenly (*Symposium,* 180D). It is the heavenly that is the pure *erōs.* Cf. also the two horses in the figure employed by Socrates (*Phaedrus,* 253C ff.). Plato speaks of love as "desire" and "a kind of madness" (*Phaedrus,* 237D, 265A), and also as a tyrant (*Republic,* 573B). Clearly he sees many possibilities in *erōs.*

"between" these two.[27] It may be used to refer to love among people, but it may also refer to a love for things. But whatever the object, the implication is always that *erōs* is the love of the worthy and the attractive, coupled with the desire to possess.

Now this kind of love is not necessarily a bad thing. I have said that the term is not found in the New Testament, but I do not want it to be thought that I am drawing a picture of an inferior kind of love and preparing to contrast it with a superior Christian love. It is not a matter of better or worse, but of difference: there are different ways of understanding love. And if we are to clearly comprehend what the New Testament writers understood love to be, we must clearly understand what *erōs* is. That will help us avoid the error of confusing the two.

Erōs can be beautiful.[28] It is a valuable part of life, one that none of us can do without. In their enthusiasm for *agapē* some have written as though *erōs* is inherently evil. This simply is not so. Certainly *erōs* is not the way of salvation or the essential Christian idea of love. But that does not mean that *erōs* does not have its rightful place in the Christian life. Romantic love at its best is a wonderful, pure love, lofty and ennobling. No Christian ought to be critical of this love, considering the Bible's teaching on the subject. The Song of Songs extols it in a way that the church has often delighted to see as an allegory of Christ's love. This is surely the wrong way to interpret the book, but the fact that it has been so understood by devout believers shows quite plainly that there is nothing essentially evil about this form of love. Moreover, throughout the Bible it is always taken for granted—and sometimes put into explicit words—that love between the sexes is a good and beautiful part of normal living for God's people.

The word can be used to refer to affections other than

---

[27]An example might be the "courtly love" of the Middle Ages, "whose characteristics may be enumerated as Humility, Courtesy, Adultery, and the Religion of Love" (C. S. Lewis, *The Allegory of Love*, Oxford, 1959, p. 2). There is a good deal that is attractive in this love, but also much that is unattractive—for example, the abjectness of the typical lover and the insistence on adultery.

[28]Cf. Paul Tillich: "We have, following Plato, defined *erōs* as the driving force in all cultural creativity and in all mysticism. As such *erōs* has the greatness of a divine-human power. It participates in creation and in the natural goodness of everything created" (*Love, Power, and Justice,* p. 117).

romantic love. For example, Plato uses it to indicate the love of the good.[29] We are not criticizing a man or saying anything bad about him when we use the term *erōs* to define his attitude toward good. On the contrary, we speak well of him when we say that he sees the good as supremely worthy and that he is determined to make it his own in his daily life. Would that there were many more about whom this could be said! But, though *erōs* can be highly praiseworthy, it is not the Christian idea of love.

We should not overlook the specifically religious use of the term. Again, this is something admirable, because it points to a strong urge to rise up to God. As Ethelbert Stauffer puts it, the corresponding verb "in its highest sense is used of the upward impulsion of man, of his love for the divine."[30] This is infinitely to be preferred to the contentment with sin and the passion for the second-rate which is so often the mark of the natural man. But it is not what Christians have in mind when they speak of love. It is harmful to define Christian love as *erōs*, a passion for God's beauty and a resolve to lift oneself to it. The essence of Christianity is to be seen not in man's ascent to God, but in God's coming down to man.[31] Love is something quite different from a passionate human longing, even a longing for the good and for God.

Agapē

An interesting feature of the New Testament is that, even though so many words for love were available and in common use, the Christians preferred to use another one—namely,

---

[29]E.g., *Symposium,* 204E. There is a sense in which all men love good things. But Plato goes on to speak of the ascent of the soul to the heavenly vision (210E). "Platonic love is a disciplined, passionate commitment to all that is good and true and beautiful, and through these things, to the Goodness, Truth, and Beauty that make them so" (Douglas N. Morgan, *Love: Plato, the Bible and Freud,* Englewood Cliffs, N.J., 1964, p. 5). But Morgan also says, "*Eros* inescapably remains *self*-fulfilling, *self*-rewarding, *self*-possessive" (p. 66; Morgan's italics).

[30]*TDNT,* I, 37.

[31]E. K. Lee points out that in Plato "love is the movement of man towards ever higher things." Later he says, "The theological notion, therefore, implied by the word *erōs* conveys the idea that God

agapē. This word was not entirely new, but it was not common before the New Testament; thus Ethelbert Stauffer says, "It is indeed striking that the substantive *agapē* is almost completely lacking in pre-biblical Greek."[32] As we have seen, the word is found in the Septuagint (twenty times) and a few times also in Jewish writings like the Epistle to Aristeas.[33] Stauffer conjectures that it made its appearance in these writings because the pious translators of the Old Testament did not wish to use a term that would convey the eroticism that was so much a part of the normal meaning of *erōs* among the Greeks. He sees a strongly passionate element in *erōs:* "What the Greek seeks in

---

cannot love men; for such love would imply a downward movement from the level of Divine perfection to a lower level.... Christians could not possibly use the word *erōs* without misrepresenting the distinctive idea of love" (*ET*, LXII, 1950–51, 29).

[32]*TDNT*, I, 37. He finds no certain example among the Greeks. A. Deissmann in his *Bibelstudien* (Marburg, 1895) accepted the conjectural emendation *agapēn* in the Paris Papyrus 49 (between 164 and 158 B.C.), but in the English edition he accepted the opinion of Blass and Pierret that the word was *tarachēn* (*Bible Studies*, Edinburgh, 1903, pp. 198f.). However, he drew attention to the use of *agapē* by Philo in *Quod Deus Immut.*, 14 (pp. 198f.). He argued that Philo cannot have derived the word from the LXX, so it must have been current in Egypt in his day. W. M. Ramsay commented, "This proof is about as strong as the former discarded proof from the Paris papyrus" (*ET*, IX, 1897–98, 568). More recently there has been discussion of P. Oxy. 1380, 11. 109–10, a second-century papyrus whose text may be earlier. The editors restored the text to read *agapēn theōn*, but Dr. Stephanie West argued that this should be amended to *agathēn theon* (*JTS*, N. S. XVIII, 1967, 142–43). This was contested by Dr. R. E. Witt (*JTS*, N. S. XIX, 1968, 209–11), but reiterated by Dr. West (*JTS*, N. S. XX, 1969, 228–30). Prof. J. Gwyn Griffiths sides with Witt (*JTS*, N. S. XXIX, 1978, 147–51). This cannot be held to be convincing proof that the word *agapē* was in use among secular writers. In any case, Prof. Griffiths says, "The idea of *agapē* here, however, includes that of *erōs*, at least the sexual love that is socially acceptable within the divinely ordained context of the family. Herein lies the main difference between the Isiac and the Christian use of the term" (p. 150). It is just possible that the word *agapē* should be restored here. But it is not possible to see in it anything that leads us to the characteristic New Testament idea.

[33]It occurs in Aristeas 229; Philo, *Quod Deus Imm.* 69; Testament of Reuben 6.9; Gad 4.2,6,7; 5.2; Asher 2.4; Joseph 17.3; Benjamin 3.5; 8.1,2; Sib. Or. 2.65, 6.25; Ps. Sol. 18.4.

erōs is intoxication, and this is to him religion."³⁴ Whether or not he is right about the reason for their choice, it is a striking fact that *agapē* is very rare indeed before the New Testament, and very frequently used in it.³⁵ In fact, it is the characteristic New Testament word—almost the only New Testament word—for love.

Why should the Christians use what was for all intents and purposes a new word for love? Because they had a new idea about the essential meaning of love.³⁶ In saying this I am not claiming that the linguistics prove this point. The essential Christian idea of love is found in books where *agapē* is not used, the meaning arising because of the way the Christians used the *concept,* not the word.³⁷ I do not see a new idea of

---

³⁴*TDNT,* I, 35.

³⁵There are some places where the readings in the MSS differ, so that there are slight divergences in the statistics given by different authorities. But *agapē* seems to be used 116 times and *philia,* once. Of related words, the verb *agapaō* is found 143 times and *phileō* 25 times; the adjectives *agapētos* 61 times and *philos,* 29 times. The total for the *agapaō* words is thus 320 and for the *phileō* words, 55. Clearly, it is *agapē* and its cognates that mattered to the writers of the New Testament—although they are not used uniformly. Thus *agapē* is absent from Mark, Acts, and James, and occurs only once in Matthew and Luke, while *agapaō* is not used in Acts, Philippians, I Timothy, Titus, or Philemon.

³⁶Alan Richardson thinks that the New Testament use of *agapē* is not as strikingly new as is often maintained, for he sees a similar idea in the Old Testament. The difference between the Testaments he sees as "an attempt to organize *agapē* into codes of law" in the Old, while the New regards it "as an eschatological reality." He further says, "But in OT and NT alike, *agapē* differs from *erōs* in that the latter is brought into action by the attractiveness of the object loved, whereas *agapē* loves even the unlovable, the repellent and those who have nothing to offer in return. It is thus a word which exactly describes God's attitude of free and utter grace in his dealings with Israel, old and new" (*An Introduction to the Theology of the New Testament,* London, 1958, p. 269, n.1). There is something to this proposition, as we have seen. But Richardson does not do justice to the New Testament link between love and the cross. That is new.

³⁷A. Nygren is often criticized for making too sharp a distinction between *agapē* and *erōs.* Thus Geraint Vaughan Jones says, "There are enough exceptions, however, and examples of overlapping, to show that the hard-and-fast distinction upon which Nygren and others insist cannot be maintained, and the infrequency of the use of *agape*

love in the New Testament because *agapē* is so characteristic; it is exactly the other way around. The early Christians had a new idea of love in whatever words they expressed it,[38] but their novel use of *agapē* is significant. The older words were not suitable vehicles for conveying the new meaning because they aroused associations the Christians did not intend; thus they used the new noun.[39]

Perhaps I should make it clear that the newness is in the noun, not the verb. The Christians did not produce a new verb but employed one already in common use—namely, *agapaō*. Even here they used a distinctive approach, because they used

---

in the Synoptic Gospels is striking; *agapao* is often used in the sense of *phileo*" (*ET*, LXVI, 1954–55, 3). But see Philip S. Watson's article, "Some Theological Implications of Agape and Eros" (*ET*, XLIX, 1937–38, 537–40). Amos N. Wilder holds that *agapē* "is in effect a Christian creation. Greek-speaking Judaism took over the commonplace pagan term to translate Hebrew words expressive of the love of God and the love of neighbor, and the church then filled it with the meanings implicit in the Christian experience" (*IB*, XII, 280). Whatever the merits of this account of the history of the word, the last point is significant. What matters is the content Christians put into the word.

[38]B. B. Warfield denies that the Christians deliberately selected *agapē*: "The simple truth is that the New Testament writers use *agapan, agapē* to express the idea of love because it was the word for love current in their circle and lying thus directly in their way" (*PTR*, XVI, 184). I doubt that this is adequate. But in any case it is the idea expressed and not the choice of word that is important. As Warfield says later, "It is not the variety of the vehicles for the expression of love for which the New Testament is notable, but the depth and height of the conception of love which it is able to express through its fundamental terms, *agapan* and *agapē*" (p. 202). C. C. Tarelli similarly argues that *agapē* was the common word for love in New Testament times, though the New Testament writers give new meaning to the idea of love (*JTS*, N. S. I, 1950, 64–67). See also R. Joly, *Le Vocabulaire Chrétien de l'Amour: Est-il Original?* Brussels, 1968.

[39]Cf. M. C. D'Arcy: "Christianity has made a special contribution by its doctrine of charity, the new and startling doctrine, that is to say, of God's manner of loving man and man's graced response to that love" (*The Mind and Heart of Love*, London, 1962, p. 8). D'Arcy does not stress the newness of the word, but here it is the distinctiveness of the teaching that is important. He thinks that Christians have understood *agapē* in a remarkable variety of ways (p. 180).

this word much more than they did *phileō,* and they did not use verbs such as *eraō* at all. The verb *agapaō* was used quite frequently in pre-Christian times, but when the Christians used it they gave it a deeper meaning. Stauffer thinks that in secular Greek in general, *agapaō* was normally used in a more colorless sense than either *erōs* or *phileō.* He sees it as characteristically having a meaning something like "prefer"[40] and therefore a verb suitable to convey the idea that God prefers one man to another. Stauffer also asserts that *agapaō* makes distinctions. It denotes "a free and decisive act determined by its subject," whereas *erōs,* among other things, "seeks in others the fulfilment of its own life's hunger."[41] He also sees *agapaō* as having "little of the warmth of *philein.* Its etymology is uncertain, and its meaning weak and variable."[42] But this is not true of the way it is used in the New Testament. There it certainly has a rich, positive meaning.

The fact that *agapaō* was in common use meant that the first readers of the New Testament would have had no difficulty understanding the general meaning of *agapē* when they first came across it. Its kinship with *agapaō* was obvious, and *agapaō* they knew. They would not immediately comprehend

---

[40]C. Spicq also thinks *agapaō* means "prefer," and comments on its use in Matthew 6:24: "Because the substitution of *philein* for *agapan* would make this text unintelligible, the verse is one of the strongest in the Bible in favor of the distinction between the two verbs. *Philia,* no matter what its preferences, is not exclusive, and admits several persons at one time to participation in friendship" (*Agape in the New Testament,* I, p. 17, n.1). But if the argument is to rest on the usage of the cognate noun, it should be pointed out that *agapē* is not exclusive, either.

[41]*TDNT,* I, 37. Stauffer uses a series of contrasts to make his point: "*Erōs* is a general love of the world seeking satisfaction wherever it can. *Agapan* is a love which makes distinctions, choosing and keeping to its object. *Erōs* is determined by a more or less indefinite impulsion towards its object. *Agapan* is a free and decisive act determined by its subject. *Eran* in its highest sense is used of the upward impulsion of man, of his love for the divine. *Agapan* relates for the most part to the love of God, to the love of the higher lifting up the lower, elevating the lower above others. *Erōs* seeks in others the fulfilment of its own life's hunger. *Agapan* must often be translated 'to show love'; it is a giving, active love on the other's behalf."

[42]*TDNT,* I, 36.

the full idea the new faith was conveying, but they would perceive that love of some sort was being indicated. As they came to know more about the new faith, they would understand more of what it meant by love.[43]

Perhaps as good a way as any of grasping the new idea of love the Christians had is to contrast it with the idea conveyed by *erōs*. As we have seen, *erōs* has two principal characteristics: it is a love of the worthy and it is a love that desires to possess. *Agapē* is in contrast at both points: it is not a love of the worthy, and it is not a love that desires to possess. On the contrary, it is a love given quite irrespective of merit, and it is a love that seeks to give.

---

[43]A. Nygren has often been criticized for making too sharp a distinction between *agapē* and *erōs*. So perhaps I should repeat that I am not basing my argument on the linguistics, though I find them interesting and see in them a pointer. The main thrust of the argument depends on what the New Testament writers meant when they used the love words, not on their terminology. John A. T. Robinson has written a penetrating criticism of Nygren in which he argues that there is something of unfulfilled desire (*erōs*) in *agapē* and of movement away from the self in *erōs* ("Agape and Eros," *Theology*, XLVIII, 1945, 98–104).

CHAPTER SEVEN

The God of Love and the Love of God

"*H*EREIN is love," wrote John, "not that we loved God" [we will never understand what love means if we start with human response[1]], "but that he loved us and sent his Son to be the propitiation for our sins" (I John 4:10). It is the cross that brought a new dimension to religion, that gives us a new understanding of love.[2] The New Testament writers saw everything in its light, finding their ideas about love revolutionized by what the cross meant.[3] The cross was the means

---

[1]Many do reason this way. For example, J. A. Baker bases his argument on an analysis of man and his environment: "If God's world makes sense only from the standpoint of this commitment which we call love, then this must be the standpoint of God as well.... We love by natural inclination. We are thus driven to suppose that if God made an environment for love, if he established the evolutionary process which endowed us with an innate impulse to love, then love must be an inner reality for him, too. He must be freely committed to it" (*The Foolishness of God,* London, 1970, pp. 132f.).

[2]Cf. James Moffatt: "One of the surprising results yielded by any close examination of Christianity as revealed in the NT literature is that apart from the redeeming action of the Lord Jesus Christ the early Church evidently saw no ground whatsoever for believing in a God of love" (*Love in the New Testament,* London, 1932, p. 5). Modern men take it for granted that God is a God of love. The early Christians saw nothing axiomatic about this proposition, but the cross gave them certainty.

[3]This point seems to be missed in Daniel Day Williams's interesting discussion, *The Spirit and the Form of Love,* to which I have already referred. He does not notice the importance of the cross when he says things like, "I use the word *agape* for God's love which the Bible sees taking form in God's election of Israel, and which is finally manifest in the story of Jesus" (pp. 2f.); and "Love is being, the very

the loving God used to deal with the problem of man's sin. On the cross Jesus died to atone for this sin and thus, as this verse reminds us, he came to grips with the wrath of God.[4]

This aspect of God's activity receives little attention in much recent writing, but it is important throughout Scripture and specifically in this place. The whole Bible bears witness to God's strong opposition to everything evil. The animal sacrifices of the Old Testament and the cross of Christ in the New Testament bear continuing witness to the truth that God never forgives sin with a wave of the hand. He takes sin too seriously to do that, a fact pointed up by the use of *propitiation* in the verse just cited, a word that means "that which averts wrath."[5] Modern treatments of the New Testament that avoid the concept of wrath are not doing justice to the language of passages like this one. We might feel more comfortable denying God's anger, but that is our idea—one we should not read into Scripture, because the Bible makes clear God's anger in response to evil.[6] Anger may not be the ideal word to describe this response, but so far no one seems to have come up with a better

---

being of God in an eternally outgoing, creative life. The spirit makes itself manifest as the form of personal communion. This is as far as our language can reach" (p. 36; he goes on to speak of the expression of love in the life of Jesus; see also pp. 46, 155, 204, 210, etc.). He expressly distinguishes "human loves" from "God's love as *agape*" (p. 3). This is true insofar as *agapē* is not to be understood from the human standpoint, but it overlooks the fact that the New Testament consistently refers to the love Christians are to show as *agapē*. Another to overlook the New Testament view of love is John Burnaby, who says, "If perfect love is spiritual communion..." (*Amor Dei*, p. 307). Is it?

[4]"God cannot and will not contradict Himself. Even as the God of love He cannot deny His wrath. His activity in the world, His law, and the *opera aliena* are all really, and not apparently, His work. This He will not renounce. But at the same time He wills to save the Creation.... The objective aspect of the Atonement, therefore, may be summed up thus: it consists in the combination of inflexible righteousness, with its penalties, and transcendent love" (Emil Brunner, *The Mediator*, London, 1946, p. 520).

[5]See the discussion in my *The Apostolic Preaching of the Cross*[3], London and Grand Rapids, 1965, pp. 144–213.

[6]Cf. D. D. Williams: "Love and wrath are woven together in the divine character as constituents of God's righteousness" (*The Spirit and the Form of Love*, p. 22).

one. Until someone does, it is preferable to continue to use the old word and accept its meaning rather than to lose an important truth simply because we do not like a word. John is saying that men were the objects of God's wrath because of their sin,[7] but that Christ's death delivered them.[8] It is only as we see the spotless Son of God crucified, John is saying, that we can see what *agapē* means. It is not a love given to the worthy or to those God charitably assumes to be worthy; it is lavished on sinners. When we see man for what he is, the wrath of God for what it is, and the cross for what it is, then and only then do we see love for what it is.

This is implied, though not explicitly stated, in the preceding verse in which John leads up to this saying. "In this God's love was made known among us," he writes, "that God sent his only Son into the world so that we might live through him" (I John 4:9). The word order puts some emphasis on "his Son"[9]: it was *his Son*, no less, that God sent[10] into the world. None less would do. The point of the sending is not brought out in this verse, but the words certainly imply that man was in so much spiritual trouble that it required no less than the Son

---

[7] J. L. Houlden translates *hilasmos* in the passage under discussion not as "propitiation" but as "sacrificial offering," and refers to his note on the same word in I John 2:2. There he says that the term "may well carry the more specific idea of 'propitiation,' and its association with the term *paraklētos* ... in *v.* 1 confirms the presence of that idea here" (*A Commentary on the Johannine Epistles*, London, 1973, p. 62).

[8] J. R. W. Stott comments, "There can be no expiation of man's sin without a propitiation of God's wrath. God's holy antagonism to sin must somehow be turned away if sin is to be forgiven and the sinner restored" (*The Epistles of John*, London, 1966, p. 87).

[9] Cf. B. F. Westcott: "The order of the words in the whole clause is most impressive: 'in this that His Son, His only Son, hath God sent into the world,' into the world, though alienated from Him" (*The Epistles of St. John*, Cambridge and London, 1892, p. 149).

[10] R. Bultmann points out that the verb "gave" appears in John 3:16 instead of "sent," but "the meaning of course is identical." He proceeds to notice that *monogenēs*, which is used in both passages, "is both a predicate of value and designates the unique one as beloved at the same time." He adds, "The historical event can and must also be understood as the eschatological event, insofar as the question of life and death is decided by one's disposition to it" (*The Johannine Epistles*, Philadelphia, 1973, p. 67).

of God to get him out of it. We see this also in the memorable words of John 3:16: "God so loved the world that he gave his only Son so that every one who believes in him should not perish but have life eternal." John does not go into detail, but it is obvious that he thinks the sinner is in serious trouble. And here the dreadful possibility of the sinner's perishing is explicitly mentioned. In the context of Scripture it cannot be doubted that the hand of God is in that "perishing." This is inevitable, because God has created a moral universe such that those who sin must in due course reap what they have sown (Gal. 6:7). True, God's will is to save men (I Tim. 2:4; 4:10), but that does not mean that he abandons all concern for moral realities. His love brings men to eternal life, but not without proper recognition of the desert of sin. So deliverance comes by way of the cross.

LOVE FOR SINNERS

Paul brings out much the same truth in an important passage in Romans. He tells his correspondents that "the love of God is poured out in our hearts through the Holy Spirit that was given us." But that leads to the reflection that it was "while we were yet helpless, at the right time" that "Christ died for ungodly people." Paul goes on, "For scarcely for a righteous man will one die; for perhaps for a good man[11] someone dares to die; but God shows plainly his love for us in that while we were still sinners Christ died for us" (Rom. 5:5–8). Notice the way the objects of God's love are described. They

---

[11]It is not certain whether a distinction should be made between *dikaiou* and *agathou*. C. K. Barrett thinks that Paul perhaps dictated the second part of v. 7 as a replacement for the first, and that Tertius didn't omit the unwanted words. This makes the two nearly synonymous (*A Commentary on the Epistle to the Romans*, London, 1957, p. 105). Others take *agathou* as neuter, meaning "for a good cause." Others see *dikaiou* as "a just man" and *agathou* as "a benefactor." Even for such not many would be ready to die. A. Deissmann draws attention to a papyrus written some time after 150 B.C. which says of a certain man, "For the most beloved of his relatives or friends he would readily stake his neck" (*Light from the Ancient East*, London, 1928, p. 118). Such devotion is rare and it is directed only to those one esteems. God's love is different: it is constant and extended to all.

are "helpless"[12] and "ungodly"; they are "sinners" and, in verse 10, "enemies." Merit is expressly excluded. We do not easily understand the force of this, because we are sinners, we have always been sinners, and sin does not seem so very terrible to us. But even sinners like us find some sins repulsive. We cannot tolerate child abuse, cruelty, egotism, or gluttony. Such sins repel us.

All sin repels God: he does not have the complacent attitude toward some forms of wrong that we have. Thus the prophet Habakkuk prays, "Thou who art of purer eyes than to behold evil and canst not look on wrong..." (Hab. 1:13). It is that God of whom Paul is writing. Yet God does not merely tolerate the sinners who constantly choose evil over good—he loves them.[13]

God's love is not some vague, theoretical thing, a woolly benevolence. It took the hard way: it meant the cross.[14] Paul is saying that it is the cross—and nothing less—that shows[15] us

---

[12]Paul's word is *asthenēs,* which is often translated as "sick," a term used in the modern idiom for those who are morally rather than physically diseased. This is not a bad way of understanding Paul's meaning. Instead of exercising a healthy moral uprightness, sinners are "sick."

[13]Cf. Roger Bowen: "Even a father who goes on loving a rebellious son is not an adequate illustration of God's love for us, because (a) the fact that the son is his own child arouses the father's love; (b) Paul never said that human beings are God's own children (although He created us); he taught that we *become* God's children *as a result of* His love for us, shown in Jesus Christ. God's love is therefore different from all kinds of human love. We have turned against Him, and there is nothing in us which can attract Him. But His love is like a spring of water; it flows from Him because this is His nature; He is love" (*A Guide to Romans,* London, 1975, p. 68).

[14]Walter Harrelson can say, "What, then, is the distinctive difference between the Old Testament view of God's love and that of the New Testament? The most obvious and the most important difference—in fact, the only significant difference—is the Cross." He goes on to quote Romans 5:8 (*JR,* XXXI, 1951, 173f.).

[15]C. E. B. Cranfield comments on the tense: "The use of the present tense is noteworthy: the event of the Cross is a past event (*apethanen*), but the fact that it occurred remains as a present proof." He also points out that *heautou* ("his") "is emphatic, God's love being contrasted with that shown by men (v.7)" (*A Critical and Exegetical Commentary on the Epistle to the Romans,* I, Edinburgh, 1975, 265).

what God's love is. God does not love us because we are fine, attractive people—not at all. Paul emphasizes that God sees us for what we are: sinners. But God loves us despite that fact.[16]

This thought is brought out in Ephesians, where we read, "But God, being rich in mercy, on account of his great love with which he loved us, made us live together with Christ, though we were dead in our trespasses" (Eph. 2:4f.). Although the cross is not explicitly mentioned, it is certainly suggested here. But what is emphasized is the demerit of the saved over against the love of God.[17] The chapter begins with a reference to those dead in trespasses and sins and goes on to remind the recipients of the letter that they used to live in a worldly, evil manner. They were "by nature children of wrath" (v. 3). Not the slightest doubt is left about the serious faults of men in general and of the recipients of the letter in particular. But God's love and grace are stressed just as strongly—in fact, the phrasing strongly emphasizes God's love.[18] Expression upon expression underscores the truth that salvation is due to no merit in the saved. In verses 8–9 we find that it is "by grace" that "you have been saved" (not "you saved yourselves" or the like), that it is "through faith" and "not of yourselves,"

---

[16] Cf. F. J. Leenhardt: "Love does not justify itself by pointing to the value of the beloved object; it does not rest on the basis of an exchange. God loves without rational justification. It is that very fact which proves that He loves. His love is intended to give to those whom He loves precisely what they have not in themselves, and what they could not in any way acquire, since they have nothing to give in return. By the death of Christ on the cross God has therefore conspicuously manifested His compassionate will towards mankind" (*The Epistle to the Romans*, London, 1961, pp. 136f.).

[17] Cf. Markus Barth: "At any rate, Eph. 2:4 treats the love of God as motivated by neither the attractiveness of his (dead!) human partners nor a weakness in his own nature. For his own sake God showers love upon man (Deut. 7:6–9). This love is manifested through the love of the Messiah, who out of love delivers himself into death for man's sake" (*Ephesians*, I, New York, 1974, p. 219).

[18] T. K. Abbott points out that the addition "with which he loved us" after the reference to God's great love, "being not necessary to the sense, gives great emphasis to the expression of the Divine love. Nor is *autou* to be neglected, 'His love' marking more distinctly that it is from Him alone and His attitude of love that this mercy proceeds" (*A Critical and Exegetical Commentary on the Epistles to the Ephesians and to the Colossians*, Edinburgh, 1953, pp. 46f.).

that it is "God's gift," a result "not of works," that there is no boasting. The recipients of God's grace have no merit at all. If we are to understand the love of God as this writer sees it, we must see it as something that does not proceed from any attractiveness in those God loves.[19]

The passages that describe Christ's death on the cross show plainly that God's love is not to be thought of as sentimentality. They reveal both God's revulsion against sin and Christ's readiness to suffer all pain necessary to defeat that sin. Such passages make it clear that suffering is not necessarily an unmitigated evil; in fact, it can be the source of good. The principal proof of this truth is Christ's suffering, because through it men are saved.

Accordingly, it is not surprising that we come across a similar idea: that God sometimes lets men suffer because he loves them. For example, the writer to the Hebrews quotes Proverbs 3:11–12 to emphasize the thought that God actively chastens his people: "For whom the Lord loves he disciplines, and he scourges every son whom he welcomes" (Heb. 12:6). Those saved by the cross see suffering in a new light, because it has brought them the greatest good. They see meaning in their own suffering, interpreting it as God's discipline at work. It is not evidence that God does not love them; it is precisely because he loves them that he goes to the trouble of disciplining them.[20] If he were merely sentimental about them, he

---

[19]C. K. Barrett notes that there are many New Testament passages that emphasize the truth that it was for sinful men that Christ died. He lists Mark 14:24; John 10:11; 11:50ff.; Rom. 8:32; 14:15; I Cor. 11:24; 15:3; II Cor. 5:15, 21; Gal. 1:4; 2:20; Eph. 5:2, 25; I Thess. 5:10; I Tim. 2:6; Titus 2:14; Heb. 2:9; 10:12; I Pet. 2:21; 3:18; I John 3:16 (*A Commentary on the Epistle to the Romans*, p. 106). This is a formidable list, one that shows that the thought of God's love for those without merit is a dominant theme in the New Testament.

[20]C. S. Lewis refers to the "intolerable compliment" that God pays us: "Over a sketch made idly to amuse a child, an artist may not take much trouble: he may be content to let it go even though it is not exactly as he meant it to be. But over the great picture of his life—the work which he loves, though in a different fashion, as intensely as a man loves a woman or a mother a child—he will take endless trouble—and would, doubtless, thereby *give* endless trouble to the picture if it were sentient. One can imagine a sentient picture, after being rubbed and scraped and re-commenced for the tenth time, wishing that it were only a thumb-nail sketch whose making was over in a

would not care. The writer is thus pointing out that God cares enough to do the unpleasant thing for the sake of his beloved.[21]

GOD IS LOVE

The New Testament, then, teaches that God strongly opposes sin and at the same time loves sinners. The reason for his love accordingly is to be sought not in men but in himself. This is emphasized in the Johannine literature; indeed, twice we are assured that God *is* love.[22] This means more than that God is loving; it means that love is of the essence of his being.[23] God loves—but not in an incidental or haphazard fashion. He loves because it is his nature to love, because it is his nature to give himself unceasingly in love. "He who does not love does not know God," writes John, "because God is love" (I John 4:8).

---

minute. In the same way, it is natural for us to wish that God had designed for us a less glorious and less arduous destiny; but then we are wishing not for more love but for less" (*The Problem of Pain*, London, 1943, pp. 30f.).

[21]In modern writing the stress is sometimes moved from Calvary to Bethlehem. Thus Denis de Rougemont says, "The incarnation of the Word in the world—and of Light in Darkness—is the astounding event whereby we are delivered from the woe of being alive. And this event, in being the center of the whole of Christianity, is the focus of that Christian love which in Scripture is called *agape*" (*Love in the Western World*, Philadelphia, 1953, p. 62). But this is not what the New Testament is saying. There the cross, not the incarnation, is central. Of course, both go together and neither makes sense without the other. But there is no doubt where the emphasis lies, and there is no justification for shifting it from the cross to the birth.

[22]Of this statement Geddes MacGregor says, "Either it is nonsense, to say nothing of maudlin humbug, or else it is by far the most exciting statement about God to be found in either the Bible or any other literature in the world" (*He Who Lets Us Be*, New York, 1975, p. x).

[23]J. R. W. Stott points out that it may also be said that "God is light" (I John 1:5), that "God is spirit" (John 4:24), and that he is "a consuming fire" (Heb. 12:29, quoting Deut. 4:24). He agrees that "God is love" is "the most comprehensive and sublime of all biblical affirmations about God's being.... Nevertheless, it is important to hold these assertions about God together." He later says, "Far from condoning sin, His love has found a way to expose it (because He is light) and to consume it (because He is fire) without destroying the sinner, but rather saving him" (*The Epistles of John*, pp. 160–161).

To speak of knowing God with knowing love is clearly ridiculous.

C. H. Dodd holds that "the proposition 'God is love' is clearly intended to go further than the proposition 'God loves us.' "[24] He proceeds to examine the meaning of the former proposition and comes to this conclusion about the statement "God loves":

> [It] might stand alongside other statements, such as "God creates," "God rules," "God judges"; that is to say, it means that love is *one* of His activities. But to say "God is love" implies that *all* His activity is loving activity. If He creates, He creates in love; if He rules, He rules in love; if He judges, He judges in love. All that He does is the expression of His nature, which is—to love.[25]

A little later John says, "We have known and we have believed the love which God has in us. God is love, and he who abides in love abides in God and God abides in him" (I John 4:16). Once again the thought is reiterated that love is closely associated with the being of God. To abide in love of the kind John has in mind is to abide in God. John is not saying that love is God;[26] he is saying that God is love, love concerned with giving rather than with seeking worthiness. It is that love, John says, that we have known and have believed, and to abide in that self-giving love is to abide in God. Love is the basic fact about God's nature.

Sometimes John refers to the love the Father has for the Son (the verb is used in this way in John 3:35; 10:17; 15:9; 17:23, 24, 26; the noun is so used in John 15:10; 17:26; there is also an occurrence of the verb in Ephesians 1:6 and of the noun in Colossians 1:13[27]). Once we read that Jesus loves the Father

---

[24] *The Johannine Epistles*, London, 1961, p. 107.

[25] *The Johannine Epistles*, p. 110 (Dodd's italics). J. L. Houlden sees the words as "the summit of our writer's whole doctrine" (*A Commentary on the Johannine Epistles*, p. 113).

[26] R. Bultmann points out that "the sentence cannot be reversed to read, 'Love is God.' In that case, 'love' would be presupposed as a universal human possibility, from which a knowledge of the nature of God could be derived" (*The Johannine Epistles*, p. 66).

[27] Literally this passage refers to "the Son of his love." This may mean "his beloved Son" (RSV). Or it may mean that the nature of God is love and that, accordingly, Christ is Son of that love. J. B. Lightfoot comments, "As love is the essence of the Father... so is it

(John 14:31). These passages show that *agapē* can be directed toward a worthy object. The fact that it denotes a spontaneous, unmotivated love does not mean that it can be directed only toward the unworthy. We tend to emphasize this meaning because it is only thus that we sinners experience love. But because this love is spontaneous it is exercised irrespective of the object's worthiness, and may be directed toward the worthiest of objects as well as those that are unworthy.

Now this stress on love is not purely Johannine. Paul speaks of love often. Indeed, he speaks of it more often than does any other New Testament writer. In the Pauline corpus *agapē* occurs seventy-five times (I John uses it eighteen times); *agapaō,* thirty-four times (John uses it thirty-seven times); and *agapētos,* twenty-seven times (I John uses it six times). This makes a total of 136 uses of the love words, which is a large proportion of the New Testament total of 320 uses (the love words are used a total of 112 times in the five Johannine writings). Clearly, the idea of love is of great importance to Paul. He links it with Christ: to be "rooted" in Christ (Col. 2:7) is much the same as being rooted in love (Eph. 3:17). In addition, he speaks of God as "the God of love" (II Cor. 13:11; he adds, "and peace"),[28] so that it is fair to say that he sees God and love as closely related. His terminology is different from that in I John, but the thought is much the same. If God is to be characterized, it is love that is the proper term with which to do it. The addition "and peace" does not alter this, because the peace that matters so much to Paul is the peace that comes from the ultimate expression of God's love: his bringing salva-

---

also of the Son" (*Saint Paul's Epistles to the Colossians and to Philemon,* London, 1884, p. 142). Origen refers to "the Son of the Father's love" (*Cels.* 5:11), and Augustine says, "The phrase 'Son of his charity' means simply 'his beloved Son'—in fine, the Son of his substance.... The Son of his charity is no other than the offspring of his substance" (*De Trin.* xv.19; *LCC,* VIII, 166).

[28]This is the only place in the New Testament where God is called "the God of love." C. K. Barrett notes this fact and adds the comment, "The meaning appears to be not only that God is himself characterized by love and peace, but that he supplies love (cf. Rom. v.5) and peace" (*A Commentary on the Second Epistle to the Corinthians,* London, 1973, p. 343). J. J. Lias comments on "the great Christian fact that all love is His love, whether manifested *by* Him or *in* man" (*The Second Epistle to the Corinthians,* Cambridge, 1890, p. 137).

tion to men who had made themselves his enemies. It is love that is basic.

We should probably apply this understanding to the benediction we read a few verses later. This is the well-known and much-used "grace": "The grace of the Lord Jesus Christ and the love of God and the fellowship of the Holy Spirit be with you all" (II Cor. 13:13). We should not differentiate too sharply between the Persons of the Trinity, and we should certainly not reason that love is strictly the Father's attribute, while grace and fellowship are the attributes of the Son and the Spirit respectively.[29] But it is nevertheless worth noting that "love" and "God" are linked once more;[30] in fact, it is difficult not to think that for Paul they belong together. A similar remark might be made about his prayer for the Thessalonians: "May the Lord direct your hearts into the love of God . . ." (II Thess. 3:5).[31] Love and God go together, and it is God's love that matters. Paul wants his friends to experience that love more fully. A further "love and peace" passage is found at the end of Ephesians: "Peace to the brothers and love with faith from God the Father and the Lord Jesus Christ" (Eph. 6:23). This adds little to what we have seen in the other passages, but

----

[29]Augustine, of course, linked love particularly closely with the Holy Spirit. He quotes the words "Hereby we know that we dwell in him, and he in us, because he hath given us of his Spirit" (I John 4:13), and proceeds: "Thus the Holy Spirit, of whom he has given us, makes us dwell in God, and God in us. But that is the effect of love. The Holy Spirit himself, therefore, is the God who is love" (*De Trin.* 15.31; *LCC*, VIII, 160).

[30]"Behind *the grace of the Lord Jesus Christ,* which is known as an observable event in history (cf. viii.9), stands *the love of God,* which, though commended in time in the action and especially in the death of Jesus (Rom. v.8), is an eternal fact" (C. K. Barrett, *A Commentary on the Second Epistle to the Corinthians,* p. 344).

[31]Some understand the genitive as objective with the meaning "love for God." But Paul normally refers to God's love for men when he uses this expression (e.g., Rom. 5:5; II Cor. 13:13). E. Best points out also that if Paul "had intended to say that men should love God, an infinitive after 'direct' would have been much more natural (cf. II Chron. 12.14; 19.3; Ps. 118(119).5). Moreover, the rendering 'God's love' is not without meaning in the context: if the Thessalonians continually remember how God loves them, their hearts will be steeled to keep the instructions he has given" (*A Commentary on the First and Second Epistles to the Thessalonians,* London, 1977, p. 330).

it is noteworthy that once more love is so closely linked with God.

We see this yet again in the words Paul uses to describe God in a prayer: "Now our Lord Jesus Christ himself and God our Father, who loved us and gave eternal encouragement and good hope in grace . . ." (II Thess. 2:16). It is not easy to separate the Father and the Son in this passage, but there is no real need to do so, because to Paul the cross demonstrates both the love of the Father and the love of the Son. Neither is excluded, and certainly we need both for any adequate understanding of the way our salvation was secured. But in the present passage it is worth noticing that the participle translated "loved" is singular, and that it immediately follows the reference to "God our Father," so that grammatically it must be taken as referring to him.[32] Clearly, it is natural to speak of God in terms of love.

So is it when Jude exhorts his readers, "Keep yourselves in the love of God" (Jude 21). He might have referred them to the greatness or the holiness or the majesty of God. But when he selects one quality to characterize the Deity, it is love. This follows naturally from the fact that Jude has greeted his correspondents as "loved by God" and has prayed that love be multiplied to them (vv. 1, 2). J. N. D. Kelly explains this passage well: "What the writer means by this is, not that they are loved by himself with a love rooted in God, but rather that they are loved by God and that His love enfolds them. As a result of being called, they have fellowship with Him, and in that fellowship experience His love."[33]

---

[32]Cf. G. Milligan: "The two participles under the vinculum of the common art. belong to *ho theos* alone, and the use of the aor. shows that the reference is to the definite historical act in which the Gospel originated" (*St. Paul's Epistles to the Thessalonians*, London, 1908, p. 108). J. E. Frame, it is true, thinks that the words refer "to both Christ and God" (*A Critical and Exegetical Commentary on the Epistles of St. Paul to the Thessalonians*, Edinburgh, 1960, p. 286). W. Neil agrees with Milligan: the words "seem grammatically to apply to God alone" (*The Epistles of Paul to the Thessalonians*, London, 1950, p. 185).

[33]*A Commentary on the Epistles of Peter and of Jude*, London, 1969, p. 243. There are some problems in the opening verse. The later MSS read "sanctified" where the earlier have "loved," but most agree that this reading is to be rejected. "Loved" is certainly right. Another difficulty arises from the dative and the *en*. Michael Green points out that "there is no place in the New Testament where Chris-

When Paul greets the Romans as "God's beloved ones" (Rom. 1:7), we have yet again the thought that the first thing to be said about the recipients of a letter is that God loves them. His love is what matters most. Perhaps we should add John's words, "We love, because he first loved us" (I John 4:19),[34] because again divine love is primary. Finally, under this heading, let us notice John's other words: "Look what love the Father has given us, that we should be called 'God's children'" (I John 3:1). We see God's love not as a reward for our attractiveness or achievements, but as a gift: he made us his children, took us into his family. That we may now call him "Father" is a consequence of his love, not of our merit.[35]

LOVE GIVES

I have said that *agapē* contradicts *erōs* in two ways. First of all, it is not a love of the worthy, of the meritorious. Secondly, it does not share with *erōs* the desire to possess. There is, of course, a sense in which God desires us; the entire Bible expresses this truth. But in *erōs* the desire to possess is crucial—it is the only way to gain satisfaction and fulfill-

---

tians are said to be 'beloved in God the Father.'" He sees the rendering of the NEB, "who live in the love of God the Father," as a "dubious paraphrase," and goes on to notice the suggestion of Westcott and Hort that perhaps the "in" is misplaced and that we should read, "beloved by God the Father and kept safe in Jesus Christ." He goes on, "Perhaps Jude originally left a gap after the 'in' for the appropriate place-name to be inserted, when the messenger brought his short letter round the various towns and villages where the incipient heresy had begun to spread. We could then translate, 'to those in_____, beloved by God the Father, etc.'" (*The Second Epistle General of Peter and the General Epistle of Jude*, London, 1968, p. 156). However we resolve the problem, it is clear that Jude is referring to his readers as beloved by God, and that this is the first thing to be said.

[34]It is possible to take *agapōmen* as a hortatory subjunctive, but most agree that the indicative should be understood. C. H. Dodd comments, "Our very capacity to love, whether the object of our love be God or our neighbour, is given to us in the fact of our being loved by God" (*The Johannine Epistles*, p. 123).

[35]"That Christians enjoy this status is the result of God's love (cf. iv.19). Salvation is wholly the result of his initiative: man is helpless to save himself" (J. L. Houlden, *A Commentary on the Johannine Epistles*, p. 89).

ment. The young man in love *must* have the woman who is the object of his *erōs*. Without her, life stretches before him like a barren desert. He tells her that he cannot live without her, that he needs her. *Erōs* means need, need that only the loved one can fulfill.

There is nothing of this in God's love for men, because when men come to God they cannot bring him anything. "All things come of thee, O God," we sometimes sing as an offertory prayer, "and of thine own have we given thee" (words taken from I Chron. 29:14). This points to an important truth. We make our offerings to God, but what do we bring him that we did not first receive from him? There is nothing intrinsically our own that will make God's life fuller and richer. We cannot add to his riches.

Scripture makes it clear that God is pleased when men repent of their wickedness and come to him (e.g., Luke 15:7, 10). But this is something quite different from the delirious happiness of *erōs*. It is a joy, indeed, but the joy of giving, a joy brought about partly at least because now we have entered the state in which we can receive more of the blessing that God is eager to give us. We sinners are not the kind of people we ought to be; we cut ourselves off from many of the good gifts God would give us. When we turn from our evil ways we do become more able to receive these gifts. But we are all wrong if we think that we are conferring some great favor on God by coming to him. *Agapē* is not *erōs*. We do not bring anything valuable to God—in fact, we acquire value only because we are the recipients of his love. *Agapē* is creative (a truth to which we shall return). It makes us into different and better people who are valuable—valuable not because of what we are intrinsically or because of what grace has made us, but because we are the repositories of God's love.

Why does God love sinners? I have been arguing that he loves them because it is his nature to love, because he is love. Unceasingly he gives in spontaneous love. He loves not because of what we are, but because of what he is: he *is* love. This is a new and distinctive idea in Christianity, though in parts of the Old Testament (notably in Hosea) we read about something very much like it. But it is not found in the non-biblical religions.[36] Dominated as they were by *erōs*, the love

---

[36]Emil Brunner says, "The message that God is Love is something wholly new in the world. We perceive this if we try to apply the statement to the divinities of the various religions of the world: Wotan

for what one does not have but longs for, they could not imagine that God loved man. Of course, they thought it right that man should love God, but what could a God who has everything desire from man? They thought of God as serene and detached, passionless and unmoved.

We do not know *agapē* apart from the Christian revelation. "We love," writes John, "because he first loved us" (I John 4:19). A number of manuscripts read, "We love God" or "We love him." This is, of course, true: our love for God is always a response to his love for us. But that is not what John is saying. He is saying that we love, in the sense of *agapē*, only because of God's great love for us.[37] We would not know what *agapē* is were it not that Christ died for sinners. "In this we have come to know love, that he laid down his life for us" (I John 3:16).[38]

Without the cross we would never have known what *agapē* is, let alone have experienced it. But the cross shows us what love meant. There the sinless Son of God laid down his perfect life for sinners, there he died for men without merit. That is *agapē*. It is not a love drawn from God by attractiveness in men; it is the expression of his own innermost nature. It comes natural to him to love because he is love.

Emil Brunner finds a parable of this in the element radium.[39] It is possible to point out all sorts of things about

---

is Love; Zeus, Jupiter, Brahma, Ahura Mazda, Vishnu, Allah is Love. All these combinations are obviously wholly impossible. Even the God of Plato, who is the principle of all Good, is not Love. Plato would have met the statement 'God is Love' with a bewildered shake of the head. From the standpoint of his thought such a statement would have been utter nonsense" (*The Christian Doctrine of God,* London, 1949, p. 183).

[37]Long ago R. S. Candlish wrote, "We have now a divine faculty of loving; we love with the love which is of God; which is God's very nature" (*The First Epistle of John,* II, 1870, 157).

[38]"There is no need to supply a genitive, *tou Christou* or *tou theou.* The true nature of love was manifested in such a way that men could learn to realize it, with abiding effects on their character and life" (A. E. Brooke, *A Critical and Exegetical Commentary on the Johannine Epistles,* Edinburgh, 1912, p. 95).

[39]He says that God's "Being as Subject is 'for-some-end,' it is Being which goes forth from Itself, Being which communicates Itself. To use a parable: We cannot grasp or describe the nature of radium without speaking of radio-activity. Radium is the radiant element— that is its very nature" (*The Christian Doctrine of God,* p. 192).

radium: its physical and chemical properties, the compounds it forms, its molecular structure. But if one omits to say that radium is constantly radiating away, one has omitted its truly distinctive characteristic. And if one speaks about God, stressing his holiness, his greatness, and his goodness but omitting the fact that he is constantly giving himself in love, one has omitted the thing that really matters. Moreover, we should not simply list love as part of a string of divine attributes, because without it God would not be God. God is love.

THE LOVE OF CHRIST

We have been concerned so far with passages that speak expressly of God's love. But because "God was in Christ," the references to Christ's love are just as relevant for our purpose. The New Testament writers do not see Christ's love as somehow different from and separate from the love of God; the Father and the Son are one in their love. Thus we read, "Therefore be imitators of God as beloved children, and walk in love as Christ loved us and gave himself for us, an offering and a sacrifice to God for a sweet-smelling fragrance" (Eph. 5:1f.). We are to be "imitators of God" by following Christ's example (by walking in love as Christ did). The passage indicates no difference between God's love and Christ's love.[40] The context has referred to being "forgiven" (Eph. 4:32), so it is obvious that the issue is God's love for the completely undeserving.

We were in desperate trouble, unable to save ourselves. But out of love Christ offered himself as a sacrifice to save us. Again it is plain that divine love is love for the undeserving. And, though the cross is not specifically mentioned, the references to forgiveness and to sacrifice demonstrate once again that it is the cross that teaches us what love is.

It is the same with Christ's love for the church, about which we read in a later passage. Men are exhorted to love their wives "as Christ loved the church, and gave himself for it, so that he might sanctify it, having cleansed it . . ." (Eph.

---

[40]Cf. Charles Hodge: "The apostle makes no distinction between our being the objects of God's love and our being the objects of the love of Christ. We are to be imitators of God in love, for Christ hath loved us" (*A Commentary on the Epistle to the Ephesians,* London, 1964, p. 277).

5:25f.).[41] Appearing again is the thought that the church had no merit. It needed sanctifying and cleansing. Clearly, the love that brought salvation under those circumstances was a love for the unworthy.

Again, Paul writes movingly of "the Son of God who loved me and gave himself for me" (Gal. 2:20). The context stresses the impossibility of salvation by the law. Paul is talking about both his unworthiness and his salvation through Christ's love. It is impossible to empty the passage of either thought.

In another well-known passage Paul tells the Corinthians that "the love of Christ constrains us" (II Cor. 5:14). Some, it is true, have understood this as an objective genitive, interpreting it as a reference to man's love for Christ. But this is unlikely, because both the context and the words used work against this idea. Thus there is force in C. K. Barrett's contention: "The fundamental thought here must be that of Christ's love for us, since this alone can provide a suitable introduction to what follows." He goes on, "God's (Christ's) love for men is proved by the death of Christ."[42] The apostle immediately relates God's love to the cross. It is clear that it is this that proves the love in question, that provides the motivation for Christian action. And Barrett is surely right in seeing this love as that of both God and Christ. It is not possible to separate them. The connection of love with the cross is noteworthy.

We should add to these a group of passages which do not specifically refer to the cross, but which refer to the need of men or the like. Thus there is a prayer that the Ephesians "might be strong to apprehend, together with all the saints,

---

[41] Cf. Markus Barth: "The Messiah in person (cf. 2:14) and he alone is the origin and criterion of marital love. Instead of a love principle, the Prince of Love is set forth; instead of a daemonic power (eros, libido), the Friend is praised who died for his friends; rather than paint a rose-colored cloud, Paul calls to mind specific events in the history of God and man. By benefiting and drawing from the fact, mode, intention, and achievement of Christ's love, a husband shall learn what is the essence of love" (*Ephesians*, II, 623f.).

[42] *The Second Epistle to the Corinthians*, p. 167. He notes the view of Robertson that the construction is a subjective genitive and that of Lietzmann that "it has a mystical double meaning." He does not dismiss the thought that there may be a reference to our love for Christ, but this is not the dominant thought. A little later he says, "Love for Christ may play its part, but it is Christ's love that sets in motion such behaviour as Paul's" (p. 168).

what is the breadth and length and depth and height, and to know the love of Christ which is far beyond knowledge'' (Eph. 3:18f.).[43] The Ephesians are not pictured as self-reliant and meritorious but as dependent on Christ's love, a love without limits. Paul again stresses Christian love when he mentions that he was ''formerly a blasphemer and a persecutor and insolent; but I received mercy because I did it ignorantly in unbelief; and the grace of our Lord superabounded with faith and love which is in Christ Jesus'' (I Tim. 1:13f.; the passage goes on to speak of Christ as coming into the world to save sinners). So, too, Paul exhorts Timothy to follow ''the pattern of sound words'' he has heard ''in faith and love which is in Christ Jesus'' (II Tim. 1:13). In none of these passages can it be said that Christ's love is drawn out by the worthy or the attractive. In all of them it seems that the basic New Testament idea of love prevails: Christ loved sinful men and died to bring them salvation.

This is clear also in the salutation in the opening chapter of Revelation: ''To him who loves us and loosed us from our sins in his blood'' (Rev. 1:5).[44] It is probably implied also in a later verse: ''I will make them come and worship at your feet and know that I have loved you'' (Rev. 3:9; quite evidently the people to be worshipped were lightly regarded—thus it would be a great discovery that they were the continuing objects of Christ's love).[45]

---

[43]The words stress the limitlessness of divine love. ''The love of Christ is infinitely greater than man can fully know or imagine, and it is also much more than any object of knowledge; it is superior to knowledge (I Cor. viii.1), even to spiritual knowledge (I Cor. xiii.2). It must find expression in experience, in sorrows and joys, trials and sufferings, in ways too deep for the mind of man to fathom, or for human language to express'' (F. Foulkes, *The Epistle of Paul to the Ephesians*, London, 1963, p. 105).

[44]G. R. Beasley-Murray comments, ''If the love was revealed above all in the death of Jesus, it is remembered that the death reveals an eternal love, which lies ahead of us as well as behind us'' (*The Book of Revelation*, London, 1974, p. 57). He sees the reference to loosing from sins as ''the conception of redemption as a new exodus of the people of God.''

[45]W. Klassen points out that this book ''does not give up the idea of loving the enemies, for the dominant symbol of the book, the Lamb, overcomes by absorbing suffering and conquers his enemies by the Word of his mouth (Rev. 19:13–15). The followers of the Lamb

All this has to do with the love of the risen and ascended Lord. But we should notice also that the Bible refers a number of times to Jesus' love for individuals. In the Synoptic Gospels we should notice the rich young ruler whom Jesus is said specifically to have loved (Mark 10:21).[46] In the Fourth Gospel it is mentioned that he loved the members of the little household at Bethany (John 11:5). Notice that Jesus "loved Martha and her sister and Lazarus." John is not speaking of a general love for mankind or even for the family as a whole, but of a love for each individual member of it. Similarly, there are several references to his love for his disciples (John 13:1, 34; 15:9, 12); so great is his love for them that it can be compared to the Father's love for him (John 15:9). He speaks also of people whom he will love or who continue in his love or the like (John 14:21; 15:9, 10).[47] We cannot perhaps draw the same far-reaching conclusions from such passages as we do from those that speak of the love that brought Christ to the cross. But it is important that in his earthly life Jesus loved those whom he knew.[48] Particularly intriguing is the mention of a special disciple "whom Jesus loved" (John 13:23; 19:26; 20:2; 21:7, 20).[49] Discussions of this man tend to center on his identity and on the

---

are to overcome in the same way (12:11). Vengeance here, as throughout the NT, is left entirely in the hands of God" (*IDB*, V, 558).

[46]C. E. B. Cranfield comments that this is love "regardless of the worthiness or unworthiness of its object" (*The Gospel according to Saint Mark*, Cambridge, 1966, p. 329).

[47]J. A. F. Gregg argues that John 15:9 should be understood to mean "Abide ye in love for me" (*ET*, XLVII, 1935–36, 91f.). But the context and the normal meaning of "my love" favor a reference to Christ's love for his followers.

[48]John R. Gray, in his article "Whom Jesus Loved" (*ET*, LXII, 1950–51, 291–94), examines the passages in which Jesus is said to have loved people. He sees in them evidence of Jesus' real humanity: "Can a man be truly man who has no friends? Could Christ have been human if He had never been particularly drawn to some one as He was to the Rich Young Man in St. Mark's Gospel?" (p. 293).

[49]J. C. Ryle comments, "Let it be noted that the general special love with which our Lord loved all His disciples did not prevent His having a particular love for one individual.... It is quite clear that special friendship for one individual is consistent with love for all" (*Expository Thoughts on the Gospels, St John*, III, London, 1957, 38). The verb in 20:2 is *phileō* and in the other places, *agapaō*, but there seems to be no difference in meaning.

possibility that he referred to himself in this way. But for our present purpose the important point is that Jesus loved him. (In fact, this is said repeatedly, further reminding us of Jesus' love for an individual.)

To sum up our argument thus far: the consistent teaching of the New Testament is that the love of God in Christ is prior to any love in man. Of course, God will respond with love to any love in man; yet, as the New Testament views it, the origin of love is always in God. In the religions of the Mediterranean world popular at the time of the rise of Christianity, it was an accepted idea that a man ought to revere—and possibly even love—the god of his cult. It was expected that this expression of devotion would draw from the deity some form of approval. But this is not the Christian idea. It cannot be emphasized too strongly or too often that the distinctive Christian understanding of love is based squarely on the proposition that "God is love." It is in God and in God alone that we come to understand what love is.

LOVE IN THE TEACHING OF JESUS

Because we began this study with the term *agapē*, our approach led us to the Epistles, in which the term is used often in passages that show plainly what the term meant for the early Christians. Although the term occurs infrequently in the Gospels, we should not be misled by this fact. It is the word that is rare, not the idea. In fact, until we understand that *agapē* underlies all Jesus' teaching, we cannot correctly understand it. Jesus consistently talked about God and man and his saving mission in a way that makes no sense apart from the love that gives freely for the unworthy. He did not confine his activities to those safely in the fold, but sought out sinners. He pointed this out himself when he said, "I came not to call righteous men but sinners" (Mark 2:17). Anders Nygren comments, "With these words He turns the entire scale of Jewish values upside down. He could hardly have expressed in stronger terms what was bound to be felt as an assault on the traditional outlook."[50] (Because the Jews believed that God loved the righteous and abhorred sinners, Jesus' attitude was revolutionary.) We should notice Jesus' use of the word *came*. He related his calling of sinners to his mission, thus emphasizing

---

[50]*Agape and Eros*, London, 1953, p. 68.

God's gracious intent, God's purpose. He is not saying that his attitude is a purely human one; he came to call sinners because the Father sent him to do so.[51] We have seen that this teaching was taken up by writers like Paul and John.[52] For them *agapē* is God's unmotivated love for sinful men. It is obvious that they adopted Jesus' teaching, because the "good" religious people of that day were offended by such ideas.[53] For them God's attitude toward sinners was one of condemnation and judgment, not love. But Jesus was saying something new about love, not simply in his words but in his way of living. The tax-collectors and sinners who so often drew near to him he saw as the recipients of God's love—and his love.

He repudiated those who did no more than love the people who loved them. Where is the merit in that? "Even sinners [in Matthew, 'tax-collectors'] love those that love them" (Luke 6:32; Matt. 5:46).[54] Being a follower of Jesus means much more than that: it means following his example and doing good to people who do no good to us.[55] It means lending without

---

[51]D. E. Nineham makes the point that "for St. Mark, Jesus' exceptional conduct at this point rests not on some new general principle, but *on his unique status as Messiah*" (*The Gospel of St. Mark*, Harmondsworth, 1963, p. 97). Being what he was, he acted as he did, exhibiting behavior atypical of mere men.

[52]Robert Kysar quotes E. Haenchen: "John has seen the entire earthly life of Jesus as the revelation and realization of this divine love" (*The Fourth Evangelist and His Gospel*, Minneapolis, 1975, p. 196).

[53]Cf. Mekilta Ex. 18:1: "The sages said: Let a man never associate with a wicked person, not even for the purpose of bringing him near to the Torah" (ed. J. Z. Lauterbach, II, Philadelphia, 1933, 166).

[54]Matthew goes on to refer to "the Gentiles" and their readiness to greet their brothers. In this connection M. Bouttier draws attention to a relevant passage in Hesiod: "Call your friend to a feast; but leave your enemy alone. . . . Be friends with the friendly, and visit him who visits you. Give to one who gives, but do not give to one who does not give" (*NTS*, 25, 1978–79, pp. 129f.; Hesiod, *Works and Days*, 342–355; Loeb edn.). But Hesiod exhibits a cautious attitude even toward friends: "Let the wage promised to a friend be fixed; even with your brother smile—and get a witness; for trust and mistrust alike ruin men" (370–372). Hesiod's attitude may be worldly-wise, but it is a long way from the generous love of which Jesus is speaking.

[55]W. F. Arndt deals with the entire passage, Luke 6:27–38, in the light of the demands that Christian love makes on us. He points out in connection with this verse that "our love and helpfulness should man-

hope of return. It means loving our enemies (this is stated imperatively—"Love your enemies"—in Luke 6:27,[56] 35). It means praying for those who persecute or revile us (Matt. 5:44; Luke 6:28),[57] and blessing "those who curse us" (Luke 6:28). It means turning the other cheek when we are physically assaulted and have a good case against the other (Matt. 5:39; Luke 6:29). It is in this way that we become "sons of the Most High," because he is kind to the ungrateful and evil. He makes the sun shine on the evil and the good; he sends his rain on the just and the unjust (Matt. 5:45).[58] The love men see in God is not the general benevolence towards friends that we so often see on earth. It is a love that is poured out unceasingly even in the face of the most intransigent behavior.[59]

All this points to a decisive reversal of accepted human values. Jesus is not saying that his followers ought to love as

---

ifest itself toward those who either cannot or will not repay kindness with kindness" (*The Gospel according to St. Luke*, Saint Louis, 1956, p. 191). Cf. J. C. Fenton: "To return love for love is only another form of *an eye for an eye*. It does not involve doing anything more than what those who are outside even the old Israel (*the tax collectors*) do. Therefore it merits no reward" (*The Gospel of St. Matthew*, Harmondsworth, 1963, p. 94).

[56]Cf. C. Spicq: For Luke, "the whole Gospel can be summarized in one word: the command 'Love!' " (*Agape in the New Testament*, I, 79); thus he begins the Sermon in this way and repeats the command in v.35.

[57]"Jesus demolishes all the fences into which men would confine love of neighbor" (Eduard Schweizer, *The Good News according to Matthew*, London, 1976, p. 133).

[58]A. B. Bruce emphasizes the *hoti* that introduces the clause: "*hoti*, not -*hōs*; but meaning 'because': for so your Father acts, and not otherwise can ye be His sons" (*The Expositor's Greek Testament*, I, *The Synoptic Gospels*, London, 1897, 114).

[59]C. C. Torrey sees this in the words generally rendered, "Be perfect even as your heavenly Father is perfect" (Matt. 5:48). He says the exhortation should read, "Be therefore all-including (in your good will), even as your heavenly Father includes all." In a note he argues that "the explanation of the false rendering lies, very obviously, in the fact that the form of *g'mar* (certainly used here) was active, not passive, in signification." He argues for the meaning " 'be all-including ,' making no exception in your kindliness" (*The Four Gospels*, London, n.d., p. 291). Even if his argument is not accepted, it is not unlikely that the words point to a wide-ranging benevolence. How else can one be "perfect" like the heavenly Father?

the world loves[60]—not even as the world at its best loves. He is saying that they should love everybody because God loves all men, the ungrateful and the wicked as well as the righteous. God's love is not an emotion conditioned by the kind of people we are. The duties he requires of us tell us something about the kind of God he is and the kind of love he feels for men.

This love is suggested even in many places where none of the words for love is explicitly used.[61] The very name "Jesus" points to one who would save people from their sins (Matt. 1:21; cf. Luke 2:21). At the threshold of the gospel is the sad fact of human demerit (our sins) and the joyful promise of one who would save men. What can this mean but God's love? Also indicating love are the Father's gifts to evil people (Matt. 7:11; Luke 11:13). God acts in love to all,[62] even though they do not reach his standards or even try very hard to do that. God is kind even to the thankless and wicked (Luke 6:35). "Freely you received, freely give," commanded Jesus (Matt. 10:8), and the saying points to the priority of divine love. So it is with the compassion shown in Jesus' healings throughout all the Gospels. Jesus is moved not by the merit of the sick but by their need and his great love. Matthew records the fulfillment of Isaiah's prophecy that "he will not break a bruised reed, nor will he quench a dimly burning wick" (Matt. 12:20), words that are inexplicable apart from divine compassion and love. Similar is his description of Jesus' healings: "He himself took our weaknesses and carried our diseases" (Matt. 8:17). Precisely interpreting these words is difficult, but clearly they point to a deep concern. Not to be overlooked is Jesus' identification with sinners, which he showed in his actions, such as

---

[60]O. J. F. Seitz sees this in the parable of the Good Samaritan (Luke 10:30-37). "No human being can be excluded from the scope of the divine command to act in love" (*NTS*, XVI, 1969-70, 46).

[61]We have already noticed that the words for love are rare in the Synoptic Gospels—for example, that *agapē* occurs once only in Matthew and Luke and not at all in Mark. But in these gospels very little makes sense unless we see the love of God as the great, undergirding reality.

[62]Eduard Schweizer sees in the best human love no more than a reflection of God's great love: "Because God infinitely surpasses all fatherhood or motherhood, it is true to say that one can see his love reflected in the love of earthly fathers or mothers" (*The Good News according to Matthew*, p. 174). It is the love of God that is basic.

his accepting a baptism meant for sinners (Matt. 3:13ff. and parallels). Throughout his ministry he was criticized for such things as eating with sinners (Matt. 9:10f.). Indeed, his business was with sinners, not righteous people (Matt. 9:13;[63] Luke 15:1f.; 19:7; etc.). How are we to explain all this apart from love?

Prophecies of the passion (Mark 9:12, 31; 10:33f.) point to the divine purpose of love in the cross. Furthermore, the Master bade his followers take up their cross daily (Luke 9:23). At first this may seem simply a difficult task. But it is in fact so difficult that it is beyond our strength and, as John Knox points out, "accepting the Cross means relying finally upon the love of God, the love poured out in Christ and symbolized inevitably and forever by his bitter death."[64] We see this compassion also in the references to the forgiveness of sins (Mark 2:5; cf. Luke 7:36ff., the passage about the woman who had been forgiven much and who loved much; may we not reason that she was loved much?[65]). So it is with the strong element of grace in the program Jesus outlined in the synagogue at Nazareth (Luke 4:18ff.). And the great songs in the early part of Luke all bring out the truth that God intervenes to deliver sinful men.

John has his own way of saying all this. When he speaks of Jesus as "full of grace and truth" or of "grace and truth" as coming through Jesus (John 1:14, 17), he is drawing attention to divine love.[66] Similar in emphasis is his reference to heaven as being opened in the ministry of Jesus (John 1:51). Why should God trouble to open heaven to men unless he loved them? This love is also implied in the frequent references to his sending of the Son and to his gifts of life, living water, and the

---

[63]"It is for 'the lost sheep' of Israel that he has come (see 10:6; Luke 15:4–7). It is toward them that his tenderness and his love carry him" (Suzanne de Dietrich, *Saint Matthew*, London, 1962, p. 56).

[64]*The Death of Christ*, New York, 1958, p. 171. He goes on, "The obligation of which I have been speaking is so great only because it is an obligation laid on us by so great a love. One cannot know how much God asks of us except as one knows in that same moment how much he loves us."

[65]Cf. John R. H. Moorman: "Forgiveness comes from love"; "out of their experience of the love of God their own love grows" (*The Path to Glory*, London, 1963, p. 86).

[66]It is generally agreed that "grace and truth" are intended as equivalents of the Hebrew ḥesedh wā'emeth, and, as we saw earlier, ḥesedh is an important word for love in the Old Testament.

like. Jesus speaks of the new birth (John 3), which from another angle points us to God's love. Why else should he renew us? Also expressing this love is the Good Shepherd, a well-known and well-loved figure from this gospel whose characteristic is that he gives his life for the sheep (John 10:11, 14f., 17).[67]

Much could be quoted along these lines. Very little in any of the Gospels makes sense unless we see it as somehow reflecting God's love in Christ. That is the stupendous fact that gives meaning to what the evangelists have written. Unless they had been seized with the importance of this great love, it is hard to see why they should have written as they did.

THE PRODIGAL SON

God's love clearly underlies all Jesus' teaching. This love is never seen as commonplace, nor as the kind of thing we see among men. Anders Nygren complains that A. Jülicher went seriously astray because he did not see this. For example, when he deals with the prodigal son, Nygren informs us that Jülicher takes up the position that

> "that is how it really happens in life." Then he is forced to go on and draw the conclusion: Therefore, God cannot deal otherwise with the sinner; He must receive him and give him His forgiveness. In this Parable, God's forgiveness to the sinner, His will to forgive, is "not merely illustrated, but seriously proved." For just as no one can take exception to a human father's acting in the way here described, so "the application to the Father in heaven is self-evident."[68]

Nygren counters by firmly denying that one can interpret the parables with "that is how it really happens in life." Jesus is not teaching routine human commonplaces, but something radically new. Nygren points out that the position taken up by Jülicher might well be countered by someone with a story of

---

[67]Walther Lüthi says, "It is not our strength, nor our riches, nor our goodness that attracts Him: quite the contrary; it is our poverty and need, our imperfection and weakness: in a word, our sin. It is our sin that urges Him to be our Shepherd. What a strange Shepherd! He does not think of His own advantage, but of the lost condition of the sheep" (St. John's Gospel, Edinburgh and London, 1960, p. 133).

[68]Agape and Eros, p. 82.

another prodigal who, when he returned home, was met with parental firmness. The father in this story demanded that the son prove the genuineness of his repentance: "My house is closed to you until by your own honest work you have earned a place for yourself and so made amends for the wrong you have done." The son followed this advice and in due course was able to thank his father for the strictness that had led to his amendment of life. We cannot deny that this kind of thing sometimes happens,[69] but we cannot reason that therefore God acts like this stern father.

The parable of the prodigal son is not a proof based on universal human activity; it is an illustration, in earthly terms, of divine love. The prodigal son had no merit, no money—nothing.[70] When he went back he was returning to a home to which he had forfeited all rights—yet he was welcomed with open arms. Through this story Jesus assures us that God's love is an unconditional gift to sinners who have nothing. God does not demand that we reach a certain standard before he will accept us. Out of sheer love and grace he provides for our salvation, salvation that is a free gift from a God who is love.[71]

THE LABORERS IN THE VINEYARD

This is seen in another parable, that of the laborers in the vineyard (Matt. 20:1-16). In this well-known story Jesus speaks of a man who hired laborers to work for him at the

---

[69]*Agape and Eros,* pp. 83f. Cf. A. M. Hunter: "The story is told of a certain prodigal son who, on turning up in 'the far country' of another parish, was advised by the minister there to go home and 'his father would kill the fatted calf for him.' The prodigal obeyed; and, months after, meeting the same minister again, was asked, hopefully: 'Well, and did he kill the fatted calf for you?' 'No,' came the rueful reply, 'but he nearly killed the prodigal son!' " (*Interpreting the Parables,* London, 1960, p. 13, n.).

[70]Cf. E. Earle Ellis: "The meaning for Luke's readers is simply that God loves the world—the common, mixed-up, moral-immoral, devil-may-care world. Jesus' mission expresses that love. His joy with 'that gang' is not an approval of their ethic—it *is* low (13, 15f.). Nor is it a social-work humanitarianism. His joy is that sinners respond to his message and, penitent, are brought back into fellowship with God" (*The Gospel of Luke,* London, 1966, p. 196).

[71]"A loving God is looking for [the sinner's] return. So is God, Jesus says, so incredibly good" (Wilfred J. Harrington, *The Gospel*

standard rate of a denarius a day. At the third hour he found idle men in the marketplace, and he sent them to his vineyard with the word, "You go to the vineyard, too, and I will give you what is right." He repeated the exercise at the sixth and ninth hours. At the eleventh hour he sent others to work, saying simply, "You go into the vineyard, too." He instructed his manager to pay the men, beginning with those last hired and ending with those first hired. All received a denarius. Those who had worked all day complained, "It's not fair! These last have worked for one hour and yet you have made them equal to us who have borne the burden of the day and the scorching heat." The householder replied to one of them, "Friend, I'm doing you no wrong. Didn't you agree with me for a denarius? Take what belongs to you and go. I'm willing to pay this last man just what I pay you. Isn't it lawful for me to do what I want with what belongs to me?"

Most of us feel that the complainers made a fair point. They had worked much longer and had endured the midday heat, yet they got no more than men who had done only one hour's work—and that in the comparative coolness of late afternoon. It wasn't right.

I do not know how better to bring out the teaching of this parable than to contrast it with a parable that the Rabbis told:

> ... a king... had hired many labourers, one of whom so distinguished himself by industry and skill that the king took him by the hand and walked up and down with him. In the evening the labourers came, and the skilful one among them, to receive their pay. The king gave them all the same pay. Wherefore those who had worked the whole day murmured, and spake: We have worked the whole day, and this man only two hours, and yet he also has received his whole pay.[72]

This parable is clearly very similar to the one Jesus is telling. In both is a contrast between those who worked hard and long and one who had worked but a short time. In both the

---

according to St. Luke, London, 1968, p. 197). We do not deduce this from men. God is "incredibly" good.

[72]Cited from the Jerusalem Talmud, *Berak.* 2.5c, by A. H. M'Neile, *The Gospel according to St. Matthew*, London, 1915, p. 285. The parable is repeated in Ecclesiastes Rabbah and in Song of Songs Rabbah, so clearly the Rabbis liked it and valued the point it made.

long-term workers complain about unfairness. The significant difference between the two stories is in the punch line. In the parable of the Rabbis, the king replied, "This man hath wrought more in two hours than you in the whole day."[73]

The Rabbis' parable is an excellent illustration of the way the mind of the natural man instinctively turns to merit. We take it for granted that we can win God's favor by doing what is right. No heresy is more popular than that summed up in the saying, "If you lead a good life you will go to heaven when you die." We all like to think that we can earn our salvation, that a man will be rewarded according to his works.

But that is precisely what Jesus is denying. The point of his parable is that the way the laborers were treated was not fair, but God does not deal with sinners simply on the basis of fairness. If he did, we would all end in hell. Instead, God deals with us on the basis of grace.[74] Perhaps no parable emphasizes this point more strikingly than that of the laborers in the vineyard.

T. W. Manson makes an important point in his comments on this parable. He reminds us that it would have been quite possible for the householder to have paid each of the laborers exactly what he had earned—in fact, there was a coin that could have been used for payment for one hour's work: "There is such a thing as the twelfth part of a denar. It was called a *pondion*. But there is no such thing as a twelfth part of the love of God."[75] That is the wonderful point that Jesus is making. All of God's love in its infinite richness is lavished freely on every man. God does not love because of merit or in proportion to merit. He loves all men without discrimination because he is a loving God.

THE GOD WHO SEEKS

Other parables make essentially the same point. Luke links the parables of the lost sheep (Luke 15:4–7) and the lost coin

---

[73]The Jerusalem Talmud in A. H. M'Neile, *The Gospel according to Saint Matthew*, p. 285.

[74]"God is depicted as acting like an employer who has compassion for the unemployed and their families. He gives to publicans and sinners a share, all undeserved, in his Kingdom. So will he deal with them on the Last Day. That, says Jesus, is what he is like" (Joachim Jeremias, *The Parables of Jesus*, London, 1963, p. 139).

[75]*The Sayings of Jesus*, London, 1949, p. 220.

(Luke 15:8–10) with that of the prodigal son (Luke 15:11–32).
The first two forcefully bring out the truth that God actively
seeks sinners. Indeed, some students of Judaism and Christianity see in these parables the main difference between the
two religions. Judaism knows something very much like the
search for the lost coin, but interprets it with regard to the
"words of the Torah":

> If a man lose a *sela'* or an *obol* in his house, he lights lamp
> after lamp, wick after wick, till he finds it. Now does it not
> stand to reason: if for those things which are only ephem-
> eral and of this world a man will light so many lamps and
> lights till he finds where they are hidden, for the words of
> the Torah which are the life both of this world and of the
> next world, ought you not to search as for hidden trea-
> sures?[76]

Again, this is a parable that superficially resembles the one that
Jesus told but has a very different meaning. The Rabbis were
concerned with works of human merit; Jesus, with the divine
love that seeks the lost.

Perhaps the parable of the lost sheep is even more significant. It eloquently declares God's concern for sinners as it
pictures the ninety and nine left alone while the Shepherd
searches ceaselessly for the one that is lost.[77] C. G.
Montefiore, that great Jewish scholar, says about this parable,
"The virtues of repentance are gloriously praised in the Rab-
binical literature, but this direct search for, and appeal to, the
sinner, are new and moving notes of high import and significance. The good shepherd who searches for the lost sheep, and
reclaims it and rejoices over it, is a new figure."[78] This clear
recognition of the novelty of Jesus' teaching is important. He is
not passing on a commonplace idea of the teaching of his day.
He is saying something of which his contemporaries knew
nothing as he proclaims the truth that God is a seeking God,
one who reaches out in love to the sinner and brings him home.

---

[76] *Song of Songs Rabbah*, I.i.9 (Soncino translation).

[77] Cf. H. G. G. Herklots: "The religious leaders had, very largely,
given these people up for lost. Jesus knew that they were lost; but he
knew that they could also be found—found to bring rejoicing to God's
heart; for he knew that there was more 'joy in heaven over one sinner
that repenteth than over ninety and nine just persons which need no
repentance.' In this outgoing towards the lost there was something
new" (*Publicans and Sinners*, London, 1956, p. 36).

[78] *The Synoptic Gospels*, II, London, 1927, 520.

God's love comes through once more in the parable of the wicked husbandmen (Matt. 21:33ff.; Luke 20:9ff.). Again we have a parable that does not depict ordinary human conduct. The tenants mistreated the owner's servants one after another, so the owner reasoned, "What shall I do? I shall send my dearly loved son; perhaps they will have respect for him" (Luke 20:13). In real life it is unlikely that a man would act like this. He had the law on his side and could demand and get strong retributive action (cf. v. 16). "But Jesus is depicting a God who loves beyond measure and is compassionate where He has every right to be severe."[79]

Similar are Matthew's parable of the wedding feast and Luke's parable of the excuses. Since those invited did not come to the feast, messengers were sent out to bring in others: "Those servants went out into the streets and gathered all whom they found, both bad and good" (Matt. 22:10). The last words show clearly that Jesus is not championing human merit. Once again it is God's great love which seeks out all sorts of people.[80] There is similar determination in the story in Luke. When the servants could not find enough banquet guests among the underprivileged in the city, the master sent them out "to the highways and the hedges" (Luke 14:23). Luke describes another kind of unlikely human behavior in the parable about the master who returns to find vigilant servants waiting for him. He will gird himself and serve them while they sit at table (Luke 12:37). This is improbable as a record of human conduct, but magnificent as a picture of a God who cares.

Love is Sovereign

The fact that God is not bound by the kind of consideration that influences men is brought out in many ways. Paul has a striking quotation from Malachi: "Jacob I loved, but Esau I

---

[79]Leon Morris, *The Gospel according to St. Luke*, London, 1974, p. 285.

[80]Cf. W. Barclay: "In the last analysis God's invitation to us is the invitation of grace. Those who were gathered in from the highways and the byways had no claim on the king at all; they could never by any stretch of imagination have ever expected an invitation to the wedding feast, still less could they ever have deserved it. It came to them from nothing other than the wide-armed, open-hearted, generous hospitality of the king. It was grace which offered the invitation, and grace which gathered men in" (*The Gospel of Matthew*, II, Edinburgh, 1958, 296).

hated'' (Rom. 9:13; the words are from Mal. 1:2–3). With it he emphatically underscores the point that God does what he wills. C. K. Barrett elaborates on this point when he says, "God's freedom is absolute. No antecedent ancestry, and no subsequent virtue or sin, controls it. Whatever happens, God's purpose, which operates on the basis of election, stands firm.''[81] Because we probably would not use Paul's phrasing, we may be uncomfortable when we read what he has written. But the central truth is one that the Bible affirms repeatedly: God is sovereign. Neither his love nor his hate[82] is to be explained by the way men act. Of course, this is just as well for us, because we are sinners and can never merit that love. In fact, it is a blessing that God loves as he wills, and that he wills to love and to save sinners.[83] Similar to this passage is one that Paul quotes soon after: "I will call . . . her beloved who was not beloved'' (Rom. 9:25; the words are from Hos. 2:23). Emphasized again is God's sovereign freedom, his bestowing his love where he wills.

In a number of passages love is related to election. From one point of view Israel may be God's enemies, but "with respect to the election they are beloved for the fathers' sakes''

---

[81]*A Commentary on the Epistle to the Romans*, London, 1957, p. 182. William Barclay makes a similar comment: "Everything is of God; behind everything is the action of God; even the things which seem arbitrary and haphazard go back to God. There is nothing in this world which moves with aimless feet'' (*The Letter to the Romans*, Edinburgh, 1957, pp. 136f.).

[82]The meaning to be attached to "hated'' is debated. John Murray speaks of "holy hate'' and thinks the passage must be understood "in the sense that an attitude of positive disfavour is expressed thereby'' (*The Epistle to the Romans*, II, Grand Rapids, 1965, 23). Charles Hodge argues that "in this case the word *hate* means *to love less, to regard and treat with less favour*'' (*A Commentary on Romans*, London, 1972, p. 312). F. J. Leenhardt notes that this exegesis is now out of favor, but "we think it valid'' (*The Epistle to the Romans*, p. 250 n.).

[83]Karl Barth quotes Steinhofer: "This and other passages . . . are two-sided. To the believers who trust in the love of God, they have a tender and delightful meaning: to those, however, who prefer to confide in their own works, they appear as a dark cloud. The more a man finds these texts to be harsh, the more is he wedded to his own righteousness. Inasmuch, however, as he is able to live quietly with them, his heart rests altogether in grace'' (*The Epistle to the Romans*, Oxford, 1933, pp. 349f.).

(Rom. 11:28). The fact that they are enemies and yet are beloved shows us yet again that the apostle is stressing a love for the undeserving. Enemies though the Israelites may be, God loves them.[84] Paul links love with election in other passages, too: "knowing, brothers beloved by God, your election"; "we ought always to give thanks for you, brothers beloved by the Lord, because God chose you..." (I Thess. 1:4; II Thess. 2:13). In such passages we see the same underlying thought. God wills to love men and he loves according to his own purpose of election, not according to the actions of men.

Sometimes the outcome of God's sovereign love is the main idea as the writer contemplates the impossibility of anyone resisting God's purposes. Perhaps the outstanding passage illustrating this idea is the one in which Paul assures the Romans that "in all these things we are more than conquerors through him who loved us." He goes on to maintain that there is no force that "will be able to separate us from the love of God which is in Christ Jesus our Lord" (Rom. 8:37, 39).[85] God's love triumphs.

THE PERFECTING OF LOVE

God's love has its effects. We have just noticed that it means triumph, a triumph sometimes expressed in the life the beloved believer lives here and now.[86] "Truly the love of God is perfected in anyone who keeps his word" (I John 2:5). This

---

[84]Cf. John Murray: "Israel are both 'enemies' and 'beloved' at the same time, enemies as regards the gospel, beloved as regards the election. This contrast means that by their rejection of the gospel they [had] been cast away and the gospel had been given to the Gentiles, but that nevertheless by reason of election and on account of their relation to the fathers they were beloved" (*The Epistle to the Romans,* II, 100f.).

[85]Charles Hodge exults in the security that this promises: "How wonderful, how glorious, how secure is the gospel! Those who are in Christ Jesus are as secure as the love of God, the merit, power, and intercession of Christ can make them. They are hedged around with mercy. They are enclosed in the arms of everlasting love" (*The Epistle to the Romans,* p. 293).

[86]"Love alone discovers and possesses the highest good that is in all things human and Divine.... To love the least of our brethren is to enrich the soul from the treasury of God. To love is to live" (Robert Law, *The Tests of Life,* Edinburgh, 1909, p. 240).

does not mean that men may keep God's commandments in their own way and receive perfect love from God as a reward. It means rather that God's love is primary. When it reaches men it not only brings them safety from eternal loss, but enables them to be obedient here and now. Clearly, this love does not leave people unchallenged or unchanged. This is a truth on which this writer insists again and again: "If anyone loves the world the love of the Father is not in him" (I John 2:15).[87] In this spirit the same writer asks incredulously, "Whoever has this world's good and sees his brother in need and shuts up his compassion from him, how does God's love live in him?" (I John 3:17).[88] The thing is impossible: if God's love has come to a man, then he cannot be indifferent to the needs of the unfortunate.[89] His response is the evidence that God's love lives in him. The writer comes back to the thought of perfection when he says that our love for one another is the perfecting of love in us (I John 4:12).[90] We might add the point that the writer to the Hebrews quotes Scripture to show that the Son "loved righteousness and hated lawlessness" (Heb. 1:9). Clearly, it is out of love for his people that he looks for similar attitudes of love and hate in them.

John reveals another view of this perfecting when he says, "In this is love made perfect with us, that we may have confidence in the day of judgment, because as he is so are we in this world" (I John 4:17). His "in this" almost certainly refers to

---

[87]The thought is not unlike that in the sayings "No man can serve two masters" (Matt. 6:24) and "The friendship of the world is enmity with God" (James 4:4). But it is expressed in John's characteristic way.

[88]C. H. Dodd comments, "It is the willingness to surrender that which has value for our own life, to enrich the life of another" (*The Johannine Epistles*, p. 86).

[89]This is sometimes misunderstood. Thus George Orwell speaks of "the Christian pessimism, which implies a certain indifference to human misery" (*Inside the Whale and Other Essays*, Harmondsworth, 1972, p. 26). It is unfortunately true that some who profess to be Christians have manifested such indifference. But neither Orwell nor anyone else has been able to find this mentioned in the New Testament or document it as part of authentic Christianity.

[90]The genitive (*hē agapē autou*) might be subjective when the meaning would be that God's love reaches its intended target when those he loves love others. If it is objective, the meaning will be that men's love for God is complete only when they love other people.

the preceding words, which speak of the believer abiding in God and God abiding in him. When this happens, love has reached its goal. And it does this, John says, so that (*hina*) we may have confidence in the coming day. It is important that God's people not be terrified at the prospect of judgment, and God's love eliminates this fear. John adds that we are as he is in this world, which suggests that we are like Jesus when he was on earth—that we share his special designation as God's beloved.[91] John may also be suggesting that we should try to define our lives by love, as Jesus did when he was on earth.

It is this thought of the transformation love brings that is before us when we are exhorted, "Be, therefore, imitators of God, as beloved children, and walk in love even as Christ also loved us and gave himself for us" (Eph. 5:1f.). Love does not leave us as we were; it demands that we live in the spirit of selfless love. This is again the message in the instruction "Put on therefore as God's elect, holy and beloved, compassion..." (Col. 3:12). Here love is linked with election and with sanctification. All three impel the beloved to Christ-like living. A specific aspect of the Christian life is before us in the enthusiastic exclamation "God loves a cheerful giver" (II Cor. 9:7). So often our giving is done in a grudging and formal way. But if we are gripped by love, our giving is different: it becomes a joyful privilege. God's love transforms us, so that we are eager to help other people with our gifts.

Elsewhere we find the idea that the evidence of love[92] is that we keep the commandments of Christ (John 14:21). Jesus declares that "if anyone loves me he will keep my word and my Father will love him" (John 14:23). Certainly this does not mean that obedience is to be set over against love. Love inevitably leads to obedience; obedience is evidence of the presence of love.

---

[91]Cf. J. R. W. Stott: "Jesus is God's beloved Son, in whom He is well pleased; we too are God's children (cf. iii.1) and the objects of His favour. If He called and calls God 'Father,' so may we. We are 'accepted in the beloved' (Eph. 1.6); we can share His confidence towards God" (*The Epistles of John*, p. 169).

[92]"Among all other loves, charity is distinguished in the respect that it declares itself, it acts, it gives proof of itself. It cannot remain hidden in the heart. It is imperative—it is its very essence—that it reveal itself and translate itself in the most expressive fashion possible" (C. Spicq, *Charity and Liberty*, New York, 1966, p. 32).

THE BOUNDLESS LOVE OF GOD

We conclude this section of our study by going back to a few of Jesus' parables that stress the greatness of God's love for sinners. We sometimes miss the point of the parable of the Pharisee and the publican (Luke 18:9–14) because we are too ready to criticize the Pharisee. His prayer repels us: "Thank you, God, that I am not like the rest of men—extortioners, unjust, adulterers—or even like this tax-collector. I fast twice a week; I give tithes of all I get." We tend to dismiss the man, taking it for granted that he was exaggerating grossly. But the sting in the parable lies in the fact that he was being honest. His prayer was certainly in questionable taste, but what he said was true. He was not like other men. His religious observances of fasting two days each week and of faithfully giving his tithe represent an earnestness in approaching God that many of us are far from reaching. His trouble was not that he was not far enough along the road, but that he was on the wrong road altogether. He was seeking God by his own merit, trying to rise up by way of *erōs*. Unlike him, the tax-collector simply cast himself on God's grace. He struck his breast and said, "God be merciful to me, the sinner." And it was this man rather than the Pharisee who was "justified." Once more Jesus is teaching that God's love reaches out to sinful men.[93]

God's boundless love underlies the parable of the unmerciful servant (Matt. 18:23ff.). His debt was so great that he had no way of paying it—just as the sinner has no way to compensate for his unworthiness. But in the story this man was freely forgiven just as the sinner is forgiven by God's unlimited and unconditional love.

That is the wonder of it all. This is not a love familiar to mankind, one that stresses human merit, as *erōs* does. In

---

[93]A. Nygren sees this also in the parable of the sower: "The spontaneity of Christian love means that it is directly opposed to all rational computation and calculation. Agape gives and sacrifices even where rational calculation would suggest that any sacrifice was useless. Agape sows its seed in hope, even when there seem to be no grounds at all for hope. When the Sower goes forth to sow (Mark iv.3ff.) he knows that by far the greater part of the seed will be lost and yield no fruit; yet he takes no account of that, but sows broadcast in the carefree manner of love. The spirit of Agape breathes through this Parable" (*Agape and Eros*, pp. 90f.). Nygren's main point will stand even if we do not agree that the main part of the seed will be lost.

agapē God takes the initiative. He loves with a love that springs from his own nature. It is not a love won by something attractive that he has found in us; it is a love that proceeds from the fact that God is who he is. He loves because he is love.

> *I stand all amazed at the love Jesus offers me,*
> *Confused at the grace that so freely he proffers me.*
> *I tremble to know that for me he was crucified,*
> *That for me, a sinner, he suffered, he bled, he died.*
> *O it is wonderful, wonderful to me.*

CHAPTER EIGHT

Love is Creative

THERE is something profoundly disturbing about *agapē*. No one can ever be quite the same after seeing what love really means. This is not the case with *erōs*. As long as we see love as some form of *erōs* we may surrender to it or resist it. We may find it worth pursuing, or we may prefer not to give ourselves over to its passionate embrace.

But *agapē* is different. To come to see that God's love is a deep, warm love—a love constantly lavished on us quite irrespective of our merits, a love that cost the cross—is to reach a turning point. It is impossible to experience this love and remain unchanged. A man may respond to it with all his being, saying, in effect, "This is tremendous. Deep down this is what I have always wanted." He will then open his heart to God's love and respond with an answering love. On the other hand, he may reject this self-sacrificing love, thus joining the succession of those who put Christ on the cross. What he cannot do is remain neutral. Attempting to remain neutral in the face of such love is itself a rejection, for love like this cries out to be received.

Notice how it operates in the best-known text in the entire Bible: "God so loved the world," we read, "that he gave his only Son so that everyone who believes in him should not perish but have life eternal" (John 3:16). Here is *agapē*, God's gift to a world of sinners who were ready to perish. The gift is not made to any meritorious group, to those who love God or who lead good lives or who worship devoutly. God's love is for "the world."[1]

---

[1]Cf. R. Schnackenburg: "The plan of salvation which is realized in the way of the Son of Man through the Cross into glory, stems ultimately only from God's incomprehensible love for the 'world,' that is, for the world of men, which is estranged from him, bereft of divine life and the object of his anger (cf. v. 36)" (*The Gospel accord-*

165

We rejoice in this, the most wonderful thing that God does for us. What we do not always stop to consider is that John immediately goes on to show that this love divides men. "God did not send the Son into the world to condemn the world," John writes, "but that the world should be saved through him" (v. 17). Salvation, not condemnation, is the divine purpose, but John goes on to point out the separation that love inevitably brings about: "He who believes in him is not condemned;[2] he who does not believe has been condemned already because he has not believed in the name of the only Son of God" (v. 18). Clearly judgment is involved here, a judgment that divides men. The man who responds to God's love has nothing to fear. But also possible is that a man may be condemned already. John's perfect tense indicates that he is talking about a condemnation that has already taken place. Here he is not referring to the future judgment he speaks of elsewhere. Here his point is that the man has already passed judgment on himself.[3] He goes on to say, "This is the condemnation, that the light has come into the world and men loved the darkness rather than the light because their works were evil" (v. 19). Such a man suffers continuing condemnation because he lives in a continuing state of unbelief. John is talking about a present reality, not saying that the man will one day be judged because he loved darkness. To love darkness *is* the judgment, the condemnation. The man is offered entrance into the light, the enjoyment of blessing and love and fellowship with God. But because he chooses darkness instead, he must accept its consequences.

Paul speaks of people who "did not receive the love of the

---

ing to St. John, I, New York, 1968, 398); "The 'world' is not simply the place where men live, but sinful mankind which has turned away from God" (p. 399).

[2]Here is a dilemma: whether to translate *krinō* as "judge" or "condemn." I have opted for "condemn" because the context seems to show that this is in mind here. It should be borne in mind that John does not use the verb *katakrinō*. We must expect accordingly that *krinō* will sometimes have the meaning "condemn."

[3]"How can death result from a choice set before men by the God whose love gave his only begotten Son in order that all who believe might live?... John's answer to this is to reassert that God's act is one of love, and of universal benignity. The condemnation to perish is not the act of God, which is simply the giving of his only Son. Condemnation does not follow from God's action, but from man's" (John Marsh, *The Gospel of St. John,* Harmondsworth, 1968, p. 183).

truth so that they should be saved" (II Thess. 2:10). Here, as in a number of places, we should bear in mind that the New Testament writers closely link truth with Jesus. He is the truth (John 14:6) and truth is in him (Eph. 4:21). From another point of view "the truth of Christ" is in Paul (II Cor. 11:10). There is a reference to "the truth of the gospel" (Gal. 2:5), and "the word of truth" is equated with "the gospel of your salvation" (Eph. 1:13). Thus the rejection of "the love of the truth" must be understood as a rejection of God and of what God has done in the Gospel. God looked for love in men to whom the Gospel came, but found none. *Agapē* means that God offers the world the love of the cross and never withdraws it—but that does not mean that all men will be saved. There are always those men who will reject God's love, preferring their comfortable sins and their selfishness.

True love is not simple and soothing like a lullaby; it is demanding. To see love for what it is—the reckless self-giving so wonderfully shown on Calvary—is to realize that selfishness is not an option.[4] No one can persist in seeking the best for himself while he keeps before him what Christ has done for him on Calvary. Love does not mean that there is no judgment; love guarantees judgment, because it points up the ugliness of sin like nothing else does. Sin against one's fellowman or against oneself is bad enough, but sin against the sacrificial love of God is infinitely worse. The man who spurns the love he sees on Calvary writes a damning judgment against himself.

TRANSFORMING LOVE

In this study, however, we are primarily interested in those who welcome God's love, not those who reject it. When we open our hearts to God's love, we discover that love is creative. It takes us, loveless and selfish as we are, and re-makes us.[5] It re-makes us so that to some extent we who are the

---

[4]C. E. Raven speaks of "a love that is both utterly sensitive and utterly sincere, a love devoid alike of all power to hate the wrongdoer and of all condoning of the wrong" (*Jesus and the Gospel of Love*, London, 1931, p. 274).

[5]Cf. Emil Brunner: "God's fire sets our hearts aflame. We cannot be touched by the fire of God's love without ourselves being set afire with the same love" (*Faith, Hope, and Love*, London, 1957, p. 74).

recipients of God's love come to see other people as God sees them, as those for whom Christ died. We begin to love not because it has been our good fortune to come across a particularly attractive lot of people, but because in our own limited way we have become loving people. The more fully we respond to God's love, the more fully we show love. When we respond wholeheartedly, love becomes the basis of all of our living. We are then "rooted and founded in love" (Eph. 3:17).[6] With Paul we can say, "The love of Christ constrains us" (II Cor. 5:14).[7]

This is not a human achievement. "We love, because he first loved us" (I John 4:19). Left to ourselves, we do not know the kind of love of which the New Testament speaks. We know several kinds of *erōs* and some other loves like *philia* and *storgē,* but only Calvary enables us to know what *agapē* means. Only there do we come to understand a little of "the breadth and length and height and depth and to know the love of Christ that passes knowledge" (Eph. 3:18f.). It is only

---

[6]It is possible to take "love" with the preceding to mean "that Christ may dwell through faith in your hearts in love . . . in order that having your roots and foundations firm . . ." (so F. R. Barry says in *A Philosophy from Prison,* London, 1935, pp. 86f.). But most agree that love is to be taken as the root and foundation of the Christian life. R. W. Dale sees this meaning in this passage: "Love will not be an intermittent impulse, or even a constant force struggling for its rightful supremacy over baser passions; its authority will be secure; it will be the law of their whole nature; it will be the very life of their life" (*The Epistle to the Ephesians,* London, 1900, p. 250).

[7]Cf. P. E. Hughes: "The great compelling motive force in his life since conversion is that of love; not, however, love originating, far less ending, in himself, but the love which originates and ends with God in Christ. His conduct, however it be judged, is dictated by the love of Christ (not so much his love for Christ—though that inevitably is involved—as Christ's love for him, which is prior to and the explanation of his love for Christ, and which is supremely manifested, as is clear from what immediately follows, in Christ's atoning sacrifice of Himself for mankind). It is this love (*agape*) and none other that shuts him in, confines him as between two walls, to one purpose which may be summed up in the terms of the preceding verse as being to live selflessly 'unto God' and, within the framework of that supreme allegiance, to his fellow-men ('unto you')" (*Paul's Second Epistle to the Corinthians,* London, 1962, p. 192).

through God's transforming love that we are able to love.[8] As Ethelbert Stauffer puts it, Jesus

> proclaims and creates a new world situation. He proclaims the mercy of God, not as a disposition which God always and in all possible ways expresses—pardonner, c'est son métier—but as an unheard of event which has the basis of its possibility in God alone, but which now places man in a completely different situation. Jesus brings forgiveness of sins, and in those who experience it a new and overflowing love is released.[9]

The New Testament does not say in specific terms that God's love "creates" love, but this is surely its meaning. When God's love comes to anyone, it creates an answering love that spills over into love for one's fellowmen. This love for man is emphasized in the New Testament, but we should not overlook the all-important call to love God.

LOVE FOR GOD

The first and great commandment is that we love the Lord our God with all our heart (Matt. 22:37, etc.). The Pharisees are censured for passing over "judgment and the love of God" (Luke 11:42). Similarly, people who love God only with their lips are blamed (Mark 7:6). Men should love God truly, not demean that love with shallow responses or a vain concern with appearances. The consequences of a heartfelt love for God are

---

[8]Emil Brunner points out that *agapē* is "unmotivated love," which poses the question "What is its origin?" He goes on, "The answer that the New Testament gives is that the origin of this paradoxical love is God. You *can* love so only because God makes you love, by his love. Therefore we have to speak of God's love in order to understand *agape*" (*Faith, Hope, and Love*, p. 65).

[9]*TDNT*, I, 47. For "released" I would prefer "created"; this kind of love is never regarded as pent-up in man and simply awaiting an outlet. Cf. T. W. Manson: "A new power has come into human life from heaven, a new insight into life is ours, a new attitude to God and man has become part of our nature. And what effects this change is the love of God. Love is no longer a laborious business of doing the right thing by your neighbour: it is a new spirit in which you approach him and it finds out its own way of treating him" (*On Paul and John*, London, 1963, p. 106).

great; indeed, "for those who love God he works all things together for good" (Rom. 8:28).[10] In a similar way Paul writes to the Corinthians of the things "which God has prepared for those who love him" (I Cor. 2:9). Later in the same epistle this idea takes an interesting twist. Pointing out that love builds men up, Paul proceeds, "If anyone thinks he knows something, he does not yet know as he ought to know; but if anyone loves God, _____." We expect him to finish this thought by saying something like "he has real knowledge." Instead, Paul says, "this man is known by him" (I Cor. 8:1–3). In other words, it is God's knowledge of man that matters, not man's knowledge of God. Notice further that Paul is speaking not of God's knowledge of all men but of his knowledge of the man who loves him—something very special. As Herman Ridderbos puts it, it "refers to the gracious and loving electing act of God; 'to be known' by him in this way means the same as to have been chosen by him and loved by him. . . . This divine love works itself out in the love of those known by him. Therefore the love of the church is a gift of God."[11]

It is interesting that Paul rarely speaks of man's love for God. It may be significant that while he quotes the command to love the neighbor (Rom. 13:9), he does not quote the command to love God with all one's heart. He does frequently mention God's love for man, but among human responses the one that most interests him is love for our fellowmen.[12] When he refers to the Christians' attitude toward God, he prefers to speak of faith. Faith is our trustful response to what God has done in

---

[10]The words may be understood as "all things work together for good" (so the AV has it). But it is unlikely that Paul is thinking of things as somehow cooperating. It is God who brings about the good of which he writes, even if "all things" be held to be the subject of the verb.

[11]Paul, Grand Rapids, 1975, p. 294.

[12]C. Spicq holds, though, that "the early Gospel catechesis united the two loves so intimately that to mention one always implied the other." He sees "the entire 'moral section'" of Romans as governed by the opening words of chapter 12, which refer to offering a sacrifice "pleasing to God" (Agape in the New Testament, II, St. Louis and London, 1965, 58); "Although the love of God is not mentioned in these two texts (i.e., Rom. 13:8–10 and Gal. 5:14), nevertheless it remains the soul, the source, and the end of fraternal love" (p. 98). Even if this is accepted, it is still true that Pauline usage emphasizes love for man, not for God.

Christ. It is not love, but it is a companion of love; indeed, Paul often links the two. Clearly, he thinks both are necessary, and does not regard faith as a preferred alternative. Paul frequently declares the Christian message by speaking of people as believing in God and loving their fellowmen. But we should not then overlook the fact that Paul does on occasion refer to love for God (e.g., Rom. 8:28; I Cor. 2:9).[13] Faith is certainly characteristic, but love's warmth and wholeheartedness are also important. The two responses must unite and reinforce each other if the believer is to respond appropriately to God's love.

James says that God has promised "the crown of life" to those who love him (James 1:12), and says again, later on, that God has promised these people "the kingdom" (James 2:5). Neither of these good gifts is spelled out, but clearly the writer holds that God blesses those who love him. Similarly, the writer to the Hebrews assures his correspondents that "God is not unrighteous to forget your work and the love which you have showed for his name" (Heb. 6:10). What God will do as a result of this remembrance the writer does not say, but clearly he, like James, looks for blessing.

In none of these latter passages is the writer concerned to bring out the idea that men must love God. In each case he assumes this love as fact and is more concerned with its consequences. But we should not miss the implication that love for God is expected, as it is by all biblical writers.

Love for Christ is of course an element here, because the New Testament doesn't strongly differentiate between loving God and loving Christ, which is made plain in passages like John 14:21. There Christ declares that "he who loves me will be loved by my Father." Ephesians finishes with a prayer that "grace" be with those who love Christ (Eph. 6:24). We read that love for Christ brings joy when Christ goes to the Father (John 14:28); that people who have God for their Father love Christ (John 8:42); that this influences their conduct, because those who love him must keep his commandments (John 14:15, 21, 23). By contrast, anyone who does not love him does not

---

[13]"Although Paul does most frequently speak of man's response as faith, there are several references, some of them of crucial importance, to man's love for God"; "the word 'faith' obviously does not express the fulness of man's love to God" (Walter Harrelson, *JR*, XXXI, 1951, 175). For a discussion of the relationship of the two terms, see below, pp. 189f.

keep his words and is reminded that his word is that of the Father (John 14:24). The importance of loving Christ is obvious here—as it is elsewhere. For example, Peter was asked about his love for Jesus and repeatedly affirmed it (John 21:15–17). And in his first epistle he refers appreciatively to those who have not seen Jesus but who love him nonetheless (I Pet. 1:8).

LOVE FOR PEOPLE

Throughout the New Testament the believers' love for their fellowmen is emphasized. This thought is particularly stressed in I John. We understand the essence of love not through our love for God, but through his love for us (I John 4:10). The love of God shown on the cross impels us to love one another (I John 4:11). In fact, John cannot recognize a love for God that is not shown in love for our fellowman (I John 4:20).[14] It is God's commandment that the man who loves God love his brother, too (I John 4:21);[15] indeed, love to God and love to men and the keeping of God's commandments are all wrapped up together (I John 5:12). This insistence on love for our fellowmen is a salutary reminder of what love means. Of course, we are all prepared to love God in a nebulous, "spiritual" way, because that is a love that no one really knows about other than ourselves. It is only as demanding as we are prepared to let it be, and it cannot be tested in practice. But love for our neighbor is quite another thing. It is tremendously demanding, requiring of us all kinds of service, much of which we naturally do not like and would rather not perform. And this love can be tested: it is obvious to all whether or not

[14]Cf. A. E. Brooke: The love "which He has called out in us must find an object. If it fails to find out the nearer object, it will never reach the further" (*A Critical and Exegetical Commentary on the Johannine Epistles,* New York, 1912, pp. 125f.).

[15]Cf. V. P. Furnish: "When the double commandment of the Synoptic tradition is invoked in vs. 21, but using the word 'brother' instead of 'neighbor,' the conclusion to be drawn is not that this writer is thereby limiting love's scope. The more accurate conclusion is that, for this writer, the term 'brother' can be used as a synonym for 'neighbor,' and that in I John there is indeed some specific acknowledgment of one's responsibility to love all men" (*The Love Commandment in the New Testament,* Nashville and New York, 1972, p. 154).

we engage in acts of love and service to others. In short: we commend the gospel and the Lord who made the gospel possible not by some secret love that we say we have for God, but by what we do, by the open way in which we show love for our neighbor.

By contrast, those who have not "the love of God" in them are condemned (John 5:42). It is possible to interpret this as referring either to God's love for man or man's love for God. The context seems to favor the latter, but we should bear in mind the discussion by E. A. Abbott in which the grammatical points at issue are examined closely and the conclusion is reached that the meaning is "the love that God gives to man," "the love *that proceeds from God*."[16] It is human love, but not love of human origin. The passage is to be added to those that look for men to respond to God's love by showing love for their fellows.

The derivative nature of our love is brought out emphatically in the First Epistle of John. We have already noticed that John says plainly, "We love, because he first loved us" (I John 4:19). F. D. Maurice makes an insightful comment on this verse:

> Let no one cheat you of the simple force of these words by persuading you to understand the Apostle as saying that we love God out of *gratitude* for the love He shows to us. Some ethical writers are wont to talk much of the motives, to which, they say, man's nature is subjected; this motive of gratitude, they affirm, is one of the chief. I do not wish to argue the point with them; but I say they have no right to impute these notions to the Apostle, to make him put *motives* in the place of *God*. And which is the most elevating doctrine, theirs or St. John's? *They* would make me the slave of a certain set of influences which I feel I ought to control. *He* represents God as acting upon me that I may be free....[17]

---

[16]*Johannine Grammar*, London, 1906, pp. 84–89. Douglas N. Morgan says, "Plainly this Biblical teaching is that love must radiate back toward God from men, just as it has come down toward men from God" (*Love: Plato, the Bible and Freud*, Englewood Cliffs, N.J., 1964, p. 107).

[17]*The Epistles of St. John*, London, 1881, p. 245 (Maurice's italics). Similarly, Robert S. Candlish says, "'We love.' It is not merely that we have a natural faculty of loving, and exercise it by letting it go forth on things and persons naturally attractive to us. But

We should clearly understand this point. John is not speaking of our love as an imitation of what we see in God, nor is he referring to gratitude or some kindred emotion. He is saying that God's love is creative: it produces its like in believers.

This is all of a piece with the way the New Testament writers see the Christian life. Christians have been born again (John 3:5, 7f.), they have been converted (Matt. 18:3), they have been buried with Christ in baptism so that they walk in newness of life (Rom. 6:4); their old selves been crucified (Rom. 6:6), and they have put off their old natures (Eph. 4:22; Col. 3:9). They have been crucified with Christ (Gal. 2:19) and raised with him (Col. 3:1); they live by faith in the Son of God (Gal. 2:20). They have put on the new man (Eph. 4:24; Col. 3:10); they have been renewed in the spirit of their mind (Eph. 4:23; cf. Rom. 12:2). And there is much more. The New Testament envisages a thoroughgoing change when people become Christians, a change brought about by the power of God within them.[18] The first part of the fruit the Spirit produces is wholehearted love (Gal. 5:22). Paul points out that "the love of Christ constrains us" (II Cor. 5:14), and goes on to refer to the cross. The cross shows us the self-sacrificing love that has made us Christians, the kind of love that is looked for from us.[19] This kind of love is not the achievement of the natural

---

we have now a divine faculty of loving; we love with the love which is of God; which is God's very nature" (*The First Epistle of John*, II, Edinburgh, 1870, 156f.; he goes on to speak of loving persons "as they are attractive, not to us, but to him"; I do not think that attractiveness of the persons loved comes into it, but the stress Candlish puts on loving with the love which comes from God is welcome).

[18]Karl Barth says of I Corinthians 13, "The unique feature of this chapter is that Paul here really ventures to make man the subject of predicates, from which the inference immediately suggests itself: here is another man, a new creature; 'the old is passed away, behold the new is come' (2 Cor. v.17)" (*The Resurrection of the Dead*, New York, 1933, p. 87).

[19]Cf. C. Spicq; "To love (*agapan*) and to die (*apothnēiskein*) are one and the same thing.... By nature an active and manifest love, *agape* finds its proper means of expression in Jesus' example: to die to self as Christ died for God and his brothers" (*Agape in the New Testament*, II, 315); "*Agape* is an heroic virtue which implies complete sacrifice of self for the sake of others and corresponds exactly to God's profuse gift of love" (p. 113).

man. True, the natural man feels certain kinds of love, but *agapē*, love as the New Testament writers understand it, is not among them. It is brought about in man by God himself, a most important part of the transformation that turns a worldly man into a Christian.[20]

CREATIVE LOVE IN I JOHN

The thought that God's love is creative runs through I John 4. John addresses his readers here as "Beloved" (I John 4:7), a term about which Karl Barth says, "In this passage we cannot explain the fact that they are called *agapētoi* merely as a convention of rhetoric. Those who are exhorted to love are already loved (above all by God), and in respect of what they are to do they are urged and claimed on this basis."[21] John goes on to say, "Love is of God," clearly indicating that love is of heavenly—not earthly—origin.[22] John proceeds, "Everyone who loves has been begotten of God and knows God." The presence of this kind of love in a man is evidence that God has been at work in him. He has been "begotten" of God. Like the "new birth" teaching of John 3, this passage brings out the

---

[20]The connection of *agapē* with newness of life is sometimes overlooked. Thus M. C. D'Arcy criticizes Nygren because he "thinks that only by divine Agape can the soul be unselfish." D'Arcy proceeds, "It would seem more likely that below the divine Agape there is to be found a movement in the anima which balances the egocentric and centripetal urge by a centrifugal love which carries it beyond what reason can clearly delineate" (*The Mind and Heart of Love*, London, 1962, p. 265). This location of love somewhere in the human anima is not the New Testament teaching. That is rather that we do not know what *agapē* is until we see the cross. It is not a question of whether the soul can be unselfish in the way Nygren says or not, but rather of what the New Testament means by *agapē*. D'Arcy does not give sufficient attention to the cross. He does, it is true, refer to the cross from time to time (e.g., p. 324). But he does not make it the decisive thing; the New Testament does.

[21]*Church Dogmatics*, IV, 2, Edinburgh, 1958, 754.

[22]Cf. J. R. W. Stott: "Because God is the source and origin (*ek*) of love and all true love derives from Him, it stands to reason that *everyone that loveth*, that is, loves either God or man with that selfless devotion which alone is true love according to John's teaching, *is* (literally, has been) *born of God, and knoweth God*" (*The Epistles of John*, London, 1966, p. 160).

truth that *agapē* is divinely inspired.[23] John brings out the same thought by putting it negatively: "He who does not love does not know God, because God is love" (v. 8). It follows from what has been said and also from the fact that God is love that anyone who is not displaying this characteristic does not know God. How can a man possibly know God, who is love, when he displays no love in his own life? If he really knew God, he would have experienced the miracle of love.

From this John proceeds to associate life and love with the cross. As ever, he can recognize love only from the cross: "The love of God was manifested among us in this, that God sent his only Son into the world so that we should live through him. In this is love, not that we loved God but that he loved us and sent his Son as the propitiation for our sins. Beloved, if God so loved us, we too ought to love one another" (vv. 9-11). First, John brings out the incarnation and mission: God sent his Son into the world. Our life as Christians is derived from this, because we are dependent on what God has done in Christ. Next, John stresses the display of love on the cross, where we see expressed both the fact of God's love and its meaning. We should possibly see in the aorist tense a glance at the once-and-for-all act of love on the cross, an act that is central. For John it is crystal clear that we would not know love at all were it not for that great act of propitiation.[24] As John has been writing about knowing God, he has had sinful men in mind. But the reference to propitiation makes it clear

---

[23]Cf. A. E. Brooke: "The true nature of love cannot be appreciated unless it is recognized that its origin must be sought beyond human nature" (*A Critical and Exegetical Commentary on the Johannine Epistles*, p. 118). B. F. Westcott sees the negative clause in v. 10 ("not that we loved God") as "brought forward to emphasize the thought of man's inability to originate love" (*The Epistles of St. John*, Cambridge and London, 1892, p. 150).

[24]Cf. I. Howard Marshall: "This is what God has done for rebellious mankind: he pardons their sins against himself at his own cost. To remove this element from the biblical teaching on the nature of God's love is to water down the concept of love beyond measure. It is true that some writers have denied that a loving God needs to be propitiated for human sin and have suggested that this makes him less than loving. They have not realized that the depth of God's love is to be seen precisely in the way in which it bears the wounds inflicted on it by mankind and offers full and free pardon" (*The Epistles of John*, Grand Rapids, 1978, p. 215).

that he is not thinking of a God who is ready to condone anything. God's integrity is such that he takes sin seriously; his
whole nature is antagonistic to it. The fact that he loves so
deeply means that he is necessarily opposed to all that is evil in
the beloved, to all that degrades them and causes suffering.
Precisely because he loves them he will be angry with them.

John sees the cross as the expression of a love that takes
wrath seriously. He does not work out a theory of atonement,
but what he says must enter into our theories if they are to be
at all satisfactory. That Jesus is the propitiation for our sins
means that God's forgiveness goes hand-in-hand with his
wrath against evil, which is taken seriously and not overlooked
in sentimental fashion. It is important to see that John is talking
about love, not sentimentality. In modern times we do not
always observe the distinction.

From this John moves to the obligation that rests on those
so loved to love one another (v. 11). Once again he sees our
love as flowing from the love with which God has loved us—
clearly not a human achievement.[25] In verse 12 he brings out
this idea from another point of view. It is axiomatic that nobody has seen God, but men sometimes look for visions: they
seek God through mysticism. At times in the history of the
Christian church believers have stressed the importance of a
mystical love for Christ. With this emphasis quasi-spiritual
emotionalism can develop, characterized by a deep piety of an
otherworldly kind. But this is not what the New Testament
teaches. We find God not through mysticism but through love.
As James Moffatt puts it, "The organic tie between love for
Christ and love for fellow-Christians precludes the idea that
one comes nearer to the Lord by sinking into the depths of
oneself in subconscious reverie or rapture than by the activities of service towards those whom Christ loves."[26] Those

---

[25]"A person cannot come into a real relationship with a loving
God without being transformed into a loving person. John does not
explain how this transformation comes about. He speaks of it as an
obligation in verse 11, but he also implies that the love of God takes
control of our natures and transforms us" (I. Howard Marshall, *The
Epistles of John*, p. 212).

[26]*Love in the New Testament*, London, 1932, p. 278. Moffatt
goes on, "In fact, the entire Johannine theology of love, in this aspect,
is an equivalent to the conception in Paul and others of covenant
(*diathēkē*)—i.e., of a bond involving a relationship to the Lord which

activities of loving service are of primary importance. When we cease seeking some beatific vision and concentrate on the business of loving our brothers, we find that God lives in us and fills us with love.

This section of John's letter is a sustained argument that develops his point that God's love produces changes in believers. To respond to God's love means to become loving people. John comes back to this idea a little later when he points out that we (emphatic, meaning we Christians, not men in general) have known and believed the love God has in us.[27] He goes on, "God is love, and he who abides in love abides in God and God abides in him" (v. 16). When God's love reaches us, he dwells in us and we dwell in him. This means that we never get away from love, that we never cease to be loving people. If God lives within us, how can it be otherwise?

NO LOVE, NO LIFE

Elsewhere John brings out the same truth by considering some negatives. He says, for example, that "he who does not love abides in death" (I John 3:14).[28] The fact that he shows no love is enough to prove that he is dead. Now throughout his epistle John presupposes that life is the gift of God, so it follows that when God gives the gift of life, the gift of love follows. Thus John asks of the man who has this world's goods and refuses to help a brother in need, "How does the love of God abide in him?" (I John 3:17). Clearly, the reasoning is that if God's love were in him, he would love other men. This idea

---

is created by His actions of grace in the history of the People; these actions are shown to run up into a climax in the revelation of Jesus the Christ, whereby the People are awakened to the full meaning and value of life, the source and standard of which is the divine love with its claim for reciprocal love and its manifestations of the sphere in which that love finds an adequate expression."

[27]Or, "among us" (*en hēmin*). John may be referring to God's love in sending his Son to be among men.

[28]James Moffatt cites Voltaire's comment on the Jesuits and the Jansenists, who contended "for a century which party loved God most suitably, and which could most effectively harass and torment the other" (*Love in the New Testament*, p. 300). Unfortunately, Christians have too often left such an impression. Vigorous advocacy of a cause is part of the Christian way, but it is no substitute for love.

is a sequel to one of John's great sayings about love: "In this we know love, that he laid down his life for us; and we ought to lay down our lives for the brothers" (I John 3:16). That is a big demand. But to be loved with the love of Calvary inspires in us a deep, self-sacrificing love, not the tepid, insipid sentimentality we so often think is love. To be a Christian means to be ready to sacrifice everything, because love's demand is total. But John is practical. He knows that a man may easily declare himself ready to lay down his life for others, because words are cheap, and such a sacrifice is unlikely to be required. What he demands is not this heroic gesture, but a daily sharing of what one has with those who have not.[29] Taking thought for the day-to-day needs of people in want is a duty John sees as a necessary consequence of the cross. The cross shows us what *agapē* is: a readiness not only to die for others but to live for others. Love is not a fragile treasure to be tucked away securely somewhere; it is a robust virtue to be practiced in everyday life.

The divine origin of love is indicated by these words: "Everyone who believes that Jesus is the Christ has been begotten of God, and everyone who loves the parent loves the child" (I John 5:1). The believer owes his position not to anything he has done, but to the fact that God has begotten him. From this thought John immediately proceeds to the fact that the believer loves—because God's creative love is at work in him. This is apparent also in references to love as being "perfected in us" (I John 2:5; 4:12, 17).[30] It is as we love that what God intends for us is realized. We should probably discern a similar thought when we read, "Look what kind of love the Father has given us, that we should be called God's children; and we are" (I John 3:1). All that this means has not yet been realized (v. 2), but what is certain is that we are sharers in the love about which this epistle says so much.

---

[29]Cf. I. Howard Marshall: "The need of the world is not for heroic acts of martyrdom, but for heroic acts of material sacrifice. If I am a well-off Christian, while others are poor, I am not acting as a true Christian" (*The Epistles of John*, pp. 195f.).

[30]The verb "perfected" is *teleioō*, which denotes reaching the end or aim (*telos*). It means perfection in the sense of having reached the end for which a person or thing is destined. See p. 161, n. 90 above for a consideration of the genitive as subjective or objective.

THE NEW COMMANDMENT

This idea is also apparent in the Fourth Gospel, though it is not dwelt on there as it is in the First Epistle. "If God were your Father," Jesus says to the Jews who did not accept him, "you would love me" (John 8:42; cf. 5:42). Obvious here is the relationship between God's working in men and men's living in love.[31] The Jews claimed that God was their Father (v. 41). If that were the case, Jesus retorts, you would love, because the two go together. This is also the point of his "new commandment" to his followers: "that you love one another; that you love one another as I have loved you" (John 13:34; cf. 15:12).[32] Jesus' love for them (which is not differentiated from God's love for them) leads to love for one another. This may be the point of the keeping of the commandments, which means abiding in Christ's love (John 15:10). Jesus himself suggested this relationship in his discourse in the upper room, in which he repeatedly links love for the Lord and the keeping of his commandments (John 14:15, 21, 23, 24). Indeed, in I John love for God may be equated with keeping his commandments (I John 5:3). What does love mean if one ignores what God wants one to do?

In a most instructive incident Jesus talks with Peter by the lake, asking three times whether that disciple loves him (John 21:15–17). Discussions often center on the fact that twice Jesus uses the verb *agapaō* in his question, to be met each time by Peter's use of *phileō* in his answer. Then in the third question Jesus uses Peter's word and the apostle retains it in his reply. But the significant thing is surely not so much the variation in the verb,[33] but the fact that Jesus is speaking about love at all.

---

[31]Cf. Sir Edwyn Hoskyns: "The love between Christians is itself to testify to the fact that they have been called into being by Him whose disciples they are" (*The Fourth Gospel*, London, 1961, p. 451).

[32]J. N. Sanders comments that what makes the commandment new "is the fact that Jesus chose it as the one necessary and sufficient principle to guide his disciples" (*A Commentary on the Gospel according to St. John*, edited and completed by B. A. Mastin, London, 1968, p. 317).

[33]I have discussed the point in *The Gospel according to John*, Grand Rapids, 1971, pp. 870ff., and have come to the conclusion that the variation is a stylistic one, not one of meaning. See also John A. Cross, *The Expositor*, IV, 7, 1893, 312–20; W. G. Ballantine, *Bibliotheca Sacra*, XLVI, 1889, 524–42, etc.

Peter's position of leadership in the apostolic band must have been at least dubious in the light of his threefold denial of Jesus. This incident, in which Peter three times affirms his love for his Lord in the presence of the other apostles, must be seen as a reinstatement. Three times Jesus commissions Peter to feed the sheep or the lambs, thus ensuring his position. But in doing so Jesus does not ask him about his faith or his courage or his ability to lead or anything of the sort. The one question that matters in this situation is the question of love.

Taught by God

Paul is no member of the Johannine school; he has his own ideas. But the idea expressed in John that love comes from God is taught in a number of places in the Pauline corpus. Paul is sure that the Thessalonian Christians have no need to be told to love each other, "for you yourselves are taught by God to love one another" (I Thess. 4:9). It is God—not Paul nor any of the other preachers—who has produced love within the Thessalonians. Later on Paul again refers to the divine origin of love in a prayer he offers for the same group of Christians: "Now the Lord direct your hearts into the love of God and into the steadfastness of Christ" (II Thess. 3:5). Here, as in a number of places, it is not easy to be sure whether "the love of God" means "your love for God" or "God's love for you." Many commentators see here a combination of the two—as I do, in fact: "If we may accept this, then the primary idea will be that of God's love to us, but there will be also the secondary idea of our love to Him. Paul's prayer, then, will be that the inner life of his friends be so concentrated on God's love for them that this will evoke an answering love for Him."[34]

A similar idea might be in mind in at least some of the references to election. Election proceeds from the love of God (I Thess. 1:4; II Thess. 2:13), but it also leads to love. Thus we read that God "chose us in him before the foundation of the world, so that we should be holy and blameless before him in love" (Eph. 1:4).[35] Clearly, love is at least part of the object of

---

[34]Leon Morris, *The First and Second Epistles to the Thessalonians,* Grand Rapids, 1959, pp. 249f.

[35]It is, of course, possible to take "in love" with the preceding "he chose us" or with the following "predestined." But most agree that "he chose us" is too far away. The connection with "predestined" is taken seriously by a number of scholars, and certainly this

the choosing. God produces love in his elect; it is certainly not their own achievement.

Certain passages relate love to the Spirit.[36] When Paul is listing the qualities he sees as "the fruit of the Spirit," he begins with love (Gal. 5:22). Again, Timothy is reminded that God "did not give us a spirit of cowardice, but of power and love..." (II Tim. 1:7). "Spirit" here may not mean "the Holy Spirit," but it is not easy to see love as other than of divine origin.[37] Similar is the reference to "your love in the Spirit" (Col. 1:8). Paul does not say explicitly that this means love that the Spirit gives, but that seems to be his meaning. He beseeches the Romans "through our Lord Jesus Christ and through the love of the Spirit" (Rom. 15:30), which may well be relevant. And there is little room for doubt when he speaks of love as "poured out in our hearts through the Holy Spirit who was given to us" (Rom. 5:5).[38] The believer cannot claim

---

linking reproduces a New Testament thought. But it does not seem to be the meaning here. The interpretation I have adopted is supported by the fact that elsewhere in this Epistle "in love" always refers to the action of believers (3:17; 4:2, 15, 16; 5:2). It is also the case that the expression "in love" goes with what precedes much more often than with what follows (3:17 appears to be the only exception). W. Hendriksen, however, takes the word with "predestined." He rejects the connection with "holy and blameless" as being "unnatural" (*New Testament Commentary, Exposition of Ephesians,* Grand Rapids, 1978, p. 79n.). Charles Hodge uses exactly the same word—"unnatural"—to characterize the connection Hendriksen favors (*A Commentary on the Epistle to the Ephesians,* Grand Rapids, 1950, p. 35); he has the further objection that it is "tautological to say: 'He hath predestined us in love according to the good pleasure of his will.'" F. Foulkes thinks that the words can be taken either way, but holds it to be more likely that they go with the preceding words: "The point, then, is that holiness of life is only made perfect in and through love" (*The Epistle of Paul to the Ephesians,* London, 1963, p. 47).

[36]This may be implied also in passages in which love is not explicitly mentioned. For example, the Ephesians are exhorted not to grieve the Spirit (Eph. 4:30). This is followed by the injunction to put away all bitterness, anger, and the like. Clearly, the kind of conduct that grieves the Spirit is unloving conduct.

[37]M. Dibelius refers here to "the charismatic virtues of strength and love, which are effected by the spirit" (*The Pastoral Epistles,* Philadelphia, 1972, pp. 98f.).

[38]Some have seen the meaning as "poured out in our hearts by a holy spirit that was given to us" (C. Spicq, *Agape in the New Testament,* II, 227).

credit for being loving. The more genuinely he loves, the more certainly he knows that this is a work of God in him and not any work of his own.[39]

Love is the very basis of the Christian life, for Christians are "rooted and founded in love" (Eph. 3:17). Love is both soil and rock, the root from which everything grows, the foundation on which everything is built.[40] This verse is yet another indication that the love in question comes from God (the words quoted are from a prayer that God would grant this gift). Another phrase emphasizing love as fundamental is that which speaks of Christians as "knit together in love" (Col. 2:2).[41] The writer is referring to fundamentals, as he goes on to refer to God's "mystery"—namely, Christ. It is thus basic that Christians be united in love. Once again we see that love is the necessary product of God's saving activity.

The importance of love is underscored when it is described as more important than intellectual achievement. Paul lived in a day when many Greeks (and others) took great pride in their academic excellence. They thought knowledge was important in man's relationship to God. Paul respects knowledge and strives to help others do the same: he writes feelingly of true wisdom, and his letters are full of teaching that would help his readers become better-informed Christians. But he objects to the idea that knowledge is all-important: "We know that all

---

[39]Cf. Karl Barth: "It is in the quickening power of the Holy Spirit, and therefore in a new act of God who is man's Creator and Lord, that in his life-act and individual actions a man can actually love in the Christian sense" (*Church Dogmatics,* IV, 2, Edinburgh, 1958, 747).

[40]Rosemary Haughton says that in Paul the Law "fades into insignificance before the power of Christ, the fully realized human spirit which inspires right conduct, not out of fear or a sense of duty but out of a fiery love that leaves no trace of other considerations, however worthy" (*The Drama of Salvation,* London, 1976, p. 20). I would not have put it quite like that, but the emphasis on "fiery love" is noteworthy.

[41]C. Spicq follows the Vulgate, which has "instructed" in love, though he admits that "united" is "very plausible." He reasons from the usage in LXX, Acts, I Corinthians 2:16, and the stress on understanding and knowledge in the immediate context (*Agape in the New Testament,* II, 249). But he goes on to argue that, understood in this way, the words "are a reference to the very essence of the Christian life" (p. 250). Thus, even if this interpretation is accepted, it does not affect the point I am making.

have knowledge," he writes to the Corinthians (i.e., knowledge is not as special as some claim). He proceeds, "Knowledge puffs up but love builds up" (I Cor. 8:1). Edification is so much more important than the knowledge that engenders pride. In fact, that kind of knowledge radically contradicts the Christian way, and Paul will have none of it. Nothing must be allowed to obscure the importance of love.[42]

Other Terms

The importance of love is clear in many passages in which the word *love* does not occur. Because love is opposed to the self-seeking life, it is implied whenever the selfish way is condemned. Several times Jesus points to the dangers of selfishly "saving" one's own life. Over against it he sets "losing" one's life for his sake and that of others, which is the real way forward. This abnegation of self in serving God and others is surely another way of referring to love (Matt. 10:39; 16:25; Mark 8:35; Luke 9:24; 17:33; John 12:25).[43]

Or consider the great judgment scene in Matthew 25:31–46. The important question is whether or not men have shown love. The word is not mentioned, but it is clear that those God chose performed loving deeds, and those he condemned did not.[44]

---

[42]After citing "beloved by God" from II Thessalonians 2:13, C. Spicq says, "Without a doubt, this teaching, so little emphasized in the Synoptics, is the chief revelation St. Paul makes in the New Testament" (*Agape in the New Testament,* II, 93); he adds later, "The believer not only is made aware of this mysterious fact (i.e., that Christ in love has sacrificed himself for men), but also is actually reborn to a new life and transformed by God's active charity" (p. 100).

[43]Cf. Geddes MacGregor: "Love *is* the abdication of power"; he proceeds to cite Simone Weil: "Love consents to all and commands only those who consent. Love is abdication. God is abdication" (*He Who Lets Us Be,* New York, 1975, p. 120). I do not want to put it quite like this, but MacGregor and Weil firmly reject the self-assertive way and assure us that love is very different.

[44]V. P. Furnish sees in the passage "an unforgettable picture of what love means and of what obedience to the Great Commandment requires" (*The Love Command in the New Testament,* Nashville and New York, 1972, p. 79; I should perhaps add that Furnish disagrees with the view that the passage is "directly representative of Jesus'

Almost the entire book of Acts may be cited to make the same point. Neither the verb *agapaō* nor the noun *agapē* occurs in this book (and *agapētos* occurs only once, in Acts 15:25). But it nonetheless reveals the love of the early Christians. People were ready to sell what they had to give to the needy. Provision was made for widows (and when a dispute arose among the Greeks, seven people with Greek names were appointed to deal with the matter). From start to finish, Acts pictures a community motivated by brotherly love and reaching out in love to those outside it. In fact, it is impossible to read about the church in Acts and not see the meaning of love in action.

THE COMMAND TO LOVE

Sometimes we read that God has commanded us to love. Such a command certainly means, among other things, that God wills that his people be loving people. It is another aspect of the great truth that he produces love in them. As we have seen, he does so by his Holy Spirit[45] and by the sacrifice of Christ for them. And he does it by commanding them to love. Love is not one among several options that the Christian may choose. If anyone responds to the love of God in Christ, he is transformed into a loving person. This love is to distinguish the followers of Jesus: "A new commandment I give you, that you love one another, that you love one another as I have loved you. All men will know that you are my disciples by this, that you have love for one another" (John 13:34f.). There is, of course, a sense in which there is nothing new about the commandment to love; it has been given long ago (Lev. 19:18). But it is radically new nonetheless, because it is linked with the love that Jesus shows for the unworthy on the cross. Thus what

---

own teaching," seeing it rather as "representative of the evangelist's own viewpoint and intentions").

[45]John Burnaby quotes Augustine: "The presence in us of the Holy Spirit means that we love God 'through God' (*amemus Deum de Deo*)." He also says, "That the love of God, our love for God, is God's gift, was his final reply to the Pelagianism which saw in the Incarnation only the *demand* of God's love that we should love him in return. *Amare Deum, Dei donum est*" (*Amor Dei*, London, 1960, p. 176; the meaning of the final Latin quotation is, "To love God is the gift of God").

is new is the quality of the love that will be characteristic of his followers.[46]

The command is repeated a little later, with a significant addition: "This is my commandment, that you love one another as I have loved you. Greater love has no man than this, that a man lays down his life for his friends" (John 15·12f.). The addition about dying for others shows clearly the new element. Jesus is speaking about the kind of love he was to show on Calvary, the kind of love that he now demands from his followers. And at least in the early church people sometimes produced it. Tertullian tells us that the heathen commented on the Christians of his day: "See, they say, how they love one another."[47] Of course, sometimes this love has been far from obvious (which must cause us to search our own hearts). But there have never been times when it has not been required of us.

The command to love is a double commandment in the Synoptics, a command to love God with all one's heart, mind, soul, and strength, and to love one's neighbor as oneself (Matt. 22:37–39; Mark 12:30–31; Luke 10:27).[48] To love God is the

---

[46]Cf. W. Hendriksen: "The *newness* of the precept here promulgated is evident from the fact that Jesus requires that his disciples shall love one another *as he loved them*! His example of constant (note: *keep on loving*), self-sacrificing love (think of his incarnation, earthly ministry, death on the cross) must be the pattern for *their* attitude and relation to one another" (*New Testament Commentary: Exposition of the Gospel According to John*, II, Grand Rapids, 1970, 253).

[47]*Apol.* XXXIX. Cf. also Caecilius: "They love one another almost before they know one another" (Minucius Felix, 9; *ANF,* IV, 177; the words are intended as criticism). Lucian of Samosata's well-known picture of Peregrinus yields impressive testimony to the same effect. The man was a charlatan, concerned only to get what he could out of the Christians. But this whole adventure was possible only because it was so well known that Christians characteristically behaved with love (Lucian of Samosata, *The Passing of Peregrinus,* 11ff.; Loeb edn., vol. V, 13ff.). As Lucian points out, "If any charlatan and trickster, able to profit by occasion, comes among them, he quickly acquires sudden wealth by imposing upon simple folk" (p. 15).

[48]In Matthew and Mark the words are spoken by Jesus, but in Luke they are the response of a lawyer to a question from Jesus, a response which Jesus approves (v. 28). In each case the words are

first obligation resting on men. Pious works, like tithing, are no substitute for love (Luke 11:42).[49] And Jesus told the Jews, "If God were your Father you would love me" (John 8:42). In other words, truly loving God necessarily means loving Christ—and both loves are expected of believers.

This can present a problem to us, because we do not see love as something that can be produced in response to a command. We "fall in love"; love is drawn from us unbidden by the attractive. But the New Testament writers are not looking for this kind of love, but for a love that is a response to Christ's love and sacrifice for us. God in Christ has done something great for us, so it is not inappropriate that he now calls on us to align our wills with his in a loving response to his loving act.[50] In understanding this response, we must not confuse love with passion or with sentimentality.[51]

---

quotations from Deuteronomy 6:5 and Leviticus 19:18. Jesus finds in them the fulfillment of all that the law and the prophets contained. Love is all-embracing.

[49]The Western text of Mark 7:6 has "loves me with their lips" in place of "honors me. . . ." It is not clear whether this reading is from a lost Septuagintal text, or whether it is due to the makers of the Western text. Be that as it may, the words are another way of indicating that love is important and that it must be genuine. Love which goes no deeper than words is not enough.

[50]R. Bultmann points out that for Christians "the care for oneself is changed into a care for one's neighbour. But since it is precisely this becoming free from the past and from oneself that is subjected to the imperative, the future that is grasped as command coincides with the future that is promised for loyalty of faith; for it was freedom from the past and from oneself that was promised to the believer. Thus the imperative is itself a gift, and this can be because it receives its significance and its possibility of realisation from the past, experienced as the love of the Revealer" (*The Gospel of John*, Philadelphia, 1971, p. 525). I do not agree with his last word: it is the love of the Redeemer rather than the love of the Revealer that is in mind here.

[51]Cf. Joseph Fletcher: "People often point out, quite reasonably and properly, that 'it is impossible to love in obedience to a command' and that to ask it of us only encourages hypocrisy, 'since all men are not lovable.' Both objections are correct. But only if we *sentimentalize* love, taking it to be a matter of feeling or emotion, could they be true objections to *agapē*" (*Situation Ethics*, Philadelphia, 1966, p. 106). I find it impossible to accept Fletcher's essential position, but this comment is worth noting. W. G. Cole understands the Hebrew

The New Testament is specific, clearly reiterating the Lord's commands in similar words. For example, Paul exhorts believers in Ephesians 5:2, "Walk in love as Christ also loved us and gave himself up for us...." Timothy is told to pursue desirable qualities, one of which is love (I Tim. 6:11). "Love one another fervently from the heart," writes Peter (I Pet. 1:22); he also urges believers to "love the brotherhood" (I Pet. 2:17). The elder writes to the "elect lady," not giving a new command but reminding her of a command that has stood from the beginning, "that we love one another" (II John 5).

Repeated often, the command is clear, new and yet old. It is the first and great duty of Jesus' followers. Some people think that it is clearly important, but that it needs redefinition: because we think of love as an involuntary emotion, they argue, we should interpret the biblical command to mean that we are to do the right thing.[52] We may not feel a warm affection for some people, but that need not stop us from being kind and considerate to them. Certainly this idea has some merit, because Christ's people should be kind and considerate. But I doubt whether this behavior adequately meets the demands of the New Testament, because it is possible to act kindly yet have motives that are anything but kind. In any case, the suggestion seems to presuppose that Christian love is something like *erōs*. Such a love depends on finding attractiveness in the beloved, and the suggestion recommends action even when nothing arouses this love.

But we must remember that the New Testament writers are concerned with *agapē*. To them, love first of all means God's spontaneous, unmotivated love for the sinner, the love that proceeds from God's essential nature. When the sinner receives and welcomes this love, he finds that God's love kindles love within him. The love that is commanded is not a love

---

idea of love as "not ephemeral emotion but steadfast concern, involving the will rather than the feelings" (*Sex and Love in the Bible*, New York, 1959, p. 67; see also pp. 69, 75).

[52]Cf. Erich Fromm: "The most fundamental kind of love, which underlies all types of love, is *brotherly love*. By this I mean the sense of responsibility, care, respect, knowledge of any other human being, the wish to further his life. This is the kind of love the Bible speaks of when it says: love thy neighbor as thyself" (*The Art of Loving*, New York and Evanston, 1956, p. 47).

that believers generate themselves;[53] it is a love that proceeds from divine love. Confronted with God's love, we may respond by accepting it or rejecting it. The right response may be commanded—the response of love. While it is nonsense to be commanded to generate a passionate *erōs,* it is not nonsense to be commanded to respond to God's love.[54]

The demand for love may be likened to the demand for faith; indeed, faith and love are sometimes linked, at least in the Pauline writings.[55] Paul wonderfully describes the Christian way as "faith working through love" (Gal. 5:6),[56] listing these qualities (with others) as the fruit of the Spirit (Gal. 5:22). We also find the two linked in a closing greeting: "Peace to the brothers and love with faith from God the Father and Jesus Christ the Lord" (Eph. 6:23). Similarly, Paul tells his readers to put on "the breastplate of faith and love" (I Thess. 5:8). Several times he refers appreciatively to the faith and love of his correspondents (Eph. 1:15; Col. 1:4; I Thess. 1:3; 3:6;

---

[53]Cf. G. Thomas C. Oden: "The clinical wisdom of psychotherapy has persuasively called our attention to just how little we know of how to love ourselves properly, and consequently how twisted is our perception of how we would wish to be loved. If we want to be loved possessively, masochistically, dependently, with a love that compensates for our guilts and reassures our anxieties, then how little are we really capable of knowing how we *need* to be loved. How insecure, therefore, is our platform for knowing how to love others" (*Radical Obedience,* Philadelphia, 1964, p. 125). I do not wish to endorse Oden's whole position, but his recognition of our inability to love others is interesting.

[54]Cf. Emil Brunner: "The meaning of *Agape* as the demand of God only becomes intelligible to one who knows the fulfillment of this law from the standpoint of Jesus Christ, in the surrender of Christ Himself; that is only to one who receives the divine gift in Jesus Christ in faith.... What the love that is commanded *is,* only he can know who has *experienced* the love which has been given" (*The Christian Doctrine of God,* London, 1949, p. 197; Brunner's italics).

[55]The two are linked 20 times in the Pauline corpus; possibly also in II Corinthians 8:7 (though this seems rather to refer to the faith of the Corinthians and the love of Paul; see below, p. 204, n. 35). They are also joined in Revelation 2:19. For the nine instances in which the two are linked in the Pastoral Epistles see below, pp. 234f.

[56]His words are, "In Christ Jesus neither circumcision nor uncircumcision is of any force, but faith working through love."

II Thess. 1:3; Philem. 5). And, of course, he links faith and love with hope as the three things that remain (I Cor. 13:13).[57]

It is not really surprising to find these two linked. To come to God we must come in simple faith, faith evoked by what he has done for us at Calvary. And Calvary is the place where we see what love is. It is not easy to see how there could be either real faith without love or real love without faith. The two belong together in the Christian way.[58]

The command to love is clear, but it is not found often in the New Testament. Part of the reason for this may be that it is not easy to see love, which finds its origin in God, as a response to a command. Anders Nygren seems to hold this opinion, because he says, "Agape is spontaneous, unmotivated love. But in relation to God, man's love can never be spontaneous and unmotivated. God's love always comes first and awakens man's love in response."[59] This may be stated too strongly. If a man has been so transformed by God's love that he becomes a loving person, then this will govern his attitude toward God just as it does his attitude toward man. But Nygren is surely right in emphasizing that this kind of love appears in man only as a response, not as a self-initiated achievement. So Nygren goes on to say, "Man loves God, not because on com-

---

[57]Some appear to make faith and love identical. Thus R. Bultmann comments on John 14:15–24, "This love in fact can be nothing other than faith" (*The Gospel of John*, p. 612). Cf. Emil Brunner: "Faith is nothing other than the vessel into which God pours his love.... Faith and love not only are inseparably related, but become one with each other" (*Faith, Hope, and Love*, London, 1957, p. 75). But this seems to be going too far. Luther relates faith to God's prior love: "If we rightly consider it, love comes first, or at the same moment with faith. For I could not trust God if I did not think He desired to be favourable and gracious towards me" (cited in John Burnaby, *Amor Dei*, p. 312). Alexander Maclaren sees faith as the spring of human love: "It is of no use to say, 'Go to, let us love one another.' That will be unreal, mawkish, histrionic. 'The faith which thou hast toward the Lord Jesus' will be the productive cause, as it is the measure, of 'thy love toward all the saints'" (*The Epistles of St. Paul to the Colossians and Philemon*, London, 1893, p. 438). Faith and love are intimately connected, but they are not the same thing.

[58]I say this despite the fact that L. Feuerbach writes, "Faith is the opposite of love" (*The Essence of Christianity*, London, 1890, p. 257; trans. Marian Evans).

[59]*Agape and Eros*, p. 213.

paring Him with other things he finds Him more satisfying than anything else [that, for Nygren, would be *erōs*], but because God's unmotivated love has overwhelmed him and taken control of him, so that he cannot do other than love God. Therein lies the profound significance of the idea of predestination: man has not selected God, but God has elected man."[60]

And that salvation is powerful, something Paul recognizes when he insists that God's love will not be defeated. "Who will separate us from the love of Christ?" he asks, dismissing the possibility with a rhetorical question: "Affliction or trouble or persecution or famine or nakedness or danger or the sword?" (Rom. 8:35). Just to mention these candidates is to show the complete impossibility of their decisively intervening between God and those God loves. This list might give the impression that God's love means that God's people are immune from the troubles that plague mankind. But the apostle quickly dispels this idea, quoting Psalm 44:22 to show that believers may in fact suffer grievously: "For thy sake we are killed all day, we were reckoned as sheep for the slaughter" (v. 36). But though such troubles are real enough, they do not remove us from God's love: "But [on the contrary] in all these things we conquer and more through him who loved us" (v. 37). It is not our natural fortitude that enables us to emerge from such troubles unscathed; it is God's love in Christ that enables us to escape defeat.[61] The climax of Paul's argument is this well-known declaration: "For I am persuaded that neither death nor life nor angels nor principalities nor things present nor things to come nor powers nor height nor depth nor any other created thing will be able to separate us from the love of God which is in Christ Jesus our Lord" (vv. 38-39). Clearly, love is all-

---

[60]*Agape and Eros*, pp. 213f. Predestination is often regarded as a harsh and forbidding doctrine, but the seventeenth of the Anglican Thirty-nine Articles maintains that it "is full of sweet, pleasant, and unspeakable comfort to godly persons... , as well because it doth greatly establish and confirm their faith of eternal Salvation to be enjoyed through Christ, as because it doth fervently kindle their love towards God...." Predestination and love go together.

[61]Cf. F. F. Bruce: "Nothing can come between His love and His people.... Mighty forces—supernatural as well as natural—are arrayed against the people of Christ, but through Him they overcome them all and remain irrevocably encircled and empowered by His unchanging love" (*The Epistle to the Romans*, London, 1963, p. 179).

conquering.[62] Paul's acknowledgment of this fact is strengthened by his personal history. He is no starry-eyed innocent, unmindful of the troubles the world can bring on men—especially God's servants. Having suffered greatly himself (cf. II Cor. 11:23ff.), he is well aware of what the world can do. But he is also well aware that God, not the world, has the last word, because God is love. And there is nothing in all this mighty creation that can separate God's people from God's love.

Love like this is incompatible with fear, as certain passages make clear: "God did not give us a spirit of cowardice, but of power and love and self-control" (II Tim. 1:7); "There is no fear in love, but perfect love casts fear out" (I John 4:18). God's great love gives the believer assurance that all will be well.[63] If believers can rely on the love God showed at Calvary, what is there to be afraid of? Because God's love is invincible, nothing can prevent its creating love in those who receive it,[64] a love more powerful than the world's opposition and than the fears that are part of man's life.

---

[62]John Murray emphasizes the connection with Christ: "The love of God from which we cannot be separated is the love of God *which is in Christ Jesus our Lord.* It is only in Christ Jesus it exists, only in him has it been manifest, only in him is it operative, and only in Christ Jesus as our Lord can *we* know the embrace and bond of this love of God" (*The Epistle to the Romans,* I, Grand Rapids, 1959, 335).

[63]Cf. R. Bultmann: "*agapē* cannot be understood other than as God's 'love with us,' and must therefore be the love of God given to us. Precisely of this love can it be said, however, that it is without fear, for fear can only be fear before God. But there can be no fear for those who know themselves to be endowed with God's love" (*The Johannine Epistles,* Philadelphia, 1973, p. 73). He cites Luther approvingly: "Fear has its own agony" (p. 74).

[64]Karl Barth says, "New and different men are needed in order that love may take place as a human act. And God creates these new and loving men" (*Church Dogmatics,* IV, 2, 777); "His love is creative love; love which does not ask or seek or demand or awaken and set in motion our love as though it were already present in us, but which creates it as something completely new, making us free for love as for an action which differs wholly and utterly from all that we have done hitherto" (p. 777).

CHAPTER NINE

Love for Other People

W_{HEN} Jesus was asked which was the greatest commandment in the Law, he replied, "You shall love the Lord your God." He did more than he was asked, because he went on, "A second is this, 'You shall love your neighbor as yourself.' No other commandment is greater than these" (Mark 12:30f.; cf. Matt. 22:39, where Jesus adds, "On these two commandments hang the entire law and the prophets"; the scribe had asked only about the Law, but Jesus replied in terms of the prophets also, indicating that the command to love is basic to Old Testament revelation).[1] The scribe who asked the question was evidently a man with some spiritual perception, because he immediately recognized the rightness of the answer, and went on to note for himself that "to love him with all the heart and with all the mind and with all the strength and to love the neighbor as oneself is more than all the burnt offerings and sacrifices" (Mark 12:33).[2] Given the importance the Jews attached to ritual observance and their universal belief in sacrifice as a divine ordinance, the answer is all the more signifi-

---

[1] The addition of a second commandment to that to love God is unexpected and highly significant. C. Spicq comments, "To love one's neighbor is a commandment equal to the precept of love of God" (*Agape in the New Testament,* I, St. Louis and London, 1963, 28; cf. 136f.). In volume III he has a long note on the question "And who is my neighbor?" (St. Louis and London, 1966, 201–4). Among other things he says, "Liberated from its social and affective limitations, the biblical concept of *plesion* becomes an absolute. In Christian language, 'neighbor' is 'everyman'" (p. 203).

[2] Cf. C. Spicq: "The Scribe in the Gospel saw that Jesus was not establishing a random hierarchy of values—mercy above sacrifice— but was setting love in an order apart, superior even to the most sacred, the cult of God" (*Agape in the New Testament,* I, 66). He also says, "A Christian can be defined as a person who loves" (p. 74).

cant. We should perhaps notice that another Jew, this time described as a "lawyer," summed up the Law in much the same way, drawing attention to the commandments to love God and the neighbor (Luke 10:27), to which Jesus replied, "You have answered rightly."[3]

The importance Jesus placed on this commandment is indicated by his reply to the rich young ruler. This man asked him what he should do to obtain eternal life. Jesus quoted some of the Ten Commandments: "You shall not kill; You shall not commit adultery; You shall not steal; You shall not bear false witness; Honor your father and your mother." Then he added, "You shall love your neighbor as yourself" (Matt. 19:18f.). One might reason that citing the Ten Commandments would be enough, because they are God's supreme requirements. But for Jesus the commandment to love was so important that it had to be added in such a case.

Some of the most important teaching in the Sermon on the Mount is about love. Jesus reminds his hearers that "you have heard that it was said, 'You shall love your neighbor and hate your enemy'" (Matt. 5:43). The Old Testament does not, of course, command hatred for the enemy, although this was evidently a popular filling out of the requirement of the Law. But Jesus makes it the springboard for an injunction: "Love your enemies and pray for those who persecute you" (Matt. 5:44). Jesus makes it clear that we must love, not hate, to be true sons of the heavenly Father. We must remember that God does not confine his bounty to those who love him: he gives his good gifts of rain and sunshine to evil and to good, to just and unjust alike (Matt. 5:45). Like him, we must love those who are evil as well as those who are good.[4] This command to love all men

---

[3]The early Christian writing called the *Didache* describes "the Way of Life" in these terms: "First, thou shalt love the God who made thee, secondly, thy neighbour as thyself; and whatsoever thou wouldst not have done to thyself, do not thou to another" (1:2; Loeb edn.).

[4]E. Schweizer has an important comment on the fulfilling of the Law in Matthew 5:18. He refers to Matthew 7:12 and proceeds, "He is saying that the entire Law, every point and every stroke of it, is contained in the commandment to love one's neighbor, as expounded by Jesus in his teaching and ministry. This is confirmed by the observation that Matthew adds this commandment in 19:19, equates it explicitly in 22:39 with the commandment to love God, states in 22:40

is a noteworthy advance beyond the teachings that preceded it. The Rabbis were prepared to extend the meaning of "neighbor," whom the Law instructed them to love (Lev. 19:18), so that it included the resident alien (cf. Lev. 19:34; Deut. 10:19), but that was the limit.[5] Jesus set no limit. Because he saw God's love given to all men, he demanded that God's people love their fellowmen.

We should not miss the revolutionary nature of this new teaching. Jesus dismissed loving those who love us; even despised people like the tax-collectors do that, he pointed out. And to greet our brothers is to do no more than the Gentiles do (Matt. 5:46–47). Jesus is not teaching his followers simply to live as the world about them lives. They are to be different and distinctive by faithfully following God's pattern—by showing love to all, even to those who do not love them. It is to this maturity that Jesus calls his followers (Matt. 5:48). For them love is a way of life.[6]

Sometimes Jesus used parables to help define the kind of love for which he was looking. Thus he told of a servant who was forgiven a great debt by the king he served (Matt. 18:21–35), but who had no mercy on someone who owed him a trifle.

---

that on these two commandments the entire Law and the prophets 'depend,' and in 9:13 and 12:7 interpolates the statement that God desires 'mercy and not sacrifice'" (*The Good News according to Matthew,* London, 1976, p. 108). Cf. V. P. Furnish: "For Matthew, it would appear, these two commandments do not just *contain* or *spawn* the law, but *constitute* it, or better, provide the decisive word about its *meaning* and thus enable its correct interpretation" (*The Love Command in the New Testament,* Nashville and New York, 1972, p. 34).

[5]Cf. H. L. Strack and P. Billerbeck: "The Synagogue at the time of Jesus understood the concept 'neighbor,' *rē(a)'*, just as strictly as the Old Testament: only the Israelite counted as *rē(a)'*, the 'others'—that is, the non-Israelites—do not come under this heading" (*Kommentar zum Neuen Testament aus Talmud und Midrasch,* I, München, 1922, 353f.).

[6]Henry Drummond cites Jesus' words about it being better to have a millstone put round one's neck and to be thrown into the sea than to offend one of the little ones who believe (Matt. 18:6), and comments, "It is the deliberate verdict of the Lord Jesus that it is better not to live than not to love. *It is better not to live than not to love*" ("The Greatest Thing in the World," *Addresses,* Philadelphia, 1891, p. 46; Drummond's italics).

The point is that the mercy shown to this man was totally unexpected and completely unmerited. He should have responded with love, not simply with love to the king (that would be expected; that is the way of the world), but with a love that would make him merciful to his fellow servant (v. 33). Obviously this love is special, set apart from the ways of the world.

Jesus also teaches about love by using what seem to be contradictions of love. For instance, Jesus said, "If your brother sins, rebuke him" (Luke 17:3). We do not usually associate rebuke with love, but this is mere thoughtlessness. The indifferent would certainly not embark on such a difficult and thankless task; only the truly loving believer would try to help an erring brother. Jesus goes on to say, "If he repents, forgive him," adding that the process is to be repeated seven times in a day if necessary (v. 4).[7]

Some of Jesus' followers obviously learned the lesson.[8] James, for example, tells his correspondents that if they keep "the royal law" they will do well. He proceeds to quote it (as Jesus did earlier): "You shall love your neighbor as yourself" (James 2:8). While he cites other commandments also ("Do not commit adultery" and "Do not murder" in v. 11), he does not attach the same central importance to them as he does to the command to love.[9] We see this also in I Peter. The writer points out that the Christian must not return evil for

---

[7]There is an interesting parallel in a Jewish source, the *Testament of Gad* 6:3: "Love ye, therefore, one another from the heart; and if a man sin against thee, cast forth the poison of hate and speak peaceably to him, and in thy soul hold not guile; and if he confess and repent, forgive him" (Charles's edn.).

[8]In the text I draw attention to important scriptural passages, but the attitude is found outside the New Testament as well. For example, Jerome cites the *Gospel of the Hebrews* for a wise saying of Jesus to his followers: "Never be ye joyful, save when ye behold your brother with love" (W. Schneemelcher, ed., *New Testament Apocrypha*, I, London, 1963, 164).

[9]V. P. Furnish cites a number of authorities who think that James sees love as central, but also some who think that to break any of the commandments is to become a law breaker (James 2:10f.), so that the love command is on much the same footing as other commands (*The Love Command in the New Testament*, pp. 177–182). He himself favors the second view. But I doubt whether he has given sufficient attention to the significance of "royal." In the first century this did not denote "being on the same level as others."

evil, because he has been called to live a different way. He is required to bless those who revile him, for, "he who would love life..." must "do right," return good for evil (I Pet. 3:9f.). Love for living spills over into love for the wrongdoer.[10] This is the typical New Testament emphasis on love, even love for the enemy who reviles the believer.

Also reproducing this teaching is Paul. He tells the Galatians that "the whole law is fulfilled in one saying, namely, 'You shall love your neighbor as yourself' " (Gal. 5:14). He has been speaking of the freedom into which Christians are called and pointing out that this is not to be seen as a means of gratifying one's desires. Rather, "in love serve one another" (v. 13). He makes it clear that Christians are not legalists, called to a way of life in which they are perpetually bound by a set of commandments that they strive to keep. They depend not on keeping commandments but on God's grace, which allows them to live in freedom. The Law does not dominate them as Paul saw it dominating the Jews. But he is equally clear that this does not mean that Christians then follow only their own desires; on the contrary, they show loving concern to others. The whole of the Law and the whole of their duty to other people they find summed up in this one commandment: "You shall love your neighbor as yourself." There is nothing in Christian freedom that does away with love.

Paul has more to say on this theme in Romans 13:8–10. Here he says, "To no man owe anything but to love one another." Love is not an option to be casually chosen by those who like it; it is part of being Christian. In fact, love is a debt that every Christian must strive ceaselessly to pay. The fact that he can never say "It is finished" does not make it any less an obligation. As W. Sanday and A. C. Headlam put it, "Let your only debt that is unpaid be that of love—a debt which you should always be attempting to discharge in full, but will never succeed in discharging.... By this pregnant expression St. Paul suggests both the obligation of love and the impossibility of fulfilling it."[11]

---

[10]Cf. C. Spicq: "Anyone who hopes to obtain the heavenly heritage must put his brotherly love into practice" (*Agape in the New Testament,* II, 358); "He does not neglect love for enemies (3:10)" (p. 381).

[11]*A Critical and Exegetical Commentary on the Epistle to the Romans,* Edinburgh, 1907, p. 373.

Paul gives a reason for this emphasis on love: "He who loves the other has fulfilled law." In other words, simply loving one's fellowman fulfills the whole law. It seems unlikely that Paul is concerned only with the law of Moses (though he certainly has that in mind, as the following words show). Actually, his point is one that is true of law in general: what any law requires will be fulfilled when we act with love towards our neighbor.

The apostle brings out this point by listing some of the commandments—"You shall not commit adultery; You shall not murder; You shall not steal; You shall not covet." Clearly, real love rules out any of these. But the command to love is even stronger than this, as Paul stresses when he says, "And if there is any other commandment it is summed up in this word, 'You shall love your neighbor as yourself.'" It is impossible to conceive of a commandment suitable for inclusion in a code of law that would not be kept by someone acting in love. The point is that "love works no evil to the neighbor; therefore love is the fulfillment of the law."[12] The comprehensiveness of love means that it covers all that law covers, and more.

SELF-LOVE

As we have seen, the command to love one's neighbor is linked with the love of self in the quotation from Leviticus 19:18.[13] Very different conclusions have been drawn from this association. Some think all love of the self is evil, and thus feel that love for one's neighbor arises only when it is overcome. Anders Nygren offers this comment about Luther's perspective: "On the basis of Christ's words in John xii.25, it is a fundamental principle for him that: 'To love is the same as to

---

[12]George Brockwell King argues that the negative form of the golden rule is important: "Men and women are forgetting that there are things they *must not do* if we are to have a stable civilization." He sees in these words of Paul evidence that "love can express itself in obedience to a negative command" (*JR*, VIII, 1928, 276).

[13]The NEB translates this as "You shall love your neighbour as a man like yourself," which means something quite different from "Love your neighbour as yourself." J. Duncan M. Derrett examines this rendering of the NEB but does not find it convincing (*ET*, LXXXIII, 1971–72, 55f.).

hate oneself.'"[14] Nygren amplifies this point in a longer comment:

> Luther has departed so far from the traditional idea, which discovers a *commandment* of self-love in the commandment of love to one's neighbour, that he finds this latter to contain a direct *prohibition* of every kind of self-love. Love to one's neighbour, he holds, has the task of completely dispossessing and annihilating self-love.[15]

D. D. Williams also cites Luther: "While love of self remains, a man cannot love righteousness or do its works, though he may pretend to do so."[16] He also holds that for Reinhold Niebuhr "self-love is the primal form of sin."[17] Similarly, Gene Outka speaks of "the historic link between self-love, pride, and sin."[18] The New Testament does not go as far as this, but it is worth noticing that self-love is not commanded (or commended) in any of the places where it is mentioned. It is simply regarded as one of the facts of life. And further, in II Timothy 3:2, 4 "self-lovers" (*philautoi*) are included among evil-doers; by contrast, they should be "God-lovers" (*philotheoi*).

A second view is that the love of self is praiseworthy or even, as James Moffatt puts it, obligatory: "The true love of self is a duty."[19] M. C. D'Arcy thinks this is essentially what Thomas Aquinas proposes. After quoting Aquinas, he explains, "The point of this is that the duality set up by love of self and love of God is a false one; a true love of oneself is a love of God, and a true love of God means that one cherishes

---

[14]*Agape and Eros,* London, 1953, p. 711.

[15]*Agape and Eros,* p. 713. M. C. D'Arcy thinks Nygren's position arises out of his view of the Fall: "It will be noticed, I hope, that Nygren's view and Gilson's differ because of their different views of the effects of the Fall. Nygren leaves nothing in man with which grace or Agape can collaborate, and so he can find no room for self-love in his concept of Christian Agape; Gilson agrees with St. Bernard and St. Thomas in holding that man is only wounded by the Fall and that therefore his high dignity remains. He naturally and rightly, therefore, loves himself" (*The Mind and Heart of Love,* London, 1962, p. 129).

[16]*The Spirit and the Forms of Love,* Welwyn, 1968, p. 78.

[17]*The Spirit and the Forms of Love,* p. 144.

[18]*Agape,* New Haven and London, 1972, p. 56.

[19]*Love in the New Testament,* London, 1932, p. 98.

oneself as part of God's purposes."[20] At a later stage of his
argument, D'Arcy maintains that self-love is a natural part of
man's advanced development: "The more definite and orga-
nized an individual member of a species is, the more self-love
must it have, and so we tend to forget that in the species below
human nature the individual never has a complete individuality
or self." Though partly animal, man is much more, and "with
the advent of the spiritual soul, a new order begins. Insofar,
however, as he is an individual, man must have this self-love,
and by reason of his new grandeur a self-love intensified."[21]

D'Arcy, then, sees a proper self-love as essential to hu-
mans: "The love of self is a true love; it is necessary for the
permanent selfhood and splendour of our finite beauty; it is not
just a part of another love; it is a co-efficient with it"; "we are
bound to accept some self-love as legitimate."[22]

Erich Fromm is another who argues powerfully for the
desirability and even the necessity of self-love. But we must
remember that he has a view of love that differs markedly from
the scriptural view of *agapē*. For Fromm, "*Love is an active
power in man*; a power which breaks through the walls which
separate man from his fellowmen, which unites him with others; love makes him overcome the sense of isolation and sepa-
rateness, yet it permits him to be himself, to retain his integrity. In love the paradox occurs that two beings become one
and yet remain two."[23] This is an interesting view of what love
is, one that Christians would do well to bear in mind. But if we
believe that we know *agapē* only through the cross, it is not
easy to go along with Fromm's essential position.

It is this understanding of love that leads him to say such

---

[20] *The Mind and Heart of Love*, p. 122. He further gives Gilson's
point of view: "The essence of the argument is this: that as man is an
image of God, in loving the image truly one loves the original, and in
loving the original one loves the image in so far as it is a true likeness
of the original"; he goes on to cite Gilson: "To love God with disinterested love is man's true way of loving himself" (pp. 130f.). He
draws attention to Aristotle's view that evil men "do not really love
themselves, for they are too depraved to seek for their true selves and
love that" (p. 142).

[21] *The Mind and Heart of Love*, p. 287.

[22] *The Mind and Heart of Love*, pp. 409 and 419.

[23] *The Art of Loving*, New York and Evanston, 1956, pp. 20f.
(Fromm's italics).

things as, "If it is a virtue to love my neighbor as a human being, it must be a virtue—and not a vice—to love myself, since I am a human being, too. There is no concept of man in which I myself am not included." Reversing this idea, he says, "Love of one person implies love of man as such."[24] He reasons that "my own self must be as much an object of my love as another person. *The affirmation of one's own life, happiness, growth, freedom is rooted in one's capacity to love*—i.e., in care, respect, responsibility, and knowledge. If an individual is able to love productively, he loves himself, too; if he loves *only* others, he cannot love at all." He goes on to argue that the selfish person does not really love himself; "in fact, he hates himself."[25]

All this may follow if we accept Fromm's definition of love, though even then doubts may arise. I am not at all convinced, for example, that the man who loves in Fromm's sense cannot love at all if he loves only other people. Be that as it may, if we see love as the New Testament writers see it, Fromm's advocacy of self-love must be modified. If love is the denial of self, the readiness to give all for others, then it is not easy to see how there is room for the love of the self. A proper self-respect is one thing; anything that can properly be called "love" is another.

There are, then, many who argue that a proper self-love is essential. They perceive selfishness as an inadequate self-love, because in satisfying his immediate desires a man is choosing the second-best. And to love one's neighbor is an integral part of any ultimately satisfying way of life;[26] love of the neighbor and self-love are inseparable in this philosophy. But sometimes this idea is supported with rather weak arguments. For exam-

---

[24]*The Art of Loving,* pp. 58, 59.
[25]*The Art of Loving,* p. 60 (Fromm's italics).
[26]Irving Singer holds that Plato, "(unlike the Calvinists or the Freudians) never admits the possibility of ultimate conflict between loving oneself and loving ideals. When modern theologians criticize Calvin for thinking that self-love prohibits the love of God, when revisionists attack Freud for assuming that the libido is directed either toward the ego or toward others but not toward both at the same time, they subterraneously return to the position Plato takes for granted. He defines love as the search for the Good and justifies this conclusion by reminding us that men always desire what is best for *themselves*" (*The Nature of Love,* New York, 1966, p. 74).

ple, Denis de Rougemont argues from the command to love the
neighbor as oneself that "loving oneself and loving one's
neighbor is one and the same act: if not, the *as* would not have
its full meaning."[27] But this reasoning is surely fallacious, because *as* will not carry this weight. The same test, if applied to
Ephesians 5:28 ("men ought to love their own wives as their
own bodies"), would mean that loving one's wife and loving
one's body (not oneself) would be "one and the same act,"
which is clearly not what the passage means.

It seems that "self-love" is being given more than one
meaning in these discussions. Some of those who advocate it
seem to be saying that everyone should have a proper self-
respect.[28] With this there can be no quarrel, because people
only harm themselves if they have a poor self-image. On the
other hand, when people have a deep and genuine concern that
they be the best that they can be, their lives are enriched. But
the question is whether this should be called "love" for themselves. Paul Tillich holds that love "presupposes a separation
of the loving subject and the loved object," and wonders accordingly "whether self-love is a meaningful concept at all."[29]
Love as the New Testament understands it includes a giving of
oneself (perhaps a passionate giving of oneself) to the other.[30]
Without this, it is not easy to see that the term *love* applies.
And with it self-love is excluded. How can one give oneself to

---

[27] *Love Declared,* New York, 1963, p. 206.

[28] M. C. D'Arcy notices the position of W. McDougall, "that the
older moralists by using the expression self-love confused two different sentiments, self-love [and] self-respect. Self-love, he says, is
fortunately rare; the self-regarding sentiment of the thoroughly selfish
man" (*The Mind and Heart of Love,* p. 295, n. 1). D'Arcy comments,
"He seems to miss entirely the fundamental nature of self-love, without which a human being would have no care for himself and no desire
to be healthy or wise." But many will feel that McDougall is right.

[29] *Love, Power, and Justice,* New York, 1960, p. 6; see also pp.
33f.

[30] Cf. J. R. W. Stott: Love in the New Testament sense "always
includes the ingredients of sacrifice and service. Indeed, *agapē* is the
sacrifice of self in the service of another.... *Agapē* love cannot be
self-directed; if it is, it destroys itself. It ceases to be self-sacrifice,
and becomes self-service" (*Christianity Today,* XXII, May 5, 1978,
978. See also the article by John Piper, "Is Self-Love Biblical?" in
Christianity Today, XXI, August 12, 1977, 1150–53).

oneself (have a passion for oneself?) and not be selfish and self-centered?[31]

We should always bear in mind, as we noticed earlier, that the New Testament does not command self-love. The command to love one's neighbor as oneself is spoken of several times (Matt. 5:43; 19:19; 22:39; Mark 12:31, 33; Luke 10:27; Rom. 13:9; Gal. 5:14; James 2:8). But the love of self is always stated as a fact, not as something that should be sought after.[32] Something similar must be said about the statement "He who loves his wife loves himself" (Eph. 5:28; cf. the explanation in v. 29, "For nobody ever hated his own flesh, but nourishes and cherishes it"). That a man loves himself can be accepted as a fact, whether it is a proper love or not. In all of these cases the imperatives concern love for God and one's neighbor; they do not carry over to the self. It would seem that the best position to hold is that a genuine self-respect is praiseworthy, but love for the self is another matter. People do love themselves, but nothing in Scripture leads us to regard this as something Christians should seek.

BROTHERLY LOVE

The New Testament has a good deal to say about a particular form of love for others—namely, love for fellow believers. "Love the brotherhood" (I Pet. 2:17) puts it simply and directly. "Above all things have fervent love among yourselves," says the same writer, and adds, "for love covers a multitude of sins" (I Pet. 4:8). He also advises his friends to greet one another "with a kiss of love" (I Pet. 5:14). In all this he is following the teaching of Jesus, who gave his followers "a new commandment"—namely, that they should "love one another" (John 13:34). The New Testament contains many

---

[31]M. C. D'Arcy draws attention to Rousselot: "What we love we become; the lover of self becomes selfish and other human beings lose their individuality and turn into 'things' which can be of use to him" (*The Mind and Heart of Love*, p. 379).

[32]Douglas N. Morgan recognizes that "it is a fair presumption that the synoptists and Jesus himself so understood it. . . . This is the basic, historic sense, I believe" (*Love: Plato, the Bible and Freud*, Englewood Cliffs, N. J., 1964, p. 123, n. 72). This is all the more significant because Morgan thinks that men ought to love themselves. But he finds no support for his view in these biblical texts.

repetitions of this precept as well as examples of its fulfillment. In fact, I have noticed twenty-three examples of the use of the verb *agapaō* to convey the idea of love within the Christian family, eighteen of the noun *agapē*, and fifty of *agapētos* (or forty-nine, if I Timothy 6:2 refers to the love of God[33]). Loving God and keeping his commandments are linked with loving "the children of God" (I John 5:2). Earlier we noted that Paul at one point tells the Galatians that they should "through love serve one another" (Gal. 5:13).[34] That this is no casual expression is shown by Paul's frequent references to love as an attitude to be expected of Christians. For example, he looks for this attitude among the Philippians (Phil. 2:2). And in writing to the Corinthians he speaks easily and naturally of "proving the sincerity of your love" (II Cor. 8:8), urging them to give evidence of their love before the churches (II Cor. 8:24).[35] He does not have to demonstrate the importance of love for one's brethren—that is taken for granted. The only question was how best to express it.

Paul not only talked about the importance of love—he lived his message by freely loving others. In the most natural way he refers to his love for those with whom he worked, such as Epaenetus (Rom. 16:5), Amplias (Rom. 16:8), Stachys (Rom. 16:9), Persis (Rom. 16:12), Timothy (I Cor. 4:17),

---

[33]The passage refers to believing slave-owners as "faithful and beloved," and the question is whether this means "beloved of God" or "of man." M. Dibelius holds that the reference must be to God: "The slaves who must be admonished to serve cannot, in the same injunction, be expected to act out of love for the masters" (*The Pastoral Epistles,* Philadelphia, 1972, p. 82). George A. Denzer cannot decide between the two (*The Jerome Biblical Commentary,* ed. R. E. Brown, J. A. Fitzmyer, and R. E. Murphy, Englewood Cliffs, N. J., 1968, *ad loc.*). W. Hendriksen sees a reference to both (*ad loc.*), while B. S. Easton translates the line as, "They who profit by the good act are believers and friends," which implies "beloved of man" (*The Pastoral Epistles,* New York, 1947, p. 159).

[34]His verb "serve" is *douleuō,* meaning "serve as a slave." Christ frees us from sin and self-centeredness. To be free is to love, and to love is to serve, even if it means taking the lowliest place.

[35]It is possible that in the same chapter Paul is listing love along with qualities like faith and knowledge as something in which the Corinthians excel (II Cor. 8:7). If this can be accepted, love is again being regarded as fundamental. The RSV accepts this view, but it is probably better to see a reference to Paul's love for the Corinthians (so Barrett, Hughes, etc.).

Tychicus (Col. 4:7), and Luke (Col. 4:14). Great people are often so committed to a cause that their relationships with others become austere, even cold. But for Paul love was not simply a fine theory—it was his way of life. In this spirit he affirms his love for all the saints in Corinth (I Cor. 16:24), insisting on the reality of this love and calling on God as a witness (II Cor. 11:11). An interesting feature of his relationship with the Corinthians is his insistence that he is ready to "spend and be spent" for them, even though "the more abundantly I love you, the less I am loved" (II Cor. 12:15). We see here something of the essential quality of *agapē*. We see something more of it when the apostle says that he wrote the "severe letter" in order that "you may know the love I have more abundantly towards you" (II Cor. 2:4). He could take the unpopular action because his loving concern for his friends' well-being overrode any possible desire for personal popularity.

Being only human, Paul's correspondents suffered some regrettable lapses in Christian love, but more than once Paul refers to the love which his correspondents have for "all the saints" (Eph. 1:15; Col. 1:4). When he describes the Colossians as "knit together in love" (Col. 2:2), certainly he is indicating their love for one another as well as Christ's love for them. The same can be said for that love for which Paul looks, love "which binds everything together in perfect harmony" (Col. 3:14, the RSV; *syndesmos tēs teleiotētos*). A special kind of love within the brotherhood is love for the leaders; they are to be loved because of their work, not necessarily because of their personal qualities (I Thess. 5:13).

In addition to such general references to Christians' love for one another, certain passages give specific examples of such love. For example, Paul writes to the Corinthians about an offender whom the church had disciplined. He had been punished enough, Paul said, and should now be forgiven and encouraged, lest he be overwhelmed by very great sorrow. "Therefore I implore you to confirm your love to him," the apostle proceeds (II Cor. 2:8). Clearly, Paul wanted to emphasize that even discipline should be loving. Notice other examples. John affirms his true love for his correspondents (II John 1; III John 1), and Paul speaks of the joy he has in Philemon's love (Philem. 7).[36] John also speaks of the way the

---

[36]J. B. Lightfoot comments, "This thanksgiving was the outpouring of gratitude for the joy and comfort that he had received in his bonds from the report of Philemon's generous charity" (*Saint Paul's*

brothers, even those who were strangers to Gaius, had testified to his love before the church (III John 6). Paul makes an interesting pair of references to the Thessalonian Christians. In his first letter he prays "that your love for one another and for all may abound and overflow," and in his second he sees it as an obligation resting on him to thank God because "the love of each one of you all for one another is growing and abounding" (I Thess. 3:12; II Thess. 1:3; he uses the same verb, *pleonazō*, both times). We have both the prayer and its answer.[37] James makes repeated use of the expression "my beloved brothers [*adelphoi mou agapētoi*]" (James 1:16, 19; 2:5). We do not usually think of this writer as creative, but he seems to have originated this interesting description of his correspondents. At any rate, it is not attested before his letter.[38]

Scholars disagree about how to interpret the "love feasts" (Jude 12)[39] of the early church, but clearly the reference is to a central act of fellowship and worship. For our present purpose the point is that what happened at the heart of worship was designated "love." A different kind of disagreement arises about Philemon's love for and faith in Christ and the saints (Philem. 5). If, as seems reasonable, the construction is chiastic, faith is related to the Lord and love to the saints,[40] though many hold that we cannot exclude a reference to love for Christ. They point out that faith and love can scarcely be separated in the Pauline writings. The difference in attitudes toward the Lord and toward the saints is indicated in the change of preposition

---

Epistles to the Colossians and to Philemon, Grand Rapids, 1970, p. 336).

[37]There are several instances of prayer relating to love—e.g., II Cor. 13:13; Eph. 1:3f., 15f.; 3:14–19; Phil. 1:9; Col. 1:3f.; I Thess. 1:2f.; II Thess. 3:5.

[38]Cf. C. Spicq, who claims the expression "has no parallel in Jewish literature" (*Agape in the New Testament,* II, 1). He also says, "The behavior of Christians to one another is a totally original expression of the loving communion of brothers who adore one Lord" (p. 18).

[39]The term is also found in II Peter 2:13 in some MSS, but the true reading there appears to be *apatais.*

[40]Donald Guthrie notes various possibilities but favors this one (*NBCR,* p. 1188). Eduard Lohse agrees that the construction is chiastic and thinks it puts love "in an accentuated position"; "the reference to 'love' gains special emphasis" (*Colossians and Philemon,* Philadelphia, 1971, p. 193).

(*pros* is used with "the Lord Jesus," *eis* with "the saints").
The revolution that God's love brought about is implicit in the
suggestion that Philemon would receive his runaway slave as
"a brother beloved . . . both in the flesh and in the Lord"
(Philem. 16). What is interesting is that Paul usually uses the
term *flesh* in a highly derogatory way. His using the term in a
positive sense may thus suggest the transformation of the
natural by the power of love.

Clearly, then, there is substantial evidence that the New
Testament writers advocated and practiced brotherly love.
Today this is sometimes seen as a defect. Some argue that we
should concentrate on the ideal of love for all—even our
enemies—that is seen so clearly in the Synoptic Gospels. They
claim that in some places, notably the Johannine writings, love
for men in general is lost sight of in the concentration on
brotherly love.[41]

To this argument more than one response can be made.
First, it is a very dubious assertion that the Johannine literature overlooks the importance of love for one's fellowman. It is
true that it emphasizes the importance of brotherly love more
strongly than do some parts of the New Testament. But it is
certainly not true that this is the only love this literature contemplates,[42] as we shall see a little later.

Secondly, we should not dismiss brotherly love as though
it were nothing other than a refined form of selfishness. A little
reflection will show that the New Testament is bringing out
something important when it refers to this kind of love. That
is, of course, inevitable, as a logical look at salvation shows.

---

[41]H. W. Montefiore finds love for all men inculcated only in the
Synoptic Gospels: "In the synoptic gospels it is demanded that all
men should show love to their neighbour, and *neighbour* is defined in
terms of any man in need; while in the rest of the New Testament a
Christian must help his neighbour who is assumed to be a fellow-
Christian to whom he is united in Christ" (*NT,* V, 1962, 165f.). But
Montefiore never gives real consideration to the facts that (a) the New
Testament writers, especially Paul and John, see the love of Christ (or
of God; the two are not sharply distinguished) in the cross where
Christ died for sinners, and (b) believers are called to love like Christ
did.

[42]Cf. C. K. Barrett: "John is certainly not guilty of restricting the
scope and quality of Christian love" (*The Gospel according to St.
John,* London, 1962, p. 81).

The gospel tells of sinners who are offered salvation through Christ's atoning work. Christians are people who are united in the convictions that they have no merit of their own to plead, that they have been bought at a great price, and that they are called to live for Christ in the midst of a sinful world. They cannot but have a warm attitude toward others in the same position: because they are united to Christ, they are united to one another. They do not see this love as a human achievement, but as something God-given, an inevitable response that displays the very meaning of Christian love. When the New Testament speaks of "the fellowship of the Spirit," it certainly suggests that the fellowship in which Christians find themselves is a fellowship created by the Spirit, a loving relationship born of shared faith.

Then, thirdly, we must remember that in the world of the New Testament brotherly love was critically important to the survival of the infant church. We are wrong if we think of that church as existing in an encouraging environment with everyone anxious to see it prosper, because the opposite was true. It is a miracle that it survived at all, let alone grew in strength, because the church of the first century was surrounded by foes. The Jews regarded the Christians as traitors and would gladly have seen the new sect extinguished. The Romans usually did not understand Christianity, but when they realized that it was distinct from Judaism, they thought it should be abolished. Worldly people everywhere disliked the holiness they saw in Christians. And polytheists saw the Christian affirmation of monotheism not as a positive doctrine, a desirable alternative, but as a denial of the many gods in whom they believed. They opposed the Christians as "atheists," seeing them as people who denied the very existence of the gods and were a threat to ordered, civilized, religious society.

The church was not a mighty organization, well able to keep dissidents in line and opponents at bay. It was a persecuted, struggling minority, always on the brink of extinction. With its strong foes without and its lack of force within, it needed a powerful link among its adherents if it was to survive.[43] To ignore the necessity of a strong bond to unify them-

---

[43]"The little pockets of early Christians survived because they cared exclusively for the love of 'the brethren' and stopped their ears to the opinion of the Pagan society all round them" (C. S. Lewis, *The Four Loves*, London, 1960, pp. 93f.).

selves in these circumstances would have been to invite disaster. Because, humanly speaking, the Christians had only each other, it was only natural that they stressed the importance of brotherly love.

In the fourth place, we should notice that brotherly love is to be valued because of the sheer joy it brings. A fellowship of love is a wonderful thing. A warmth and devotion not easily discernible in a larger group will become apparent in a small group united by a common bond. Everyone who has experienced God's love in Christ will have known something of the value of the fellowship of love that exists among the redeemed and will have responded to it. It is one of God's good gifts, one that was particularly gratifying for the small group of New Testament Christians.

Nor should we overlook the fact that brotherly love does not exclude loving people outside of the fellowship.[44] This is sometimes stated explicitly—in fact, love for one's fellowman is even linked with love within the fellowship. Paul, for example, refers to the Thessalonians' love "for one another and for all" (I Thess. 3:12). Even where this relationship is not explicit, it is implied. It may not be easy to prove that throughout the New Testament there is a uniform emphasis on loving "outsiders," but it is harder to prove that there is any other attitude.[45] And certainly nothing in the New Testament suggests the hate for outsiders we find in the Qumran scrolls. The Christians took seriously the duty of acting with love and concern toward non-Christians.

This concern frequently took the form of evangelism. Engaging in small acts of helpfulness and service could not matter

---

[44]It is well-known that Tertullian quotes the verdict of the heathen on the Christians: "See, they say, how they love one another." It is not as well-known that a little later he says, "But we are your brethren as well by the law of our common mother nature, though you are hardly men, because brothers so unkind" (*Apol.*, XXXIX; *ANF*, III, 46). For him love to the brothers did not exclude love for those outside the fellowship. Those within the fellowship are brothers in a fuller sense, but those outside are still brothers, even if they are "unkind."

[45]Cf. Herman Ridderbos: "It is evident in various ways that Paul extends the commandment of love as widely as possible and that every suggestion that this commandment holds only for Christians among themselves is entirely foreign to him" (*Paul*, Grand Rapids, 1975, p. 299).

nearly as much as presenting the gospel in an attempt to win sinful people for Christ. Study of the documents reveals no trace of "spiritual imperialism," which would suggest that the evangelists were concerned simply with building up the number of believers. Nor were they indulging their egos, showing themselves to be great leaders by the numbers they brought in. As the New Testament reveals it, Christians witnessed to non-Christians because they were deeply concerned for those "dead in trespasses and sins." Evangelism was thus a loving response to the need of the hearers, not that of the evangelists.[46]

It is important to remember that this kind of love is often suggested even when none of the words for love is mentioned. This fact is obvious in exhortations like, "Bless those who persecute you, bless and do not curse"; "to no man render evil for evil" (Rom. 12:14,17; cf. 12:19).[47] Similar is the injunction to the Galatians: "while we have time, let us do good to all men"; here the addition "especially to those of the household of the faith" should not cause us to overlook the general benevolence enjoined (Gal. 6:10). Prayer should be made for all people, including those in authority—all of whom were probably non-Christians at the time the words were written (I Tim. 2:1f.). Herman Ridderbos stresses the importance of the fact that, for Paul, love "unfolds itself in a great many 'forms of love.'" He proceeds,

> In addition to love, Paul speaks, for example, of peace (*eirēnē*), steadfastness (*makrothymia*), kindness (*chrēstotēs*), goodness (*agathōsynē*), faithfulness (*pistis*), gentleness (*prautēs*), compassion (*oiktirmos*), humility (*tapeinophrosynē*), forbearing (*anachesthai*), forgiving

---

[46]"Evangelism is implied in the Christian's love for the neighbor.... It offers the neighbor an invitation to meet with God in Christ so that he may achieve the life which God intends for him" (Elmer G. Homrighausen, *Interpretation*, IV, 1950, 414).

[47]Richard N. Longenecker points out that it is "a common human tendency" to develop "a double standard of love: one for the brethren and one for those outside the fold." He adds, "But this one-sided emphasis finds no justification in Paul." A little later he says, "This same balance of love to both Christian and non-Christian is presented in Romans 12, where verses 3-13 deal with action within the Christian fellowship and verses 14-21 with the believer's attitude toward those without" (*Paul: Apostle of Liberty*, New York, Evanston and London, 1964, p. 206).

(*charizesthai*), thinking about what is true (*alēthē*), just (*dikaia*), honorable (*semna*), pure (*hagna*), lovely (*prosphilē*), sweet-sounding (*euphēma*), obligingness (*epieikeia*). ... Of all these concepts and descriptions, some are more, others less "specifically Christian." These virtues, however, even though they occur in the same terms in the non-Christian Greek ethic, in Paul's epistles are always brought under the viewpoint of brotherly communion and the upbuilding of the church, and not, as in the Greek ethic, under that of character formation; they are always understood, therefore, as the fulfillment of the requirement of love....[48]

For Paul, love is obviously the mainspring of Christian life, manifesting itself in a variety of ways. It is impossible to reconcile attitudes like these with hostility or indifference to outsiders. They must be understood as the fruit of love.

LOVE DIVINE

We have seen that some biblical scholars deny that love for the outsider is to be found throughout most of the New Testament. These people often single out the Johannine writings as proof, claiming that they know only about love among believers. For example, John Knox says, "There is in the Fourth Gospel no sign of interest in those outside of the community"; he also claims that, in John, "*agape* is brotherly love, not neighborly love. 'The world' is given up and disregarded."[49] Similarly, Hugh Montefiore holds that "in the Johannine literature it is forbidden to love anyone outside the closed circle of the Christian community; the 'new commandment' is for reciprocal love within the Christian fellowship."[50] Obviously, these

---

[48] *Paul*, p. 297. He goes on to give special attention to humility and meekness.

[49] *The Ethic of Jesus in the Teaching of the Church*, London, 1962, pp. 93, 94. See also the article by Clayton R. Bowen, "Love in the Fourth Gospel" (*JR*, XIII, 1933, 39–49).

[50] *Awkward Questions on Christian Love*, Philadelphia, 1964, p. 107. Similarly, E. Käsemann maintains that the Johannine writings teach love for the believing group but not for the world (*The Testament of Jesus*, London, 1968, pp. 59ff.). J. N. Sanders holds that "John thus appears to restrict the scope of a Christian's love to Christ and the Church" (*A Commentary on the Gospel according to St. John*, edited and completed by B. A. Mastin, London, 1968, p. 129).

are strongly held opinions, and it is an undeniable fact that the Johannine writings place a good deal of emphasis on brotherly love. But to say that they exclude all other love is quite another thing.[51]

When we read John it is important to remember that the love Jesus asks of believers is a love like his own (John 13:34).[52] The attitude of the world is expressly repudiated (John 15:19). Nowhere do we find the thought that love among the Christians is self-generated or produced by men imitating one another; always it is the response to God's love. Throughout the Johannine writings it is divine love that is primary.[53] Are we to think that God, who loved the world sacrificially, would produce in his people a narrow love confined to their own little circle? As John depicts it, God's love is a love for the unworthy, for the outsiders, for the world: "God so loved the world that he gave his only Son so that everyone who believes in him might not perish but have life eternal" (John 3:16).[54]

---

[51]V. P. Furnish examines the entire topic (*The Love Command in the New Testament*, pp. 144–148) and concludes that in John "love for 'one another' is neither a softening nor a repudiation of the command to love the neighbor, but a special and indeed urgent form of it" (p. 184).

[52]Cf. John Painter: "With the definitive demonstration in mind, it is hard to accept the view, put forward by some commentators, to the effect that 'love one another' (13.34f.; 15.12, 17) means 'love only believers'"; "the movement of God's love, from the Father through the Son to the disciples, has the world in view. God loved the world and gave his Son" (*John: Witness and Theologian*, London, 1975, pp. 93, 99).

[53]C. E. Raven points out that John's other great concepts must be understood in relation to love: "All his dominant ideas—life, faith, knowledge, truth, salvation, unity—are conceived in relation to love. Life is not immortality: it is a loving union with God and the brethren. Faith is love in action; knowledge, love in apprehension" (*Jesus and the Gospel of Love*, London, 1931, p. 183).

[54]Sometimes this text is regarded as relatively insignificant. For example, E. Käsemann thinks it simply "a traditional primitive Christian formula which the Evangelist employed." He holds that its "sole purpose in John" is to emphasize "the glory of Jesus' mission, that is to say the miracle of the incarnation" (*The Testament of Jesus*, p. 60). But this is to ignore the context. The passage in which the words are found is concerned with judgment and salvation, not with glory and the incarnation. Moreover, Käsemann has not succeeded in proving that the words are a traditional formula. Even if they are, John would

That is quite plain, as B. B. Warfield points out: "The declaration is not that God has loved some out of the world, but that He has loved the world."[55] And this declaration is repeated in similar assurances like this one: "God did not send his Son into the world to condemn the world, but so that the world might be saved through him" (John 3:17). The idea that the Father sent the Son is one of the key ideas of the Fourth Gospel. And if we ask why the Father sent[56] the Son, the only answer we can give from this gospel is that he sent him to bring salvation[57] to sinful men at the cost of the cross. This means that God loved sinners, even if the word *love* does not happen to be used in a particular passage.

Those who think this gospel is preoccupied with love within a narrow circle point out that John reported that Jesus said, "I do not pray for the world" (John 17:9).[58] They see this

---

not have used them unless he accepted them. And the fact is that we know them only because they are recorded in John. We should notice what C. H. Dodd has said about this verse: "The statement in iii.16 is quite fundamental to our author's position, and the reader is intended to bear it in mind during the following discussions" (*The Interpretation of the Fourth Gospel*, Cambridge, 1953, p. 307). Similarly, R. Schnackenburg's comment on the verse refers to "God's immense love" and to the world as "the object of God's infinite love and mercy" (*The Gospel according to St. John*, New York, 1968, p. 399).

[55] *Biblical and Theological Studies*, Philadelphia, 1952, p. 517.

[56] Cf. C. K. Barrett: "Love for the world led to the mission of the incarnate Son" (W. Klassen and G. F. Snyder, eds., *Current Issues in New Testament Interpretation*, London, 1962, p. 214). He contrasts this with the Gnostic *Gospel of Truth*, for that document "knows little . . . of God's love for the world, which forms a second focus in the Johannine pattern of love" (p. 215).

[57] D. D. Williams says, "In the New Testament, the love of God means the complete spiritual communion for which the human image of father and son offers the most important analogy. God loves his Son and he loves the world with an unshakeable will to communion (John 3:16)" (*The Spirit and the Forms of Love*, p. 37). But John 3:16 is not about communion; it is about saving men from perishing, about the cross and eternal life. Williams has earlier said, "*Agape* is first and primordially the spirit of communion willing the divine relationship between Father and Son as the ground and pattern of the fulfilment of all things" (p. 37). But consistently he ignores the teaching of the New Testament that it is the cross that shows us what *agapē* is.

[58] H. W. Montefiore is one; he says, "It is in the Fourth Gospel that the distinction of attitude towards Christian and non-Christian is

as conclusive evidence in itself that the Johannine Jesus had no interest in the world, no concern or love for it. But they rarely notice that Jesus *did* pray for the world—twice. He prayed that the world would believe that the Father had sent him (John 17:21); he also prayed that the world would "know that you sent me and loved them as you loved me" (John 17:23). And he prefixed these prayers with a clear statement that he did not pray "for these [i.e., the disciples] only" (John 17:20; he goes on to refer to those who would believe on him, but at the time of the prayer they were not believers but worldly people). The point of his earlier refusal to pray for the world is the obvious one that it was impossible for Jesus (and it is impossible for his followers) to pray for "the world" as such. That would be praying that the world continue in its "worldliness," in its capacity as "world." The only prayer that any serious-minded person can ever pray for the heedless, self-centered world is that it cease to be what it is—worldly. And this prayer, as we have noticed, Jesus prayed. It is simply not true that the Johannine Jesus had no love for the world. He died for it (John 3:16), and he certainly prayed for it. He prayed that it might come to know that his mission was from God the Father and that the Father's love was wrapped up with that mission (John 17:23). In this passage of John, the unity of believers and their dwelling in God and he in them are stressed for their importance to the world. This is not the ghetto mentality of a group of inward-looking believers; this is concern for the world and a reaching out to it. To stop at verse nine is to miss the thrust of the prayer and to overlook some clear words of Jesus.

The incident of Jesus' contact with the woman at the well (John 4) is instructive. The woman was far from being a shining example of virtue and worth, so Jesus' willingness to spend time with her is significant in itself; he was reaching out to the unworthy. When she recognized him as the Messiah, the first thing she did was think of the needs of others—the people of her village (John 4:28ff.). At this point Jesus talks to the disciples about the waiting harvest, and about their joining the

---

most clearly marked.... In the Fourth Gospel Christ does not pray for the world, only for his disciples and those who will believe through them. In the Fourth Gospel Christ does not die for the world. He lays down his life for his friends" (*Awkward Questions on Christian Love*, p. 106). There is truth here, but left in this form it is a distortion of the teaching of the Fourth Gospel.

labors of others (John 4:35, 38). What were those labors if not some kind of help directed toward people outside the fellowship?

A similar readiness to help others is surely implied in the difficult words about the Spirit and the outflowing of living water (John 7:37–39). It seems to me that the passage ought to be understood to mean rivers flowing from the heart of the believer.[59] If so, Jesus is saying that when the Spirit comes into the disciples, they will be outgoing people; from them living water will flow to others. But even if I am wrong, the passage still inculcates concern for outsiders. The alternative view is that these rivers flow from Christ. If this is the proper way to interpret the passage, then Jesus is setting the example of being outgoing, an example his followers are expected to imitate.

Similar are the words about disciples being made free (John 8:31f.). Jesus is not referring to philosophical truth or something like it liberating the mind from its darkness; he is speaking of the truth of the gospel, which liberates men from sin (vv. 34-36), setting them free from self-centeredness, among other things.[60] This is also the message of the passage about loving life and losing it (John 12:24f.). To be concentrating on oneself is to lose life. Jesus is calling people to a fuller life, the life of the true believer who has died to his own selfish concerns.

The washing of the disciples' feet should not be overlooked (John 13:1ff.), particularly because Jesus told the disciples that what he did then was an example for them (v. 15). For our present purpose the significant point is that Judas was included. Jesus knew that Judas was in the process of betraying him (vv. 21-30), yet he did not refrain from washing Judas's feet. This surely means that those who truly follow Jesus' example must not refrain from works of service because the recipients are unworthy. In fact, serving sinners is the kind of

---

[59]See the discussion in my *The Gospel according to John,* Grand Rapids, 1971, pp. 422–28.

[60]C. Spicq cites Thomas Aquinas to bring out the liberating function of love: "*Charity makes of the slave a free being and a friend.* . . . If one acts, not through fear of chastisement but out of love of God, he does not conduct himself as a slave but as a free being, because his action is voluntary" (*Charity and Liberty,* New York, 1966, pp. 100f., n. 2).

work to which they are called; they are not to concentrate on an "in" group.[61]

A little earlier John records a comment of this same Judas that points to an interest in outsiders. When Mary anointed Jesus, Judas asked why the unguent was not sold for more than three hundred denarii and the proceeds given to the poor (John 12:5). We are usually so taken up with Judas's misunderstanding of the spirit of Mary's gift that we do not stop to reflect that even Judas took it for granted that a generous gift might be made to the poor from the slender resources of the little band (cf. John 13:29). This clearly indicates the importance of the needs of others.

The Fourth Gospel stresses the theme that Jesus came to give men life. He is "the bread of God" and "comes down from heaven and gives life to the world" (John 6:33). He came "that they may have life and have it abundantly" (John 10:10). This gift of life comes at great cost, for Jesus is the Good Shepherd who gives his life for the sheep (John 10:11, 15, 17f.). He says that men must eat his flesh and drink his blood if they are to have life (John 6:53ff.). Because Jesus' life was offered in sacrifice, believers must embrace all that this action means. John is surely saying in such teaching that Jesus' entire life, and more especially his giving of himself in a sacrificial death, is an expression of love for sinners and of his concern to bring them life.

Thus, when this gospel says that the followers of Jesus must love others as he loved them, it is not easy to see how this can be made to mean that they are to love only selectively.[62] They must pour out their love on others just as Jesus poured out his costly love on sinners. John leaves us in no doubt that love is to be the principal distinguishing characteristic of Jesus' followers. He tells us that Jesus delivered his new commandment of love and added, "By this will all men know that you are my disciples, if you have love for one another" (John

---

[61]The dialogue with Peter centers on cleansing, and J. C. Fenton comments, "The cleansing of which he speaks is cleansing from everything that contradicts love" (*The Gospel according to John,* Oxford, 1970, p. 140).

[62]John Bagot Glub speaks of "the principle that the love flows out of us, and is in no way connected with the qualities of the recipient" (*The Way of Love,* London, 1977, p. 128). He is not speaking specifically of *agapē,* but this is not a bad description of it.

13:34f.).[63] This love must be made plain to "all men," which means people outside the church as well as its members. In John 15:12,17 the command to love comes again,[64] so it is clearly important. As G. E. Ladd puts it, "It is not too much to say that Jesus' whole ethic in John is summed up in love."[65]

It is true that some of the Jews believed that love for those within the community carried with it a hatred for those outside it. Thus the men of Qumran were called on to "hate all the sons of darkness."[66] But no such equivalent exists in John's writings, and we should not read it into what he says. Believers cannot imitate the outgoing love that sent Jesus to the cross to save sinners by engaging in a selective love extended to favored friends, coupled with a hatred for others. John's whole outlook forbids such an understanding of his meaning.[67]

---

[63]C. K. Barrett comments, "John, however, more than any other writer, develops the conception of love as the nature of God himself and as the means by which the divine life, the relation of the Father and the Son, is perpetuated and demonstrated within the community (13:35)" (*The Gospel according to St. John,* London, 1955, p. 180).

[64]The command to love in John 15:12 is followed by these words: "Greater love has no one than this, that he lay down his life for his friends" (v. 13). This obviously refers to Jesus' own death for his people. Raymond E. Brown remarks that this is an incentive to self-sacrifice which "has left a greater mark on subsequent behavior than, for example, a similar sentence in Plato (*Symposium* 179B): 'Only those who love wish to die for others'" (*The Gospel according to John,* II, New York, 1970, 664).

[65]*A Theology of the New Testament,* Grand Rapids, 1974, p. 279.

[66]Cited from G. Vermes, *The Dead Sea Scrolls in English,* Harmondsworth, 1962, p. 72. Raymond E. Brown seems to me to miss an important thrust of John's teaching when he writes, "In this stress John is not far from the thought of Qumran" (*The Gospel according to John,* II, 613). F. C. Fensham points out that brotherly love was "a general characteristic of Jewish thought in those days," and he finds it in the Apocrypha and the Pseudepigrapha (specifically in *The Testaments of the Twelve Patriarchs;* see *Neotestamentica,* 6, 1972, p. 75). That brotherly love was widespread among the Jews means that we need not see a connection between John and Qumran in this respect. There is thus no reason for reading into John statements about hate found only in the Qumran writings.

[67]V. P. Furnish points out that the command to love one another "need not be regarded in itself as *excluding* love for 'neighbors' and 'enemies.' In fact, it is hard to fit such terms into the framework of this writer's theology" (*The Love Command in the New Testament,*

LOVE IN FIRST JOHN

The First Epistle of John says a good deal about brotherly love; in fact, there are those who claim that I John, like John, looks for love only among believers.[68] True, in some places the writer seems clearly to have believers in mind. This must be so, for example, in his explicit mention of love for "the children of God" (I John 5:2). Similarly, he writes, "This is the message which you heard from the beginning, that we love one another" (I John 3:11), and he records the command that "we love one another" (I John 3:23; cf. II John 5). But more often he refers to love of "the brother," a usage that makes us wonder if the term always or sometimes refers to those outside the Christian community. The term, of course, may mean "brother man" as well as "brother Christian."

The wider meaning seems demanded in a number of passages. For instance, we read, "In this we know love, that he laid down his life for us; we too should lay down our lives for

---

p. 148). Cf. W. F. Howard: "If man's love to man is determined by God's love to man, then, as that is universal in its scope, so also will the limitless claims of human need enlarge yet more and more the scope of this inspired activity of love" (*Christianity according to St. John*, London, 1943, p. 170).

[68]Thus J. L. Houlden, commenting on I John 4:21, writes, "But here, as always in the Johannine writings, 'brother' replaces 'neighbour,' and we have no reason to believe that the 'brother' of this formulation or of iii.17 represents any wider circle than 'each other' in passages like iii.11, 23; iv.7, 11, 12. . . . As we have seen, the Johannine church is conscious of itself as the enclosed community of the redeemed, and love is the cohesive moral force of its common life. This is the situation in the Gospel, portrayed above all in the Last Discourses, with their private setting, shut off from the outside world, in the room of the supper. In I John it is reinforced by the existence of schismatic and heretical members: a conspicuous element in the charge against them is their failure, from our writer's point of view (would they have said the same to him?), to preserve this cohesive bond" (*A Commentary on the Johannine Epistles*, London, 1973, pp. 120f.). H. Montefiore draws attention to passages in the Fourth Gospel that he thinks confine love to the Christian circle, and goes on, "Indeed, in one of the Johannine Epistles, it is even said that a man cannot love God unless he loves his fellow-Christians (1 John 4:20), while anyone who loves the world is a stranger to God's love (1 John 2:15)" (*Awkward Questions on Christian Love*, p. 107).

the brothers" (I John 3:16). Here believers are urged to model themselves after Christ. Now his death "for us" was not a death for the good or the faithful or anyone who could claim merit. In his death Jesus was "the propitiation for our sins, not for ours only but also for the whole world" (I John 2:2). Because Jesus died for sinners and because believers are called on to be ready to die in the same manner as he did (I John 3:16), they are plainly directed to show sacrificial love for sinners.[69] Similar is John's assertion that love is defined not by our love for God but by the fact that "he loved us and sent his Son to be the propitiation for our sins." He immediately adds, "Beloved, if God so loved us, we too should love one another" (I John 4:10f.). Again it is Christ's propitiatory death that is the standard: we are to love sinners with a sacrificial love because Christ did.[70] The writer says, "We have seen and we bear our witness that the Father sent the Son to be the Savior of the world" (I John 4:14). Once more it is made plain that divine love is directed to those outside the fold. We should probably draw a similar inference from the fact that "God gave us eternal life and this life is in his Son" (I John 5:11). Because life is God's gift, it is not a reward for merit; because it is in his Son, it depends on the Son's saving work. Passages like these make it clear that this epistle pictures God as loving sinful people outside the Christian brotherhood. And because believers are

---

[69]Reuel L. Howe reminds us that the costliness of real love is important: "We are willing to love up to the point where it begins to be inconvenient to love any more. We like the image of ourselves as loved and loving people, but we would like the benefit without the responsibilities of the role. When the response to our love presents us with demands, we may begin to hold people off" (*Herein is Love*, Valley Forge, 1965, p. 33). But the cross demands a love that is wholehearted and sacrificial.

[70]Paul W. Hoon sees the motive for *agapē* in these words: "Let us love one another.... God is love,... he loved us,... we also ought to love one another." He says, "Other motives by contrast are seen to be inadequate.... The attractiveness or responsiveness of those to be loved is an inadequate motive. The essence of Christian love is that it is to be directed precisely toward the unlovable, the unlovely, even toward the hostile (cf. Matt. 5:44–48), for such is the character of the love God has revealed to us" (*IB*, XII, 281). It is significant that, expounding I John 4:7–12, he finds the same kind of love as that in Matthew 5:44–48, where believers are instructed to love their enemies.

to model themselves after God, it is obvious that they should love people outside their circle.

"Look what kind of love the Father has given us, that we should be called 'God's children'; and we are" (I John 3:1). John notes that the world does not know God's children any more than it knew Christ, which leads to the thought that "we know that if he is manifested we shall be like him, for we shall see him as he is" (v. 2). And he is the Savior of the world (I John 4:14). Being like him must surely include loving those he loved, those for whom he died. And when John says, "We love, because he first loved us" (I John 4:19), he surely means that the love of Christians is to be like the love of God that produced it (and thus a love for outsiders) rather than a different kind of love (confined to those in the fold).[71] This may well be the implication also of the comment about being righteous "as he is righteous" (I John 3:7), because "Jesus Christ the righteous" is both our Advocate with the Father and the propitiation for our sins (I John 2:1f.). Related to this is John's test to determine who are the children of God and who are the children of the devil; he links the failure to do righteousness with the failure to love (I John 3:10).

We can also notice the importance of love for "outsiders" in a contrast John makes. He tells his readers not to be surprised if the world hates them, and immediately proceeds, "We know that we have passed out of death into life because we love the brothers" (I John 3:14). His "we" (*hēmeis*) is emphatic. But there is no emphatic contrast if Christians love their own little group in the same way that the world loves its own. He goes on, "He who does not love... ," a clause in which the absolute use is important. A. E. Brooke points out that some manuscripts add "the brother," and continues, "But it narrows down the writer's meaning unnecessarily. In his more absolute statements he shows himself fully aware that

---

[71]G. Johnston is in no doubt about this. He remarks, "John has fully grasped his Master's teaching. Some Christians love too easily their distant, unknown brethren to the neglect of those on their doorstep; others refuse to help the far-off on the ground that charity begins at home! John might have added an injunction to love the enemy and the heretic; but his statement in 19 sublimely and simply defines the obligation of love, and makes it absolute: 'We love, because he first loved us'" (Matthew Black and H. H. Rowley, eds., *Peake's Commentary on the Bible*, London, 1963, p. 1038).

the duty of love is absolute, and has a wider application than the Christian society, even as the Christ is the propitiation for the whole world."[72] This passage, then, demands that the love of the Christian be more inclusive than the love of the world.

There is a notable sequence in chapter 4.[73] We have already noted that love is not our love for God but his for us, a love expressed in his sending his Son as the propitiation for our sins. John goes on, "Beloved, if God so loved us, we too ought to love one another" (I John 4:10f.). It is not easy to understand "one another" here as meaning "Christians only," because the model is Christ, who died for sinners, and we are to love as he did. And this is the way we should understand the next words: "Nobody has ever seen God; if we love one another, God dwells in us and his love has been perfected [or has reached its aim] in us" (v. 12).[74] Because God's Son died for sinners, we give no evidence of the presence of God within us if we simply love those who love us. True Christian love is outgoing love, a love such as God showed in saving the unlovely.

Then we read that the Father sent the Son to be the Savior of the world (v. 14), and that "God is love" (v. 16). This leads to the thought that "he who abides in love abides in God, and God abides in him. In this has love been perfected with us, that we may have confidence in the day of judgment, for as he is we too are in this world" (vv. 16f.). Once again we are likened to Christ in his death for "the world." How, then, can our love be limited to the saved?

DARKNESS AND LIGHT

John draws some interesting contrasts, one of which is that between darkness and light, a contrast he sometimes links with love. For example, he says, "He who says that he is in the light

---

[72]*A Critical and Exegetical Commentary on the Johannine Epistles,* New York, 1912, p. 94.

[73]R. Bultmann finds "no doubt" that the absolute use "he who loves" (v. 7) "means the love of neighbor, even though no object is appended," and he rejects Schnackenburg's view that brotherly love is in mind in 4:7–5:4 (*The Johannine Epistles,* Philadelphia, 1973, p. 66).

[74]Augustine cites the text "God is love," and proceeds, "Why should we go speeding to the height of heaven and the nethermost parts of the earth, seeking for him who is with us, if we would but be

and yet hates his brother is in darkness until now. He who loves his brother abides in the light" (I John 2:9f.). A problem develops if "his brother" is interpreted to mean no more than "Christian brother." Is it possible for a Christian to hate his brother Christian? That is not easy to accept. It seems that John is here writing about those who are not really Christians whatever they may say, those who are "in darkness." In their hatred they are like the world (I John 3:13). When the term *brother* is used to refer to those they hate, it cannot be limited to Christians.[75] And it is scarcely possible to take *brother* in any different sense in verse 10,[76] which speaks of him who loves his brother as being in the light. Hatred and darkness are emphatically linked again in verse 11, which points out once again that to be in the light is to walk in the way of love.

This perhaps follows from the truth that "God is light and in him there is no darkness whatever" (I John 1:5). Accordingly, anyone who claims to enjoy fellowship with God and who yet walks in darkness is lying. But walking with God, who is light, means fellowship with other believers, and it means that the blood of Jesus cleanses us from sin (vv. 6-7). In view of the way the cross is regarded throughout this epistle, it is impossible to doubt that love goes with light here just as it does in I John 2:10.

In a similar way the contrast between hatred and love may be linked with that between death and life: "We know that we have passed out of death into life because we love the brothers; he who does not love abides in death. Everyone who hates his brother is a murderer" (I John 3:14f.). Here life is linked with love, and death with hatred.[77] John speaks first of "love of the

---

with him? Let none say: 'I do not know what I am to love.' Let him love his brother, and he will love that same love" (*De Trin.* 8.11f.; LCC, VIII, 52).

[75]Cf. V. P. Furnish: "When it is said that such a person 'hates his brother' the term *brother* is being used in a general sense to mean 'fellowman.' No common faith binds the hater and the hated together" (*The Love Command in the New Testament,* p. 153). Cf. also Paul W. Hoon: "Love for one's fellow men is life" (*IB,* XII, 263).

[76]Cf. R. Bultmann: "'Brother' means, as in 3:15 and 4:20, not especially the Christian comrade in the faith, but one's fellowman, the 'neighbor'" (*The Johannine Epistles,* p. 28).

[77]Paul W. Hoon thinks that implicit here "is the recollection of a time when the author and his fellow Christians were in death, and the

brothers," but when he goes on he says, "He who does not love," not "He who does not love the brother."[78] With this general statement the writer seems to be referring to the person whose habitual attitude is hate. That man is a murderer, abiding in death; love is the essence of life.

THE WORLD

One passage confidently quoted to show that John has no notion of love outside the brotherhood is that in which he says, "Do not love the world nor the things in the world. If anyone loves the world, the love of the Father is not in him, for all that is in the world, the lust of the flesh and the lust of the eyes and the vainglory of life, is not of the Father but of the world" (2:15f.). This passage is often contrasted with "God so loved the world..." (John 3:16). The conclusion is that love for the world is not found in I John.

But this epistle speaks of the Father sending the Son to be the Savior of the world (I John 4:14). The objection overlooks the fact that "the world" may have any one of several meanings. The term may refer to the universe or to this physical earth. Or it may refer to all of the people in the world, to most of the people in the world, or to the people who set their hearts on this world and oppose God. Or it may mean the world as a round of pursuits opposed to God, what we might designate as "worldiness." This latter is surely the meaning of the term in the passage we are considering.[79] It is the world of various lusts that John deprecates. Indeed, his list of lusts comes close to defining the world in the sense in which he is using the term. To love that world is to be lost. We read, for example, of the defection of Demas, "in love with this present world" (II Tim.

---

life they experience through ethical love is so different and so possessively real that only hyperbolic language can describe the contrast" (*IB*, XII, 263).

[78]There are some MSS which include the words "his brother," but the true text seems not to have them.

[79]Guy H. King, writing a devotional study of the epistle, gives a careful treatment of the term *world* here. He points out that it is not "the world of Matter" nor "the world of Nature" nor "the world of Humanity" but "*it is all within the world that is alienated from God*—whether it be people, or things, or influences" (*The Fellowship*, London, 1954, pp. 51f.).

4:10, RSV). That is the love John opposes. The world in this sense does not know the Christians (I John 3:1); it hates them (I John 3:13). This world—this system hostile to God—is not to be loved.

But God sent his Son into the world (I John 4:9, 14). Quite plainly, John does not mean that Christ came to fraternize with the opponents of good. His mission was to die for sinful men—but it is the world of men that God loves, not the world of lusts or transitory desires. Christ is the Savior of the world, made up of sinful men (I John 4:14).[80] God's people are in the world just as Christ is (I John 4:17).

That believers are to love the world of sinners is also evident in John's view of the importance of helping those in want: "Whoever has this world's good and sees his brother having need and shuts up his compassion from him, how does the love of God dwell in him?" (I John 3:17). The writer adds, "Little children, let us not love in word nor in tongue, but in deed and in truth" (v. 18). This cannot refer only to believers. It is of course true that we cannot see God's love in someone who refuses to help a fellow Christian in need. But it is also hard to see God's love in someone who refuses to help a fellowman in need. If a man "shuts up his compassion" from a needy non-Christian, how does God's love dwell in him?

OTHER LOVES

The most important forms of love in the New Testament are God's love for man and the answering love that God's love awakens in man. We have studied several kinds of this responsive love: love for God, love for the brotherhood, and love for other men. But we should also notice that some other kinds of love are mentioned in the New Testament. For instance, Jesus says of a servant with two masters that he will "hate the one and love the other" (Matt. 6:24; Luke 16:13). This calls for no special comment, because Jesus is simply speaking about a typical human reaction. We could say something similar about the centurion who loved the nation (Luke 7:5) or about the

---

[80]J. R. W. Stott comments, "Here is the essence of the gospel. *The world* means sinful society, estranged from God and under the dominion of the evil one (cf. v. 19). Its urgent need was to be rescued from sin and Satan" (*The Epistles of John,* London, 1966, pp. 166f.).

forgiven debtors who love him who forgave them (Luke 7:42). There is also a reference to the martyrs "who did not love their life as far as death" (Rev. 12:11). With these we should perhaps group the references to loving Christ's "appearance" (*epiphaneia*, II Tim. 4:8) and to "the beloved city" (Rev. 20:9). In the last times "the love of many will grow cold" (Matt. 24:12). Sometimes men are said to love things they ought not, such as darkness rather than light (John 3:19). Demas loved this present age (II Tim. 4:10) and Balaam loved "the wages of unrighteousness" (II Pet. 2:15). The Pharisees loved prominent seats in synagogues (Luke 11:43), and there were those who loved the praise of men rather than that of God (John 12:43). We are exhorted not to love the world, because if anyone does so the love of the Father is not in him (I John 2:15). Such passages show common usages of the term *love*, references that anyone might make. They would be significant if they comprised the major usage in the New Testament, because then they would show that the New Testament sees love in much the same way as do other writings. But such references are few, and don't suggest the distinctively Christian concept of love. They simply show that sometimes the New Testament writers could use the terminology for love in ways that were common at that time.

There is, however, one group of passages that merit closer examination: those in which we read about the love of man and wife. In a way these are not distinctively Christian, because it is not difficult to find passages in all literatures that speak feelingly of love within the marriage bond. Yet they are distinctive in a most important way, as Ephesians 5:25 shows: "Husbands, love your wives just as Christ too loved the church and gave himself for it." Here, as elsewhere, the mainspring of a Christian's love is Christ's love.[81] So when the writer might easily have contented himself with a general exhortation about marital love, he instead turns quite naturally to the cross, with

---

[81]C. S. Lewis comments, "This headship, then, is most fully embodied not in the husband we should all wish to be but in him whose marriage is most like a crucifixion; whose wife receives most and gives least, is most unworthy of him, is—in her own mere nature—least lovable. For the Church has no beauty but what the Bridegroom gives her; he does not find, but makes her, lovely. The chrism of this terrible coronation is to be seen not in the joys of any man's marriage but in its sorrows, in the sickness and sufferings of a

its vivid demonstration of what real love means. The husband should love as Christ loved. H. D. McDonald explains the significance of this command:

> The call to husbands to love their wives was no less revolutionary than what Paul has to say about relationships in general. This declaration raises the wife to the position of co-partner. She is no longer a chattel; a thing to be used. Only as this statement is read in the light of I Corinthians 13 is its full significance understood. There is no question there of another's inferiority and one's own superiority. All that is gone—lost in love. And when the standard of the love as here stated is taken seriously—even as Christ loved the church—then the position of the wife in relation to the husband is all the more close and all the more intimate.[82]

A little later Paul reinforces his call for love: "Husbands ought so to love their wives as their bodies. He who loves his wife loves himself, for no one ever hated his own flesh but he nourishes and cherishes it" (Eph. 5:28f.). He reminds his readers that men naturally love their own bodies, carefully providing for their physical needs. And a man's love for his wife must be viewed as equally important, a wholehearted love. Paul goes on to refer to Christ's love for the church, so he still has the Savior's self-sacrificing love before him as the standard. He reminds his readers of the provision in Genesis 2:24 that a man should leave those nearest him, even his father and mother, and be joined to his wife so closely that they are "one flesh." There is to be no doubt about the closeness of the tie with which love binds them. Clearly there are mysteries in this description of marriage, especially when one uses it to illustrate the relationship between Christ and the church (v. 32). But later in the passage Paul clearly sums up the duty of a husband to his wife: "Let each of you individually love his wife as he does himself" (v. 33).[83] That is the significant thing.

---

good wife or the faults of a bad one, in his unwearying (never paraded) care or his inexhaustible forgiveness: forgiveness, not acquiescence" (*The Four Loves*, pp. 121f.). Christian love in a marriage is to be seen not in the fine careless rapture of *erōs* in fair weather, but in the love that is so constant in times of storm.

[82] *The Church and its Glory*, Worthing, 1973, p. 135.

[83] The expression *kath' hena* means "all without one exception" (T. C. Edwards, *A Commentary on the First Epistle to the Corinthians*, London, 1903, p. 380). J. MacPherson comments, "The care-

There is a similar exhortation to husbands to love their wives in Colossians 3:19. But on this occasion there is no elaboration or argument; husbands are simply told to love their wives and not be bitter.

*   *   *   *   *

Love for others is clearly an important New Testament conception. It is commanded; it is taught; it is lived. And the Christian community was truly permeated by love—though a few distressing exceptions were evident. "Envy, hatred, malice, and all uncharitableness" have a depressing way of turning up in human conduct, and the early church, like other communities, had members who succumbed to these negative qualities. Thus we must guard against painting an idealized picture of the church in its first days. In fact, the very emphasis that the New Testament writers gave to the importance of love may itself be an indication that some believers were not as loving as they should have been.

But, despite its shortcomings, the church emphasized love both in its teaching and in its life. It is a revolutionary thought that one shows love for God not in pious practices, but in acts of love for one's fellowmen. People still have difficulty grasping this truth. But love is still the test. To claim to love God but not to love one's fellowman is to lie. There is not and never has been a substitute for love.

---

ful way in which the counsel is addressed to each individual among them without exception shows that no plea whatever can exempt them from the discharge of this obligation" (*Commentary on St. Paul's Epistle to the Ephesians,* Edinburgh, 1892, p. 409).

CHAPTER TEN

Love, just Love

"*A*DD ... to your piety brotherly love, and to your brotherly love, love" (II Pet. 1:7). Brotherly love was very important for the early church, and it is important still. But brotherly love is not enough. The writer calls on his readers to add "love [*agapē*]" to it,[1] but he does not say to whom this love should be directed. When the phrase "brotherly love" is used, it is obvious that other members of the Christian brotherhood are to be the objects of special affection and concern. But "love" is unqualified.[2] Christians are simply to be loving people.

This way of speaking is found often in the New Testament. Quite frequently, of course, the object of the Christian's love is mentioned, as it is when he is told to love God or the brothers

---

[1]Michael Green comments, "The crown of Christian 'advance' (to return to the martial metaphor of the Stoic *prokopē* on which this list of qualities seems to be modelled) is *love*. 'The greatest of these is love' (1 Cor. xiii.13). This word *agapē* is one which Christians to all intents and purposes coined to denote the attitude which God has shown Himself to have to us, and requires from us towards Himself. In friendship (*philia*) the partners seek mutual solace; in sexual love (*erōs*), mutual satisfaction. In both cases these feelings are aroused because of what the loved one is. With *agapē* it is the reverse. God's *agapē* is evoked not by what we are, but by what He is. It has its origin in the agent, not in the object. It is not that we are lovable, but that He is love. This *agapē* might be defined as a deliberate desire for the highest good of the one loved, which shows itself in sacrificial action for that person's good" (*The Second Epistle General of Peter and the General Epistle of Jude,* London, 1968, p. 71).

[2]This does not mean that love is to be thought of as an abstract principle. Cf. James Moffatt: "There is no 'idea' of love in the NT literature. We find men loving strongly and freshly; that is the source of the conceptions about love, not any abstract principle" (*Love in the New Testament,* London, 1922, p. 53).

228

or his neighbor or his wife. But sometimes no object is specified. The noun *agapē*, for example, is used in this way fifty-five times. But it is perhaps even more significant that the verb *agapaō* is used absolutely seven times (Luke 7:47 [*bis*]; I John 3:14, 18; 4:7, 8, 19).[3] This usage, uncommon outside the New Testament,[4] is significant apparently because it indicates that the person who has felt the touch of God's love responds with a similar love, a love proceeding from the fact that the loved person is now a loving person. His habitual attitude is one of love.

An interesting example of this is provided by the story of the forgiveness of the sinful woman. When Jesus was dining in the house of a Pharisee, this woman stood behind him at his feet, weeping. With her tears she wet his feet, then wiped them with her hair, kissed them, and anointed them. When she finished, Jesus said to his host, "Her sins, many as they are, have been forgiven, for she loved much; but he to whom little is forgiven loves little" (Luke 7:47).[5] Did the woman love

---

[3]The numbers may possibly be higher, depending on the resolution of textual problems. For example, in most MSS of I Corinthians 8:3 the verb *agapai* has *ton theon* as its object, but the object is absent from P46 and Clement. C. Spicq is one who thinks this reading is to be preferred (*Agape in the New Testament,* II, St. Louis and London, 1965, 27).

[4]Thus H. G. Wood draws attention to the absolute use of *agapaō* in Psalm 113(114):1 and quotes the *Wörterbuch:* "Here the verb 'I love' has no object in the Hebrew, and it is better to retain the absolute use, in spite of its difficulty, and not to substitute words of one's own, however poetical." Wood suggests that the verb may be understood to mean "I feel the deepest thankfulness," and adds, "This removes the difficulty felt in the absolute use of the verb" (*ET,* LXVI, 1954–55, 319f.). Whatever the merits of his solution, the significant thing for us is that he finds the absolute use of the verb difficult. It seems not to have been so difficult for at least some of the New Testament Christians. Perhaps it should be added that the verse Wood is discussing is Psalm 116:1 in the Hebrew and English texts, Psalm 114:1 in LXX.

[5]Some have taken the words to mean that the woman was forgiven because of her love. Grammatically this would be possible, but as C. F. D. Moule says, this is "a non-Christian conclusion which throws the sentence into complete opposition both to the preceding parable and to the second half of this very verse." He gives the meaning as "I can say with confidence that her sins are forgiven,

God? Or Jesus? Or, perhaps, people? The Master does not say—nor does he say whom the man who knows little of forgiveness loves but little. But it is fair to say that in both cases Jesus is referring to the general attitude of the individuals involved.[6] The forgiven woman loved God and she loved Jesus, but the general use of the expression "loved much" seems to mean more: it seems to mean that she had become a loving person. Clearly, the New Testament knows nothing of a love for God that does not manifest itself in a love for people.

We have seen that the New Testament consistently sees love as originating in God, which may be expressed explicitly with the absolute use of noun or verb. "Love is of God," writes John; he also says, "Everyone who loves has been begotten from God" (I John 4:7). And, "We love, because he first loved us" (I John 4:19). In such passages the transformation that makes us loving people is God's work. People do not transform themselves, nor are they gripped by an overmastering passion; they are changed by a divine creative work.

SINCERITY

The early Christians must have been sometimes tempted to claim this kind of love when they did not have it. This becomes obvious when Paul writes, "Let love be without pretense" (Rom. 12:9), because this exhortation would be without point if

---

because her love is evidence of it" (*An Idiom Book of New Testament Greek,* Cambridge, 1953, p. 147). See also the discussion in I. Howard Marshall, *The Gospel of Luke,* Exeter, 1978, p. 313. The Jerusalem Bible translates, "I tell you that her sins, her many sins, must have been forgiven her, or she would not have shown such great love." It adds a footnote rejecting the translation "Her many sins are forgiven her *because* she has shown such great love," and comments, "The context demands the reverse: she shows so much affection because she has had so many sins forgiven."

[6]Cf. E. Stauffer: "It is striking that in this passage *agapan* is twice used without any precise indication of object, the more so as this absolute use of the verb is otherwise confined to the First Epistle of John. It brings out the more clearly what is at issue in Lk. 7:47— namely, that a new life is awakened and the person now has love, is filled with it, and is guided by it in all his actions, rather than that he is to show it to such and such people" (*TDNT,* I, 47).

there was no one who claimed to love but did not.[7] Paul further refers to his own "love without pretense" (II Cor. 6:6), and he speaks of the "sincerity [*gnēsion*]" of the love of the Corinthians (II Cor. 8:8). Genuine love is sacrificial, deeply interested in the well-being of the loved one, not in the credit the loving person might claim. The love Paul looks for is thus honest, without dissimulation. Knowing that it is easier to claim this kind of love than to produce it, John exhorts his readers, "Little children, let us not love in word nor in tongue, but in work and truth" (I John 3:18). What we say matters little. The test of love is in the things we do, the way we live.[8]

In other places it is not clear whether John has in mind people who claimed to love in this way or those who thought that this kind of love was not really necessary. For whatever reason, he assures his readers that "he who does not love does not know God" (I John 4:8; cf. John 17:3 for the connection between knowing God and life). Both to claim to have love but not to have it and to claim that love is not necessary are disastrous. A person suffering from either problem is lifeless, without any true knowledge of God. Genuine, sincere love is the essence of Christianity.

In Revelation John makes an illuminating comment on the church at Ephesus when he conveys the message of the risen Christ: "I have against you that you have forsaken your first love" (Rev. 2:4). This group of Christians is clearly going astray, as the rest of the message indicates: "Remember therefore whence you have fallen and repent and do the first works. Otherwise I am coming to you and I will remove your

---

[7]John Knox comments, "Love must be 'genuine' (literally 'nonhypocritical'). The suggestion is that it is *not* genuine if it fails to discriminate between the 'good' and the 'evil'; love is not at war with truth (cf. I Cor. 13:6). This love will manifest itself in warm 'affection,' in courtesy ('outdo one another in showing honor'), and in ardent devotion to Christ (vs. 11)" (*IB*, IX, 588f.).

[8]Cf. Clyde L. Breland: "Sheridan, in his *School for Scandal*, observes that one of his characters 'appears to have as much speculative benevolence as any private gentleman in the kingdom, though he is seldom so sensual as to indulge himself in the exercise of it'" (*Assurance of Divine Fellowship*, Nashville, 1939, p. 185). But it is both the duty and the privilege of the Christian to engage constantly in this exercise.

lampstand out of its place, unless you repent." This church is praised for a number of things: its works, its labor, its steadfastness, its refusal to tolerate evil men, its testing of false apostles and showing them to be liars, its endurance on account of Christ's name without growing weary (vv. 2f.), its hatred of the works of the Nikolaitanes (v. 6). This is a splendid list of good qualities. One might think that a church with so many credits must have a long list of demerits to justify such a serious possible punishment as the removal of its lampstand, its total destruction. But it has committed only one sin: it has left its first love.[9] Yet this single sin is so serious that the church that has committed it will forfeit its place if it does not repent.[10]

Live in Love

Many of the absolute references to love seem to show that love is a way of life, the only way for Christians. "Walk in love," we read, "even as Christ also loved us" (Eph. 5:2). Walking is a metaphor that Paul in particular uses frequently. It indicates steady and persistent—if unspectacular—progress. That Paul uses it to bring out the way Christians should live is emphasized by the NEB, which renders this exhortation as "Live in love." Among other things, this means taking care not to offend or grieve another believer. Paul points out, for example, that if a believer's eating habits offend his brother, he is "no longer walking according to love" (Rom. 14:15). Paul wants none of this; it is not the Christian way. "Let all your

---

[9]V. P. Furnish says that in Revelation "love is still hailed as a characteristic of the Christian life, indeed the vital element, the *sine qua non,* of Christian existence. When the Ephesian congregation is charged with having given up the love it had at first, the meaning is that they have fallen away from faith itself and need now to make a complete about-face" (*The Love Command in the New Testament,* Nashville and New York, 1972, p. 169).

[10]Some have found the absolute use of the term *love* impossible, and have helped out the author by supplying an object. Thus Weymouth translates, "You no longer love Me," and the TEV, "You do not love me now as you did at first." From another point of view James Moffatt renders, "You have given up loving one another." But no object is needed. The accusation is that they have ceased to be loving, and that is quite incompatible with the Christian profession.

matters be done in love," he writes (I Cor. 16:14).[11] And he offers a succinct description of the Christian way when he says, "In Christ Jesus neither circumcision nor uncircumcision is of any consequence, but faith working through love" (Gal. 5:6).

The centrality of love is also obvious in the prayer that the Ephesians may be "rooted and founded in love" (Eph. 3:17).[12] Love is to be the root of all their actions, the foundation on which their Christian edifice is built. Both pieces of imagery see love as fundamental. Similar in meaning is the injunction "And above all these put on love" (Col. 3:14). Paul has been listing a number of desirable qualities in Christians, all of which are important, but the crowning quality is unmistakable—love.

Sometimes love and good works are linked: "I know your works and love . . . ," said Christ to the church at Thyatira (Rev. 2:19). It seems that the list that follows reveals the works of which the Lord approves, and it is of interest, accordingly, that love leads all the rest (it is followed by faith, as it often is). The writer to the Hebrews calls on his readers to provoke one another "to love and good works" (Heb. 10:24). He has a strong expression for "provoke"; it is really a noun, *paroxysmos,* which usually has a meaning like "exasperation" or "irritation."[13] It is unusual to have it used in a positive sense, a usage that makes the exhortation all the more vigorous. It may be significant in two ways that the writer looks to his friends to help one another to be loving people. The first important point is that love is not a virtue that can be practiced alone. One may hope without other people, or believe, but one cannot love in

---

[11]These words follow immediately on "play the man [*andrizesthe*], be strong." As James Moffatt puts it, "Strength of conviction furnishes a special temptation to be self-assertive and dictatorial, when those who do *play the man* are unable to make others agree with their aims or methods" (*Love in the New Testament,* p. 191, n.1).

[12]See above, p. 168, n.6 for the interpretation of this verse.

[13]It is used only one other time in the New Testament—in the reference to the quarrel between Paul and Barnabas (Acts 15:39). Interestingly, the cognate verb is used in I Corinthians 13:5, where Paul says love "is not provoked." F. F. Bruce notices this passage and proceeds, "But here love *is* provoked in the sense of being stimulated in the lives of Christians by the considerateness and example of other members of their fellowship" (*Commentary on the Epistle to the Hebrews,* London, 1964, p. 253).

isolation. The other important point is that love is so essential to the Christian way that the writer does not leave it to the discretion of the individual. Each Christian should be zealous in stimulating other Christians "to love and good works."

There are some relevant passages in the Pastorals. Paul the persecutor found mercy when "the grace of our Lord superabounded with faith and love in Christ Jesus" (I Tim. 1:14). The God who saved Paul so strikingly brought good gifts to all Christians. He did not give them "a spirit of cowardice, but of power and love and a sound mind" (II Tim. 1:7). This love is the principal goal of his purpose for them: "Now the aim of the commandment is love, proceeding out of a pure heart and a good conscience and a genuine faith" (I Tim. 1:5). This emphasis is made personal for Timothy in a number of places. Paul commends the young man for having followed Paul's teaching and other things, but specifically for "following" his love (II Tim. 3:10). And more than once he exhorts Timothy to pursue desirable qualities, specifically mentioning love (I Tim. 6:11; II Tim. 1:13; 2:22). Timothy is also exhorted to be a model for the believers in a number of ways, specifically in his exercise of love (I Tim. 4:12). There is no substitute for love in a pastor.

But love is required in people other than pastors. In a passage difficult to interpret Paul talks about women being saved "through childbirth if they continue in faith and love" (I Tim. 2:15). Whatever interpretation we give of being saved through childbirth,[14] the insistence on the place of love (linked once more with faith)[15] is noteworthy. Similarly, old men are counseled to be "sound in faith, in love, in steadfastness" (Titus 2:2). Soundness matters a good deal in these epistles; in

---

[14]For a discussion of some of the suggested interpretations, see Donald Guthrie, *The Pastoral Epistles*, London, 1957, pp. 77–79. Ronald Ward comments, "We should dismiss all thoughts of attaining to salvation by bearing children; this would be a very odd form of justification by works." He understands the expression as "something like this: 'You want to teach in church and be equal to men? It is against the order of creation. You do not want marriage and a family? The pressure of the "curse" is off. Salvation will be enjoyed in the life of motherhood'" (*Commentary on 1 & 2 Timothy & Titus*, Waco, 1977, p. 53).

[15]For the connection between faith and love, see above, p. 189, n.55.

fact, it is often argued that the writer is more concerned with sound doctrine than with the abundant life that is emphasized in other parts of the New Testament. I wonder whether this does justice to the way these epistles emphasize love. Soundness, as it is understood here, includes the exercise of love; the writer is not solely concerned with theology and ecclesiastical rectitude. Of course, these are important to him, but they are not enough. Christianity is not Christianity without love.[16]

These ten[17] passages in the Pastorals, then, put a strong emphasis on the importance of love in the Christian life. The lists of Christian virtues vary in length: sometimes there is no more than a couplet, sometimes a considerable list. But ten times love is one of the virtues mentioned.[18] Indeed, it is difficult to find a list that doesn't mention love. The list of virtues sought in a widow may fit this category (I Tim. 5:10), but even this is doubtful, because the kind of conduct enjoined clearly involves love, even though it is not mentioned specifically. Throughout these epistles love has a special place. Whatever other virtues Christians may have, love is indispensable. It is not an occasional emotion but a whole way of life.

Attaining and practicing this love is a goal no Christian can reach on his own initiative. Paul speaks of it as the first of the fruit of the Spirit (Gal. 5:22). And Epaphras told him of the Colossians' "love in the Spirit" (Col. 1:8). It is only with the Holy Spirit working within them that believers develop the love about which the New Testament says so much.

LOVE AND GOOD WORKS

Love may be linked with the keeping of the law, as the Lord's two great commandments prove. In them love has specific objects, yet elsewhere the absolute use of the term *love*

---

[16]Thomas Taylor in his *Exposition of Titus* (Evansville, 1962) devotes two pages to the significance of "sound in love" (pp. 251–53). He holds that "love is sound when it has soundness in its ground, in its order, in its seat, in its work, and in its endurance" (p. 252). He leaves no doubt about the importance of being sound in love.

[17]If the reading *agapēn* is adopted in Titus 2:10, the number would be eleven. But the attestation seems insufficient, and it is probable that *agathēn* is the right reading.

[18]Faith is mentioned in all except II Timothy 1:7; steadfastness is mentioned three times.

may convey the same meaning. For example, Paul writes, "Love works no evil to the neighbor; therefore love is the fulfillment of the law" (Rom. 13:10).[19] Here a negation and an assertion work together: love does not do ill,[20] and love is a positive fulfillment of all that the law requires.[21] John similarly reminds the elect lady that "this is love, that we walk according to his commandments" (II John 6). Both positive and negative can be documented in other places too: the phrase "forbearing one another in love" (Eph. 4:2) suggests suffering for love; whereas I Timothy 1:5 seems more positive: "The end [or aim] of the commandment is love out of a pure heart."[22]

In one of his "faith and love" passages (this one also mentions hope), Paul writes to the Thessalonians that he remembers their "work of faith and labor of love" (I Thess. 1:3). We should not take "labor of love" to mean small services rendered without hope of reward (as we so often do when we use the expression). It points to wholehearted and difficult work done by a truly loving person.[23] Love gives unstintingly, something probably implied also in Paul's including in the Chris-

---

[19]Cf. Gerald R. Cragg: "Every phase of duty is adequately covered if we make sure that love will have its proper place" (*IB*, IX, 606); outside the New Testament "we find the duty of love stated incidentally—perhaps in a high form, but not with regulative force. In the N.T. it is given a central and decisive place. Love does not supply the content of one counsel among many others; it is an inclusive motive which governs the whole of life" (p. 607).

[20]T. W. Manson comments, "The first half of this verse may be taken as a warning: some of the worst mischief in the world can be caused by people who set out to do good to their neighbours but do not love them" (Matthew Black and H. H. Rowley, eds., *Peake's Commentary on the Bible*, London, 1963, p. 950).

[21]Cf. Ernest Best: "In Paul the basic element in behaviour is love. . . . The good, the beautiful and the true may become ideals to be admired; love is always active. It is not a succession of 'good deeds' but the source out of which all goodness flows" (*A Commentary on the First and Second Epistles to the Thessalonians*, London, 1977, p. 234).

[22]Cf. Patrick Fairbairn, who interprets this to mean "being put in trust with the scheme of God for the well-being of men, and so having love for its grand aim [*telos*] . . ." (*Pastoral Epistles*, Minneapolis, 1976, p. 79).

[23]A. L. Moore comments, "The Greek word *kopos*, over against the more frequent New Testament word for work, *ergon*, denotes

tian's armor "the breastplate of faith and love" (I Thess. 5:8). The military metaphor points to warfare, not the path of careless ease.

We should also bear in mind the words "truthing [*alētheuontes*] in love" (Eph. 4:15). This is normally understood as "speaking the truth in love," and this may be the sense of it.[24] But in English we do not have a verb meaning "to truth," and it is worth bearing in mind that sometimes in the New Testament truth is a quality of action as well as of speech (e.g., John 3:21). It is quite possible that the writer means that Christians are to act truly, and that if they do they will act in love. This in turn is related to growth ("truthing in love, we may grow up into him . . ."). With a slight change of metaphor we find that the "building up" of the Christian body is done in love (Eph. 4:16), not with wealth or power or influence. Paul makes a noteworthy comment on this truth when he agrees with the Corinthians that "we all have knowledge" (I Cor. 8:1). Evidently the Corinthian Christians prided themselves on their intellectual excellence, claiming that all knowledge does not reside in people like Paul. Paul agrees, but goes on to say, "Knowledge puffs up, but love builds up." Knowledge may make a person look big (and cause him to think that he is important), but a Christian of stature is a Christian who loves.[25] Growth without growth in love is not true Christian growth.

In Ephesians we also read that God chooses us "so that we should be holy and blameless before him in love" (Eph. 1:4).[26]

---

arduous, wearying toil involving sweat and fatigue (cf. especially 2 C. 6.5; 2 Th. 3.8)" (*1 and 2 Thessalonians,* London, 1969, p. 25). Ernest Best sees another possibility. He thinks that *kopos* emphasizes "either the fatiguing nature of what is done or the magnitude of the exertion required," and adds, "The latter is intended here, since the one who loves as a Christian is never wearied by his love" (*A Commentary on the First and Second Epistles to the Thessalonians,* p. 68).

[24]Francis W. Beare comments on the translation "speaking the truth": "The meaning of *alētheuō* is wider than this; it includes such senses as 'apprehending the truth,' 'living by the truth,' 'being true,' not only in speech but even more in the whole inward disposition" (*IB,* X, 694).

[25]Cf. John Short: Paul "is content to insist, and it is a favorite theme with him, that love is the really constructive force at work in the world" (*IB,* X, 92).

[26]See above, p. 181, n.35 for a discussion of this passage.

"Holy" points to being set apart for God's service, and "blameless" to the highest standard. It is very interesting that "in love" should qualify such terms. Clearly it is not possible to be really holy apart from love, and no one is blameless who lacks love.

Paul uses the interesting expression "any consolation of love" (Phil. 2:1). This points up the truth that love not only builds up the loving person and the church but also brings help to the person loved. Presumably Paul was thinking of the hardships that many of the early Christians faced. But these distressed Christians were strengthened and consoled by their fellow Christians, who lavished love on them. Paul knew about this love from personal experience; in fact, in jail he wrote about people who preached Christ "out of love" (contrasted with others who did it "on account of envy and strife," Phil. 1:15f.). Clearly, he appreciated this love.[27]

One of love's many positive consequences is that it frees people from fear. "There is no fear in love," John writes, "but perfect love casts out fear, because·fear has torment, and he who fears has not been perfected in love" (I John 4:18). This must have been a particular comfort to the early Christians, who had many reasons to be fearful. It is not easy to say whether John is concerned primarily with the love Christians receive from God or from their fellows, or whether he is thinking particularly about the love they show to others.[28] In the first and most important instance we must feel that there is a reference to God's love for us, but both the other loves liber-

---

[27]James Moffatt translates this phrase as "from love to me," on which J. Hugh Michael comments, "The words 'to me' are not represented in the Greek; still, 'love to me' is probably the correct interpretation" (*The Epistle of Paul to the Philippians,* New York, 1929, p. 39; he understands this not as "mere personal attachment to himself, but (as the next clause shows) love to him as the representative and defender of the gospel"). William Hendriksen has a similar opinion: "The essence of this *good will* was love for Paul and for the gospel which he proclaimed" (*New Testament Commentary: Exposition of Philippians,* Grand Rapids, 1962, p. 72).

[28]C. H. Dodd comments, "The love spoken of is mutual love between God and ourselves (with its corollary of charity towards our neighbours)" (*The Johannine Epistles,* New York, 1946, p. 120). This is comprehensive enough to cover most situations. Dodd goes on to say, "To live within the love of God is freedom from the ultimate fear" (p. 121).

ate, too. The love of other people for us helps us not to be afraid. And when we pour out our love on others, our concern is for them, not for ourselves, and we are not afraid. Similarly, we read, "God did not give us a spirit of cowardice, but of power and love and sobermindedness" (II Tim. 1:7).[29] Because God's love helps us rise above our own petty concerns, we are freed from fear.

Christians may use *love* in a greeting that opens a letter (II John 3; Jude 2). They speak naturally of one another's love as something important. For instance, Paul speaks of coming to the Corinthians in love, which he obviously wants to do (the alternative is to come "with a rod," I Cor. 4:21). He pleads with Philemon "for love's sake" (Philem. 9). He prays that the love of the Philippians may abound more and more (Phil. 1:9), a prayer that leads to an extraordinary catalogue of the fruits of an abundant love. Paul sees love as abounding "in knowledge and all perception, so that you approve what is excellent in order that you may be pure and blameless for the day of Christ, filled with the fruit of righteousness which is through Jesus Christ to the glory and praise of God" (Phil. 1:9–11). When love abounds, a person is enriched in every way—spiritually, mentally, and ethically he is enriched.[30] It is not surprising, then, that Paul registers his satisfaction when Timothy brings him news of the love of the Thessalonians (I Thess. 3:6).

IN PRAISE OF LOVE

But in the New Testament the most striking unqualified usage of the term *love* is probably Paul's great treatment of it in I Corinthians 13.[31] Here we find what it means to see love at

---

[29]Cf. Donald Guthrie: "The Christian gospel could never be furthered by men of craven spirit. . . . The Spirit of *love* is to all Christians indispensable, most of all to the chosen ministers of Christ" (*NBCR*, p. 127).

[30]C. Spicq holds that this passage is "the New Testament's most profound and precise statement about the influence of *agape* from the intellectual and moral point of view, in this world or the next. Eight words show the extent of its domain: knowledge, insight, judgment, uprightness, blamelessness, holiness, glory, and praise of God" (*Agape in the New Testament*, II, St. Louis and London, 1965, 277).

[31]There is an excellent summary of the exegesis of this chapter since World War I in the article by Jack T. Sanders in *Interpretation*, XX, 1966, 159–87.

work. This is the kind of conduct the apostle looks for; this is Christian behavior as he expected it to be.[32]

The chapter comes in a section of the epistle in which the apostle is dealing with the spiritual gifts (chs. 12–14). Accordingly, some see it as a digression from the argument, and think that Paul picks up the thread again in the next chapter. But Paul knew what he was doing; this section of the letter is an integral part of what the apostle is saying about the gifts.[33] Paul makes a point of mentioning love first in his list of the "fruit of the Spirit" (Gal. 5:22). He is saying something like that here. The Spirit has given many good gifts to the church, some of which Paul has mentioned in the preceding passages—but no gift of the Spirit is as important as the gift of love. This is the "more excellent way" (I Cor. 12:31), the way to be pursued diligently (I Cor. 14:1).

The object of love here has triggered debate—is it God or man? Anders Nygren cites R. Reitzenstein, who says that love for God is in mind, and A. von Harnack, who claims that love for men is meant.[34] But the question is irrelevant, because Paul is speaking of the Christian as a loving person; thus both love to God and love to man follow. When we see the love of God

---

[32]Hugh Montefiore, incredibly, sees this chapter as concerned with love "within the Christian community" (*NT*, V, 1962, 162). There is not one word about the Christian community in the whole chapter and Montefiore has to read it into I Corinthians 12:31, because it is not there. Krister Stendahl makes a similar comment: "Love, to Paul, is constant concern for the church, for one's brothers and sisters. This is the point: concern for the church, for one's fellow Christians is what love is about" (*Paul among Jews and Gentiles*, Philadelphia, 1976, p. 58). But didn't Paul give himself wholeheartedly to the hardships of a first-century missionary's life in his endeavor to bring the message of God's love to *sinners*, people right outside the brotherhood? Paul's concern for Christians is real enough, but it is quite another thing to suggest that this exhausts his concept of love. Better is Ernest Best's comment: "When Paul sets out love as that which denotes the Christian life as the fulfillment of God's purpose, it is love to all men and not to fellow-Christians alone which he intends" (*A Commentary on the First and Second Epistles to the Thessalonians*, London, 1977, p. 140).

[33]Ira Jay Martin III argues strongly that the chapter must be understood in its context: "It is the unexpected and unconscious by-product of Paul's attempt to face realistically and spiritually the problem of glossolalia in the Corinthian church" (*The Journal of Bible and Religion*, XVIII, 1950, 101).

[34]*Agape and Eros*, London, 1953, pp. 134ff.

for what it is and give ourselves over to it, we are transformed into loving people who love both God and our fellowmen. Obviously Paul has both kinds of love in mind, neither one of which excludes the other.

The apostle begins with a series of hypothetical propositions with which he draws attention to a number of qualities that men admire. He shows that none of them amounts to much if there is no love present. Paul begins with speech: "If I speak with the tongues of men and of angels, but have not love, I have become sounding bronze or a clanging cymbal" (v. 1). The "tongues of men" probably refers primarily to speaking in tongues, something on which the Corinthians apparently prided themselves. Paul does not criticize it, because it is a gift of God that should be used. In fact, Paul thanks God that he himself has it in abundance (I Cor. 14:18). But because his expression is quite general, it may be intended to include human eloquence as well; certainly Paul knew that many Greeks were fascinated with rhetoric. But Paul makes it clear that neither speaking in tongues nor the magic of well-chosen human words is meaningful if there is no love. The apostle makes his reference to speech as comprehensive as possible when he adds to this a reference to the tongues "of angels," thus bringing in the speech of heaven. If we take the best words of both this world and the next but lack love, then we make only noise. He speaks of "sounding (or echoing) bronze," which probably refers to a gong, because gongs were often made of this material—though some think that Paul has a trumpet in mind. He is not specific, but plainly he is thinking about something loud and noisy—like the "clanging cymbal," which does not have a musically attractive sound. The reference to these noisy instruments emphasizes the idea that a man without love may indeed make himself heard,[35] but he will not be saying anything important in a Christian way.[36]

---

[35]F. R. Montgomery Hitchcock drew attention to the many references in Greek and Latin literature to the use, in many pagan religions, of noisy instruments like tambourines and cymbals, which accompanied the loud voices of worshippers. He thought that Paul was making a specific contrast: "Without love, he says, a man were no better than such shrieking votaries of raging Bellona or the Mother of the Gods. Indeed, without Love, one were no better than the instruments of bronze or the noisy cymbals the pagans played, singing to their accompaniments lewd songs" (ET, XXXIV, 1922–23, 490).

[36]Clarence Tucker Craig comments, "The sound of gong and

The Corinthians were greatly taken with the spiritual gifts, but they were also deeply interested in the wisdom that so appealed to first-century Greeks. Probably for this reason Paul turns from tongues to knowledge. He begins with revealed knowledge, with prophecy (v. 2). Because the early church revered the works of the great prophets of the Old Testament, some think that Paul is referring to these men. But he appears to be speaking about contemporary people, so it is more likely that he is referring to the prophets of the early church. He has just spoken highly of them and placed them second only to the apostles (I Cor. 12:28). Clearly, he had a profound regard for them, as was proper for men who spoke God's words. But, despite his regard for them and the esteem in which they were held throughout the church, Paul makes it clear that love ranks above prophecy. A prophet without love is nothing.

Next Paul lists "mysteries." This word often makes us think of detective stories, in which painstakingly followed clues can lead to the solution of a difficult puzzle. But Paul is talking about an impossibility: a "mystery" in the New Testament sense is one we can never solve ourselves. But when the term is used in the New Testament books there is usually the further thought that God has now revealed the secret. The term is often used to refer to the Gospel, something that men would never have worked out for themselves. But at this point Paul is using the word in a general sense, referring to any heavenly knowledge that might be revealed to men. When he links this with "all the knowledge," he is referring to all heavenly knowledge plus all earthly knowledge. But put it all together without love, says Paul, and the total is nothing.

He goes on to discuss the faith that moves mountains. All Christians, of course, have faith in Christ, but the early Christians apparently had a special gift of faith. Jesus refers to it when he speaks of the faith that can transfer a mountain to the depths of the sea (Mark 11:22f.).[37] And when Paul lists faith

---

cymbal is without melody; speaking in tongues is equally without meaning" (*IB*, X, 169).

[37]R. C. H. Lenski points out that this is not "saving trust in Christ, for he who has that has the true root of all love and could never be *outhen*, 'nothing.' " It is rather the "faith" of Matthew 7:22, where it is recorded that some people boasted of having done "many mighty works" in Christ's name, only to be met with his rebuke (Matt. 7:23): "I never knew you; away from me you workers of lawlessness" (*The*

among the "gifts" in I Corinthians 12:9, he is speaking of a special gift, not of the general gift of faith that all Christians have. It is a sobering thought that a man may have great faith, faith that enables him to move mountains, and yet lack love. If he does, says Paul, he amounts to nothing; in fact, he does not exist. "Nothing am I" forms a solemn and emphatic end to the verse.[38]

Paul's third hypothetical case is possibly even more compelling, because it describes people who occupy themselves in doing good for others and who are deeply dedicated to God (v. 3). Paul obviously regards giving to others as important, because he urges the Corinthians to be generous (I Cor. 16:1). But he recognizes that it is not enough. He speaks first of the man who gives away all his possessions, a reference usually understood to mean that he gives to the poor (and it is sometimes translated that way). There is no reason to quarrel with this interpretation, because it is logical enough—to whom else would one give? But Paul does not mention the poor; he is concerned with the attitude of the giver rather than with the recipients of the gifts. His word for "giving away" is *psōmizō*, a word related to *psōmion*, the "sop" which Jesus dipped and gave to Judas at the Last Supper. Its use is probably meant to signify that the man gives away his goods in small quantities so that there are many beneficiaries. The emphasis, however, is not on the distribution of the gift, but on the fact of it, the fact that the man gives away all that he has. It is a sobering thought that a man can give to others until he is poor, yet be without any real love.[39] Of course, the deed itself is not wrong; it is wrong only when it is done out of pride rather than compassion. It is this lovelessness that Paul is repudiating.

With this kind of giving he links giving up the body.

Interpretation of St. Paul's First and Second Epistles to the Corinthians, Minneapolis, 1963, p. 550).

[38]Cf. John Short: "Loveless faith and loveless prophecy account for some of the more tragic pages in the Christian story through the ages. It has burned so-called heretics, it has stultified the sincere quest for truth, it has often been contentious and embittered; and it has often issued in the denial of Christian brotherhood to fellow believers" (*IB*, X, 170).

[39]"Charity may exist side by side with extraordinary uncharitableness" (Harrington C. Lees, *The Practice of the Love of Christ*, London, 1915, p. 58).

Though translations usually render the phrase as something like "to be burned," this reading isn't as well attested as "to have something to boast about." The difference in Greek is not great (*kauthēsōmai* and *kauchēsōmai*). Certainly the scribes would have been tempted to alter "boast" to the more spectacular "be burned"; that the reverse would happen is less likely. Although the probability is that Paul had boasting in mind,[40] giving up the body to be burned is not a bad illustration of the kind of thing that is meant.[41] Paul is saying that a man can be so dedicated to God's service that he will surrender himself to a painful death—yet if he does so out of pride, not love, it is unprofitable. If the reference is indeed to burning, Paul may have had in mind the three youths of Daniel 3, who were thrown into the fiery furnace because of their firm commitment to serving God. There is, of course, no suggestion that they were lacking in love; it is simply that their deed represents the utmost in devotion. Paul is pointing out that it is possible to be as devoted as this and yet lack love. And if this is the case, then such a death is a profitless exercise.[42]

In verse 4 Paul turns from the situation in which love is lacking to that in which it is present, and describes the characteristics of true love. First, love is long-suffering. The word Paul uses indicates having patience with people rather than with circumstances (as William Barclay notes).[43] In fact, Paul's word is the opposite of "short-tempered"; it means—if we may invent a word—"long-tempered."[44] He is affirming

---

[40]See Bruce M. Metzger, *A Textual Commentary on the Greek New Testament,* London and New York, 1971, pp. 563f. for a statement of the reasons on both sides and for the considerations that led the Committee that produced the third edition of the United Bible Societies' *Greek New Testament* to accept *kauchēsōmai.* For a statement on behalf of a group that accepted the other variant, see R. V. G. Tasker, ed., *The Greek New Testament,* Oxford, 1964, p. 436.

[41]This was not unknown in antiquity. Philo quotes a letter from an Indian called Calanus in which he says, "We burn ourselves alive" (*Quod omnis probus liber,* 96).

[42]Cf. Charles R. Erdman: "There is no virtue in merely making one's self miserable. Suffering self-inflicted because of such unworthy motives as pride or stubbornness or anger or desire for unstinted applause is utterly and shamefully profitless. Apart from love, self-sacrifice is vain" (*Paul's Hymn of Love,* New York, 1928, p. 32).

[43]*The Letters to the Corinthians,* Edinburgh, 1959, p. 133.

[44]C. Spicq says that the Old Latin translates this description as "It is magnanimous." He comments, "A patience which is so disin-

that loving people are not "short" with others; they put up with a lot. Loving people are also "kind," a word suggesting goodness as well as solicitousness. They are interested in true goodness, actively interested in the welfare of those about them. Obviously these people are doers; they do not claim good intentions but then plead helplessness because of weakness or apathy. As Lewis B. Smedes put it, long-suffering "is the power to be a creative victim. Long-suffering is not passive. It is a tough, active, aggressive style of life. It takes power of soul to be long-suffering."[45] It is possible to question the use of the word *aggressive,* but long-suffering love is certainly creative, tough, active, and powerful.

In addition, "love does not envy." Most of us do, particularly when we struggle but can't reach our goals, only to see others achieve similar goals—sometimes with relative ease. But love is never displeased when other people are successful, even if the loving person very much wants but lacks that very success. This is perhaps a way of saying that love and pride have nothing to do with each other, a thought that is certainly brought out in the next part of the verse: "Love is no braggart," writes Paul, and the word he uses for braggart means something like "windbag."[46] It points to an empty boasting that is totally incompatible with the Christian way. Paul links with this the assertion that love "is not "puffed up" (*physioutai*), a word that indicates another form of pride. He uses this verb half a dozen times in this epistle and only once elsewhere (no other writer in the New Testament uses it at all). Evidently he thought that it was especially applicable to the Corinthians and their situation, but because pride comes easily to most of us, the warning has broader applicability. We must remember that *agapē* gives, whereas pride asserts itself. But love casts out the spirit of pride.

Paul uses four negatives in verse 5 as he continues to outline

---

terested, requiring this sovereign mastery of self, without growing hard and triumphing over the evil behavior of the neighbor as well as over adversity, is a quite beautiful magnanimity" (*Charity and Liberty,* New York, 1966, p. 23, n.13).

[45] *Love Within Limits,* Grand Rapids, 1978, p. 3.

[46] The word is *perpereuetai.* The verb is a rare one, found here only in the New Testament. Jean Héring says, "It is derived from the adjective '*perperos,*' which describes a boastful and tactless nature" (*The First Epistle of Saint Paul to the Corinthians,* London, 1962, p. 139).

the kind of conduct that love renounces. The first is not easy to translate. The basic idea appears to be that love rejects what is not according to proper form (*schēma*; the verb is *aschēmoneō*). This leads to the translation of the Authorized Version: "Love doth not behave itself unseemly." More recent translations prefer something like "Love is not rude" (the RSV, NEB, and NIV) or "ill-mannered" (the TEV).[47] Because the word has a wide range of meanings, we should not try to tie it down too closely or rigidly. Paul is simply saying that there are many ways of behaving badly, and that love avoids them all.

Similarly, love "does not seek its own,"[48] which might be understood to mean "Love is not selfish" (so the TEV has it), or "does not insist on its own way" (the RSV). Though these two things are different, they are both born of self-centeredness—and it is this that love rules out.[49] Love is concerned with the well-being of the loved ones, not with its own welfare. Of course, it is sometimes important for a loving person to insist on his rights in order to help others who have the same rights but are less able to claim them. If, for example, I fail to secure my rights to a pension when I am disabled, I

---

[47]Henry Drummond thinks the expression refers to courtesy, and comments, "The one secret of politeness is to love. Love *cannot* behave itself unseemly. You can put the most untutored persons into the highest society, and if they have a reservoir of Love in their heart, they will not behave themselves unseemly. They simply cannot do it" ("The Greatest Thing in the World," *Addresses,* Philadelphia, 1891, p. 35).

[48]Philip S. Watson sees in this the characteristic differentiation of *agapē* from *erōs*: "At almost every point, Agape is the antithesis of Eros. It has nothing to do with desire and longing. It does not seek to satisfy its own needs, but to supply the needs of others. 'Agape seeketh not its own'" (*ET,* XLIX, 1937–38, 538).

[49]Krister Stendahl puts his finger on a particularly insidious temptation when he entitles a chapter "Love Rather than Integrity." He is not, of course, arguing that the loving person is prepared to abandon his integrity. But he points out that we sometimes sin against love by placing what we call "integrity" ahead of the real interests of other people. He concludes, "Love allows for the full respect of the integrity of the other, and overcomes the divisiveness of my zeal for having it my way in the name of my own integrity" (*Paul among Jews and Gentiles,* p. 67). He sees love as the criterion by which we distinguish between "those on an ego-trip" and those using their gifts to build up the community (pp. 112f.).

inflict hardship on my dependents. So wisdom must temper love's selflessness. But Paul's point is that love is never selfish.

Love is also even-tempered. We have already seen that it is "long-tempered" (v. 4), and here is a related characteristic —that it is not easily provoked.[50] Phillips translates this as "It is not touchy," which gives us a good idea of what Paul means.[51] It is easy to be so concerned with getting our own way that we become irritated with people, well-meaning and otherwise, who frustrate our best intentions.[52] But the person infused with God's love takes such frustration in stride, accepting it as part of life.

Paul's next point is that love does not, so to speak, go around with a little black book making a note of every evil thing. "Love keeps no score of wrongs," says Paul (the NEB translation). We find it hard to forget it when people offend us, often storing up such grievances.[53] But people of God should

---

[50]Cf. Henry Drummond: "The peculiarity of ill temper is that it is the vice of the virtuous. It is often the one blot on an otherwise noble character. You know men who are all but perfect, and women who would be entirely perfect, but for an easily ruffled, quick-tempered, or 'touchy' disposition. This compatibility of ill temper with high moral character is one of the strangest and saddest problems of ethics" ("The Greatest Thing in the World," *Addresses,* p. 40).

[51]Karl Barth comments, "It may be gathered from this passage that even those who were spiritually gifted in Corinth did not strike one another at once as pure angels. The neighbour can get dreadfully on my nerves even in the exercise of what he regards as, and what may well be, his particular gifts. And he can then provoke and embitter and in some degree enrage me. Love cannot alter the fact that he gets on my nerves, but as self-giving (and this perhaps with salutary counter-effects on my poor nerves) it can rule out *a limine* my allowing myself to be 'provoked' by him—i.e., forced into the position and role of an antagonist" (*Church Dogmatics,* IV, 2, Edinburgh, 1958, 834).

[52]There is, of course, a place for anger (cf. Eph. 4:26). "Righteous indignation" is part of a well-rounded life. But such a vigorous opposition to evil is not what Paul has in mind here. We must bear in mind that I Corinthians 13 is high poetry. Paul is making his points emphatically and beautifully, not putting in every possible qualification. A Christian's anger will arise out of his passionate concern for the right, not from a concern lest his own interests be neglected. Paul is dealing with this latter point, not the former.

[53]Cf. Lewis Smedes: "Resentment keeps enemy lists, files on every person who has injured us" (*Love Within Limits,* p. 69).

leave this behavior to the people of this world. True love is never interested in calculating[54] the wrongs committed against it; love does not nurture grudges.

Paul combines a negative and a positive assertion in his assurance that love "does not rejoice on the basis of unrighteousness but rejoices with the truth" (v. 6). We unhesitatingly accept this idea, yet we have trouble putting it into practice. The unhappy truth is that we do tend to rejoice in the misfortunes of others. Certainly many of our jokes prove this point (and think what happens to our clowns!). Newspaper reporting feeds our appetite for catastrophe in a similar way. Seldom does good make headlines, but evil often does. And the fact that newspapers continue to sell shows that in general we approve of this pattern—particularly when people or groups we dislike meet with misfortune. Examples of this attitude abound in every society.[55] The poor are not displeased when the rich are in trouble, while the rich take calmly the trials of the poor. The political party in government regards with equanimity the troubles of the opposition, and the opposition returns the compliment with interest. But Paul is saying that, natural though this reaction may be, it is not a loving one. Love is not happy when things go badly for others; it does not rejoice in unrighteousness.

Love is happy where the truth is. It is the progress of truth, not the misfortunes of other people, that makes love rejoice.[56] Here is the suggestion that love has a moral responsibility to

---

[54]The verb is *logizomai,* which means "to calculate." William Barclay says that the word "is an accountant's word. It is the word that is used for entering up an item in a ledger so that it will not be forgotten." He points out that "so many people nurse their wrath to keep it warm; they brood over their wrongs until it is impossible to forget them. Christian love has learned the great lesson of forgetting" (*The Letters to the Corinthians,* p. 136).

[55]Lewis Smedes explains the way of the world in these terms: "We will enjoy our disgust so much that we would be furious were we to be deprived of it. . . . Life without an occasional scandal would rob us of the joy of indignation and disgust. A well-ordered world must have some evil" (*Love Within Limits,* p. 78).

[56]Cf. Günther Bornkamm: Love "is full of joy—not the venomous, crypto-Pharisaical sort which loudly laments the evil in the world, perhaps in order to put its own self in a better light; it rejoices in the truth, particularly the truth that benefits others" (*Paul,* London, 1971, p. 218).

pursue truth. Love does not rejoice where iniquity flourishes and truth is denied. If love is to rejoice, truth must be honored.[57]

We should notice further that in the New Testament truth is often closely related to Christ himself and to the gospel Christians preach. Jesus spoke of himself as the truth (John 14:6), and Paul used the phrase "as truth is in Jesus" (Eph. 4:21). This is often misquoted as "the truth as it is in Jesus," as though the writer were saying that truth has many aspects and that he wishes to emphasize the aspect that Jesus exemplifies. Actually, he is saying something quite different: he is saying that truth, real truth, is found in Jesus. So it is that John tells us that truth (together with grace) "came through Jesus Christ" (John 1:17). And Paul uses a number of striking expressions referring to truth. He speaks, for example, of "the truth of God" (Rom. 1:25; 3:7), and he sees Christ as "a minister of circumcision for the truth of God" (Rom. 15:8). He refers to "the word of truth" (II Cor. 6:7), says that "the truth of Christ" is in him (II Cor. 11:10), and writes of "the truth of the gospel" (Gal. 2:5). More examples could be cited,[58] but this is surely enough to show that for Paul and for other New Testament writers truth was a very significant concept, one with a range of meanings wider than we grant the word today. Thus, when Paul speaks of love rejoicing with the truth, it is almost certain that he sees love as deeply concerned with the advancement of the Gospel and all that Christ stands for. Love is not really joyful unless this truth is being proclaimed.

Next Paul lists four positive achievements of love (v. 7). Most understand the first to mean love "endures all things." The verb (stegō) primarily indicates "covering," and in a secondary sense "warding off by covering." This latter meaning suggests endurance, the meaning that most students choose here (Paul uses this verb in this way in I Thessalonians 3:1, 5; I Corinthians 9:12). It seems to me that this is probably correct,

---

[57]Cf. Lewis Smedes: "Love *needs* the truth, or it turns into fuzzy-headed pathos. Without a good grip on truth—that is, on reality—love floats like dreaming desire through a fog of maudlin wishes. Truth keeps love honest, reminding it that an enemy loved is still an enemy, a sinner forgiven no less a sinner" (*Love Within Limits*, p. 80).

[58]See further the Additional Note on truth in my *The Gospel according to John*, Grand Rapids, 1971, pp. 293-96.

but we should notice that "cover" is not inappropriate in this context. Love is then seen as covering up what is amiss in another, not as dragging the worst out into the open for everyone to gloat over (cf. I Pet. 4:8: "Love covers a host of sins"). This is indeed part of the attitude of love.[59] Nonetheless, here the apostle seems to be saying something about the endurance of love, its ability to go on no matter what the opposition.

The second point in this verse is that love "believes all things."[60] It is the way of the world to believe the worst about people. Like Agatha Christie's Miss Marple, we readily assume the worst and look forward to that assumption being vindicated. But love is always ready to believe the best about people. It assumes, if there is any room for the assumption at all, that people are not as bad as they are said to be. James Moffatt translates this as love is "always eager to believe the best." This does not mean that love is gullible, easily duped by any plausible pretender. Love is not at all like the White Queen who had "sometimes believed as many as six impossible things before breakfast." Love is clear-sighted, able to recognize wrong as easily as the shrewdest evaluator of human nature. What Paul is saying is that love will always give the benefit of the doubt, because it can never assume that the worst is true.

Now Paul draws attention to love's optimism; he says that love "hopes all things."[61] The world looks for the downfall of people and assumes that they cannot survive trials. Love takes the opposite view. Of course it sees that men fail, but it can never take failure as the last word. Love always looks for something better. Because the context refers to believing *all*

---

[59]Cf. Lewis Smedes: "Love has a fine sense for when to keep its mouth shut" (*Love Within Limits,* p. 86). Allan Barr says, "The idea of 'covering' is in line with Biblical conceptions of forgiveness, and is very appropriate in a description of Christian love" (*SJT,* III, 1950, p. 422, n.1). Another variation on this theme is "always protects" (the NIV).

[60]Jean Hering does not see *panta* as the object of *pisteuei*; rather, "the accusative must be translated as an accusative of 'limitation,' expressing for once, it is true, the absence of all limits: 'at all times' " (*The First Epistle of Saint Paul to the Corinthians,* p. 141).

[61]Richard Kroner argues from this verse that "faith and hope are intrinsic constituents of that love which Paul praises, and without that love faith and hope are empty and vain" (*ATR,* XXX, 1948, 217).

things, it may be legitimate to say that Paul is looking past the trials and difficulties of this present age to the final triumph of God's cause. Certainly Christians face difficulties that, humanly speaking, seem hopeless. But love never regards such trials as insurmountable. Love does not lash out in wild rebellion against life's difficulties—love always hopes. Love knows that God will ultimately triumph through these trials.

Paul's final assurance is that love "endures all things."[62] Paul's verb (*hypomenō*) is one that indicates an active, vigorous endurance, not a passive, resigned acceptance of all that happens. It is used, for example, to describe the soldier in a keenly contested conflict who battles on undismayed. He does not allow the difficulties of the moment to rob him of strength and purpose; he fights on unflinchingly. So it is, Paul says, with love. Love's endurance is a positive acceptance of life with all its difficulties, not a passive acquiescence in things as they are. Love does more than put up with life's hardships; it grows and develops as it struggles against them. Love sees problems positively—as valuable tests that refine it and prove its worth.

Love's endurance suggests its permanence. As Paul points out, love "never falls down" (v. 8). This is usually interpreted to mean that love stands forever, an interpretation that seems to me to be right. But we ought to notice that the verb may also be used to mean "collapse" or "be ruined." Accordingly, the usage here may also suggest that love is not downed, not defeated by anything it encounters. "Many waters cannot quench love," says Song of Solomon 8:7, and this is true: love endures to the end, no matter what it encounters along the way.[63]

---

[62]James Moffatt translates this as "always patient," and connects it with the preceding: "The spirit of love prompts Christians, as they are Christians, not only to forgive but to show the man that they still believe in him and are ready to stand by him, giving him time to pull himself together (see 2 Cor. ii.5–8). Here is a special school for patience, then. It is a test of love to be 'always patient,' even under repeated disappointments, in place of becoming cynical and sharp with people who are regaining their position and endeavouring to rehabilitate themselves after a moral break-down" (*The First Epistle of Paul to the Corinthians*, New York, 1938, p. 198).

[63]"And even when it meets with no success, even when rejected and cast out and crucified, Agape does not cease to be love; it is prepared to be a 'lost love,' for even when it finds its labour lost, 'Agape never faileth'" (Philip S. Watson, *ET*, XLIX, 538).

Paul brings out love's permanence by contrasting it with some of the gifts the Corinthians valued so highly. Prophecies, he says, will cease.[64] Because prophecy is essentially a proclamation from God, it is immensely valuable here on earth, where uncertainties and perplexities abound. It helps us clearly hear God's voice among all those clamoring for our attention. But when we are all brought into God's presence, prophecy will no longer be necessary.

It is the same with "tongues," that interesting gift of the Spirit that the Corinthians valued so highly. Elsewhere in this letter Paul insists that tongues have their value, giving the Corinthians directions about how to use this gift. But, like prophecy, speaking in tongues has a temporary value, because it will be unnecessary when we all stand before God.

Now Paul turns to "knowledge," using the difficult verb *katargeō*, which he has just used to refer to prophecy. The Greeks valued knowledge very highly, and studied philosophy with relentless vigor. And no doubt some of the Corinthians shared this enthusiasm for knowledge.[65] In every age men have set a high value on education, and rightly so, because it has helped us enlarge our horizons, discover new possibilities. But at the last, Paul is saying, the knowledge we have so laboriously acquired here on earth will be of no great consequence. When we are with God and know him, we will not need the knowledge and skills of this world.[66]

---

[64]The verb *katargeō* is thoroughgoing. It is made up of the intensive prefix *kata*, the alpha-privative, and *ergon*, meaning "work," and means something like "to cause to do no work"—i.e., "to render null and void." It is translated in a great variety of ways, because there is no precise English equivalent. Hans Conzelmann understands it here as "purposely harsh: prophecy will 'be destroyed'" (*I Corinthians*, Philadelphia, 1975, p. 225).

[65]William Barclay says, "The permanent danger of intellectual eminence is intellectual snobbery. The man who is learned runs the grave danger of developing the spirit of contempt. Only a knowledge whose cold detachment has been kindled by the fire of love can really save men" (*The Letters to the Corinthians*, pp. 131f.).

[66]Cf. Karl Barth: "Here all divine revelations, and the human possibilities created by them, were they ever so significant, do *not* suffice.... Everything which man, even the man who is inspired and impelled by God, can devise here as means, way, and bridge is insufficient. And not, indeed, because the earthly, the human, is in itself so imperfect, but because the perfect comes: *Because* the *sun* rises all

The achievements and the gifts that matter so much in the life we know now have only limited validity. Of course, they have some value now and should be pursued accordingly, but Paul is arguing that we not overestimate these transitory things. Love is infinitely greater than all these achievements for a number of reasons. What he is bringing out here is love's permanence: love will endure when the value of other achievements fades.

Paul proceeds to bring out the inferiority of things men value highly—like prophecy and knowledge[67]—by comparing the part to the perfect whole, the implication being, of course, that love is perfection. Even the most sophisticated knowledge we attain here on earth is partial (v. 9). We learn to live with the frustrating realization that the more we learn, the more we recognize how little we know. It is the same with prophecy. This seems to mean that God reveals to his servants only those things that he thinks they need to know. In this life we never have God's perfect vision; we never enter into his full counsel. But one day "the perfect" will come (v. 10). This expression suggests that ultimate state for which a thing or a person is destined.[68] Perfection comes when the aim is reached. Used absolutely as it is here, the term points to the end of all things, the consummation of God's purpose for men and the universe. When that happens and God's will is perfectly done, then all this world's partial achievements will fall away, inconsequential before God's final order.

In verse 11 Paul makes essentially the same point with a contrast between childhood and manhood.[69] When he was a child, he tells us, he used to speak like a child and think like a

---

lights are extinguished" (*The Resurrection of the Dead*, New York, 1933, p. 81).

[67]"His willingness, not only to include, but to emphasize knowledge and prophecy, the gifts in which he himself was greatly interested, among the gifts that would in time be outgrown, is another instance of Paul's gracious attitude toward his opponents" (Nils W. Lund, *JBL*, I, 1931, 276).

[68]Paul's expression is *to teleion*, which derives from *to telos*, "the end" or "aim." Thus the man is the "perfection" of the boy, because manhood is that to which boyhood looks; it is its end or aim.

[69]Hans Conzelmann comments, "The antithesis between child and man is a standard rhetorical theme," and he illustrates it with reference to a number of ancient authors (*1 Corinthians*, p. 226).

child. Some translators and commentators take his verb here (*phroneō*) to mean "feel," but this scarcely seems justified. The word is related to the term that indicates the working of the mind (*phrēn*), and it refers to the thought processes in general. With this phrasing Paul contrasts the way a child thinks with the way a man thinks.[70] He goes on to say, "I used to reckon" or "to work things out" like a child. His verb (*logizomai*) conveys the meaning "calculate." Paul is proceeding from the general concept of thinking to a particular way of thinking, pointing out another difference between a child and a man. But Paul is no longer a child: "When I became a man," he goes on, "I put away childish things." His verb for "put away" is the same *katargeō* which he used to refer to prophecies and to knowledge in verse 8 and to partial knowledge in verse 10. It points to a radical repudiation of childishness, his use of the perfect tense indicating a permanent state.[71] And this change is not only an act of nature but an act of the will. The implication is that this contrast is similar to the one between this life and the next. Certain things valuable to this life have no place in the next, whereas other things remain permanently valuable. Though Paul doesn't mention love explicitly here, he no doubt has it in mind.

Paul goes on to notice that our vision here and now is at best partial (v. 12), very much like looking at things in a mirror. We easily miss some of Paul's meaning because of the high-quality mirrors we use today. But in the first century mirrors were normally made of polished metal. It is of course possible to put such a polish on a good piece of metal that it makes an excellent mirror—but it was easy for the workman to get discouraged along the way and to finish with a mirror that was far from perfect. Corinth, it is true, was noted for its good mirrors, but these were for the wealthy; ordinary people would not

---

[70]Eileen Guder comments that Paul "is concerned that we become adult in our view of ourselves and our world. . . . Children are not aware of the vast areas of knowledge outside their experience; that awareness is part of growing up. Children react simply and unthinkingly on the basis of all they know, and for them that 'all' is all there is" (*To Live in Love*, Grand Rapids, 1967, p. 157).

[71]Cf. R. C. H. Lenski, who says, "They remain thus put away" (*The Interpretation of St. Paul's First and Second Epistles to the Corinthians*, p. 568). There is no going back to them.

have been able to afford them. The Christians at Corinth, then, were accustomed to mirrors that gave only a poor reflection. In such a mirror one could see only *en ainigmati,* as Paul puts it. His word is that from which we derive our word *enigma*; it properly signifies "a riddle" or some "enigmatic" saying.[72] It was normally used to refer to obscurity in words, though here, of course, Paul is using it to refer to obscurity in vision (cf. the NEB: "Now we see only puzzling reflections in a mirror"). Here and now we see things imperfectly.[73] We look in mirrors which always distort things to some extent, if only in their reversal of right and left. At best we see a reflection; we do not see the thing itself.

But "then" it will be different. Paul does not say what he means by "then," just as he does not say with whom we will be "face to face." But there is no uncertainty. He is obviously referring to the time when our Lord will return and usher in the new order, and we will be with him. When we are face to face with him, we will be hindered by none of the things that now mar our vision.

From seeing, Paul proceeds to knowing. Under present circumstances all knowledge is partial. It is part of life that we struggle to attain more complete knowledge by the slow and laborious processes of learning—and we never do attain complete knowledge. But in the hereafter it will be different. Paul

---

[72]T. C. Edwards sees the meaning as "in a riddle" (not "darkly," as the AV has it); "that is, the phrase denotes, not the dimness of our vision, but the obscurity of the revelation. . . . The Gospel is a revelation of God, but not a full revelation" (*A Commentary on the First Epistle to the Corinthians,* London, 1903, p. 352).

[73]Samuel E. Bassett, however, holds that *ainigma* "along with its negative meaning of 'dark saying' may also have the positive signification of a real truth expressed in terms that describe a concrete instance—that is, truth clothed in the language of imagery"; "The mirror shows us only the reflection of reality. This reflection is, as it were, an *ainigma*; it must be interpreted and may not be interpreted rightly, for it is hard to interpret" (*JBL,* XLVII, 1928, 234, 236). Jack T. Sanders holds that "all such attempts, however, shatter on the contrast expressed twice in vs. 12" (*Interpretation,* XX, p. 165, n.18). He holds that J. Behm, "for all practical purposes, brings this discussion to a close" and sums up his idea by saying, "1 Corinthians 13:12 contains purely and simply a figure of speech meaning that God is seen—known—only imperfectly this side of the Parousia" (pp. 165f.).

looks forward to knowing just as he is known, and he uses an interesting change of verb to make his point clear. "Now I know" is *ginōskō*, but in both "I shall know" and "I am known" he switches to the compound *epiginōskō*. Sometimes the words aren't very different in meaning, but the compound can suggest having complete knowledge, and there is little doubt that it is used in its fullest possible sense here.[74] J. H. Moulton holds that we should understand this passage to mean "Now I am acquiring knowledge which is only partial at best: then I shall have learnt my lesson, shall *know*, as God in my mortal life knew me."[75] Paul is plainly contrasting the best knowledge of this life with the kind of knowledge that we will have in the life to come, thus showing that the former falls very far short of the latter. God's knowledge of us all is complete; we can never think that there is anything about us that God does not know. Our imperfect knowledge is not the measure of God's knowledge, nor is it the measure of the knowledge that God's people will have in the hereafter.[76]

Paul's point is that big changes await us when we depart this life. Things like prophecy, speaking in tongues, and the earthly knowledge that we value so highly will then have no relevance. Just as the things of childhood are transcended by adult life, so these earthly achievements will find no place in heaven. But Paul does not include love among these transitory achievements. We can know here and now the love that God's divine love kindles in our hearts, a love that we will still know

---

[74]Cf. T. C. Edwards: "The *epi-* expresses perfect knowledge, either because full knowledge is the result of continual *additions* to previous knowledge . . . or because it is attained by *applying* the mind *to* a subject" (*A Commentary on the First Epistle to the Corinthians*, p. 352).

[75]*A Grammar of New Testament Greek*, I, *Prolegomena*, Edinburgh, 1906, 113.

[76]James Moffatt connects this knowledge with love: "To 'see' him 'face to face' is at once the other side and the reward of having sought to 'see' him in this fellow-Christian or that, as one has imbibed the Spirit of the Lord's Body; the experience is not any lonely rapture or private ecstasy of beatific vision, but the fruition of response (in personal devotion to others) to the eternal personal interest of the Lord in them and theirs" (*The First Epistle of Paul to the Corinthians*, p. 202).

in the hereafter. We are loved by God now, and we will be loved by God then. Love surpasses all those other qualities that we so readily value too highly.[77]

So Paul comes to his conclusion (v. 13). His "now" may be understood to mean "now in this life," but this seems unlikely. Paul does not appear to be saying that faith and hope and love continue through this life, because exactly the same could be said about the other matters to which he gives attention—prophecy, tongues, and knowledge. But he is contrasting these with love and its associates, not saying that they are alike. So it seems that his "now" is to be understood to mean "now, in conclusion." To sum up his discussion of the theme, Paul lists three things which, he says, abide—namely, faith, hope, and love. The three are linked a number of times in the New Testament by Paul and by other writers as well, indicating that the early Christians must have commonly grouped these things together.[78] And Paul's verb is singular, indicating that he sees these three things as a kind of unity. His addition of "these three" after listing the three qualities sets them apart, pointing up their distinctiveness.

This is an intriguing short list. We are not surprised that it includes faith, because faith is the fundamental Christian attitude. As Paul says, "The life which I now live in the flesh I live by faith of the Son of God" (Gal. 2:20). The entire Christian life is a life of faith.

---

[77]E. M. Blaiklock draws attention to Oliver Wendell Holmes's interpretation of life as an exclamation mark over a question mark: "In the symbolism of this device he pictured an upper world and a lower world separated by the thinnest of divisions. Below is questing, questioning, search for truth, and many an unanswered problem. Above lies the astonished answer. 'He that seeks should cease not till he finds,' runs a non-Biblical saying of Christ, 'and when he finds he shall be astonished.' The words, discovered by Grenfell and Hunt in 1903 on a papyrus scrap at Oxyrhynchus, make the point of Holmes' symbol exactly." Blaiklock adds, "We shall know one day. Meanwhile we can only trust, hope, and love" (*The Way of Excellence*, Grand Rapids, 1968, p. 36).

[78]See Rom. 5:2–5; Gal. 5:5f.; Eph. 1:15–18; 4:2–5; Col. 1:4f.; I Thess. 1:3; 5:8; Heb. 6:10–12; 10:22–24; I Pet. 1:3–8, 21f. Cf. Barnabas 1:4; 11:8; Polycarp 3:2f. Sometimes faith and love are linked with steadfastness (*hypomonē*), which is similar to hope (e.g., I Tim. 6:11; II Tim. 3:10; Titus 2:2).

But it is surprising to find hope on the list.[79] Few of us would spontaneously include hope in a short list of three essential things, because these days we have reduced the blazing certainty that the New Testament calls hope to a cautious optimism that fits these uncertain times. This is an unfortunate situation, because hope is vital. Has any truly effective social or religious movement—one that really gripped people—failed to inspire hope in its followers? Certainly hope infused early Christianity. It took people like slaves, outcasts, and women—people with very little to look forward to in the society of the time—and gave them a new and living hope. And the Christian faith has repeated this miracle throughout the centuries. We cannot do without hope.

But Paul's emphasis is not there. Fittingly, the word that Paul gives primary emphasis—the word that is the last in this chapter—is love. He speaks of it as "the greatest of these." I do not think that by saying this he is trying to arrange the three things in order of importance. Because each is important in its own way, Paul is not critically comparing them.[80] Rather, Paul is saying that love is pre-eminent.[81] He is saying to the Corinthians that the things that they value most—such as prophecy

---

[79]A. A. van Ruler sees a connection between hope and love. He asks, "Which is prior, love or hope? Is it that a man hopes for God to bring things right because he loves things? Or is it that man is able to love God's creation because he expects God to make things right?" He goes on, "I doubt that there is a simple answer to this question. We can perceive here a complete reciprocation between love and hope. They are present concurrently. They melt into each other. They inspire each other. A man must hope because he has love. And a man can love because he has hope" (*The Greatest of These is Love*, Grand Rapids, 1958, p. 75).

[80]F. F. Bruce sees a reference to the fact that love will not change: "Whatever form faith and hope may take in the resurrection age, when faith as we now know it gives place to open vision (cf. 2 C. 5.7) and hope is swallowed up in realization (cf. Rom. 8.24f.), love remains unchanged in its nature even when it attains perfection; therefore 'the greatest of these is love'" (*1 and 2 Corinthians*, London, 1971, p. 129).

[81]Cf. Augustine's well-known saying, "Love, and do what thou wilt" (*Ten Homilies on the First Epistle of John*, VII, 8; *NPNF*, I, vii, 504). For him, love, properly understood, is the sufficient guide to conduct.

and knowledge and speaking tongues—are not the things that matter most. More important are the great qualities of faith and hope and love. And, he is saying, there is nothing greater than love.[82] Love matters, now and always.[83]

---

[82]Jack T. Sanders argues that the expression points to the activity of God within man: "*Agape* is primarily not a trait of human character which survives the eschaton, but is, rather, the transcendent which from time to time occurs within the sphere of the finite. Or, in other words, Paul is saying to the Corinthians that God is love—but the subject of that sentence is love" (*Interpretation*, XX, 187).

[83]Ralph P. Martin argues for this translation: "Greater than these [three] is the love [of God]" (*ET*, LXXXII, 1970–71, 120). This is attractive, but he gives no reason for holding that "the love" in this context would be understood to mean God's love. This does not seem to be its meaning in vv. 4, 8.

CHAPTER ELEVEN

The Love of Friendship

So far we have been concerned almost exclusively with the love that is indicated by *agapē* and its cognates. But because the New Testament also uses the *phileō* words, it is time to look a little more closely at them. They denote a variety of affections,[1] but basically they indicate friendship. The words have other uses, but this is the most important one.

In the New Testament the word from this group that is most important is the noun *philos,* meaning "friend."[2] Jesus was criticized for being "a friend of tax collectors and sinners" (Matt. 11:19; Luke 7:34). This need not, of itself, indicate anything more than that Jesus associated with these people. It does not necessarily point to close ties, though it certainly indicates some warmth and acceptance—something more than cool tolerance. It forms part of the New Testament evidence that Jesus was concerned with others besides the conventionally righteous. He was a friend to those with no merit (cf. Luke 5:32). It reinforces what we have seen in our earlier study— namely, that God's love is spontaneous and not evoked by attractiveness in the beloved.

Jesus sometimes called his followers his friends (e.g.,

---

[1]T. W. Manson points out that in earlier Greek the *phileō* words "are designations of love in its widest sense, every kind of normal and intellectual affection, instinctive or acquired" (*On Paul and John,* London, 1963, p. 99). But the passage of time saw a progressive diminution in the use of these words, with a corresponding increase in the use of the *agapaō* words. In LXX and New Testament use, the *phileō* words are not nearly as important as the *agapaō* words. The reverse is the case in earlier Greek (*TDNT,* IX, 116).

[2]The term is mostly Lukan. It occurs 29 times in the New Testament—15 times in Luke and 3 times in Acts. John's Gospel uses the word 6 times, and it occurs twice both in James and III John and once in Matthew.

Luke 12:4), and once he linked himself with them when he called Lazarus "our friend" (John 11:11). In the upper room he declared, "Greater love [*agapēn*] has no man than this, that a man lay down his life for his friends" (John 15:13). He went on, "You are my friends if you do the things I command you" (John 15:14). We have noticed before the link between love and the keeping of the commandments (either those of God or those of Jesus). What is new here is the reference to the disciples as "friends."[3] Jesus goes on to differentiate friends from slaves. He points out that the slave is ignorant of the purposes of his master, "but I have called[4] you friends, because all the things I heard from my Father I have made known to you" (John 15:15). Here Christ's death and his teaching are closely related, and his warm affection for those for whom he died is clear. We should add to this the fact that once in the New Testament the term is used in a reference to God. James tells us that Abraham was called "the friend of God" (James 2:23).[5]

Most of the time this word is used to refer to typical human friendships.[6] The centurion with a sick slave had friends who spoke to Jesus on his behalf (Luke 7:6). Certain Asiarchs are described as Paul's friends (Acts 19:31), and on another occasion the centurion Julius allowed some of the apostle's friends

---

[3]Gustav Stählin sees behind this usage in Luke and John "the thought that Christians, as friends of Jesus and also *philoi* among themselves, are at the same time the new friends of God . . . and that they are this as members of the *familia Dei*" (*TDNT*, IX, 162f.).

[4]The perfect tense, *eirēka*, may be significant; if so, it indicates that there is something permanent about the naming of the disciples "friends." Jesus does not use the term casually.

[5]For this term see above, pp. 13f., n.8. W. O. E. Oesterley has a long note on the term in *The Expositor's Greek Testament*, IV, London, 1910, 448f. He says, "The phrase *philos theou*, therefore, while in the first instance probably general in its application, became restricted, so that finally, as among the Arabs, 'the Friend of God,' *Khalil Allah*, or simply *El Khalil*, became synonymous with Abraham."

[6]Of the use of the term in III John 15, C. Spicq says that the writer "was using the conventional profane formula. He did not even take the trouble to Christianize it as St. Paul had done (Titus 3:15), an omission which is normal enough in so personal a letter, which is not really an 'epistle' at all, but a simple note" (*Agape in the New Testament*, III, St. Louis and London, 1966, 229). In other words, we have here an example of a typical first-century reference to good friends.

to help him (Acts 27:3). There was an occasion when Herod and Pilate made up their quarrel and became friends (Luke 23:12). In John 19:12 the term "Caesar's friend" may be used in a technical sense to indicate a person honored by the emperor with this title, but more probably it signifies an individual well-disposed toward the ruler and recognized as such. In Acts 10:24 it is mentioned that Cornelius the centurion gathered his close friends to hear Peter. All this is the very stuff of life: having friends who help us or whom we help is a very valuable part of our existence. Jesus uses this kind of friendship to indicate the greatness of the trouble that looms ahead for mankind. In those days believers' friends will betray them (Luke 21:16).

Frequently Jesus appeals to the actions of friends in his parables, as he does in the parable of the friend at midnight (Luke 11:5–8). Sometimes these parables emphasize the sharing of happiness. The shepherd who found his sheep and the woman who found her coin both invited their friends and neighbors to rejoice with them (Luke 15:6, 9), and the elder brother complained that his father had never given him a kid so that he could make merry with his friends (Luke 15:29). There is also a reference to "the friend of the bridegroom" who is happy in the bridegroom's joy (John 3:29).

Jesus counsels people to sit in a lowly place when they come to a feast. Then the host will say, "Friend, come up higher" (Luke 14:10). While discussing feasts Jesus told his hearers not to make them for their friends and relatives (especially the rich ones) who will recompense them with reciprocal invitations. Instead they should make feasts for the poor and helpless who cannot return the favor (Luke 14:12f.).[7] He urges them to make friends for themselves out of the mammon of unrighteousness (Luke 16:9), which appears to mean that they should use their money to help the less fortunate. By aiding the poor they will make friends for themselves. Concern for the poor is a typical New Testament attitude, once again indicating the basic love that characterizes those who have experienced God's love.

Two opposite uses of the term should be further noticed. It

---

[7]This injunction "stands in open antithesis to the conventions of antiquity. Here everything is based on the principle of reciprocity, whereas Jesus expressly excludes this" (Gustav Stählin, *TDNT*, IX, 160).

may be used to refer to Christians, as when John closes his letter to Gaius with "The friends greet you; greet the friends by name" (III John 15). By contrast James warns his readers that whoever wills to be the friend of the world makes himself God's enemy (James 4:4).

When we turn to the verb *phileō*,[8] the first thing that strikes us is that it is generally used to refer to the love of men in one form or another. Of its twenty-five occurrences only six refer to divine love: four refer to the love of Christ and two to that of God. Among the four is John's reference to "the disciple whom Jesus loved," which uses this verb (John 20:2; usually he employs *agapaō* in this expression). People call Lazarus him "whom you love" (John 11:3) and exclaim, "How he loved him!" (John 11:36). The risen Lord assures the church in Laodicea that "those whom I love I rebuke and discipline" (Rev. 3:19).[9] On one occasion Jesus assured the disciples that the Father himself loved them (John 16:27), and on another he told them that the Father loves the Son (John 5:20).[10] This fairly meager harvest illustrates that the typical New Testament view of love—specifically of God's love—is not indicated by this verb. The striking use of *agapaō* for God's love for the unworthy is simply not found when we turn to *phileō*.

This verb is most frequently used to indicate the love men have for Christ. This is largely accounted for by the fact that it occurs five times in Jesus' conversation with Peter by the lake. Three times Jesus asks whether Peter loves him and three times is assured that he does. On the first two occasions Jesus uses the verb *agapaō*, but switches to *phileō* the third time.

---

[8]The verb is found 25 times in the New Testament: there are 13 references in John, 5 in Matthew, 2 each in Luke and Revelation; and one each in Mark, I Corinthians, and Titus.

[9]"The Lord's censure is always a token of his seeking love; only those for whom no one cares are lost" (Hanns Lilje, *The Last Book of the Bible,* Philadelphia, 1957, p. 102).

[10]John also uses *agapaō* to say "The Father loves the Son" (John 3:35). C. Spicq argues that there is a difference: "Jn. 3:35 refers to the Father's generous and respectful love for his Son, which is the reason for his giving Christ all power." But in the other passage he thinks that "the intimacy of God's love for Christ is stressed here. The Father trusts his incarnate Son.... He treats him as a friend" (*Charity and Liberty,* pp. 86, 87). But it is more than difficult to see such a distinction, either in the way John uses the two verbs or in their respective contexts.

Consistently Peter uses *phileō* in his replies, and the author uses it too when he says that Peter was grieved because Jesus asked the question three times (John 21:15–17). As we have noted elsewhere,[11] we should probably not emphasize the change of verb but should see the incident as important for the stress it puts on love. When Peter was being restored to his position of leadership among the Twelve, the thing that mattered above all else was his love. All the rest could be taken for granted, but not love—that must be there and be declared.

There is a passage explaining what happens to those who love Jesus, and another referring to those who do not. Jesus tells the disciples that the Father loves them because they have loved him (John 16:27).[12] We should not think that this indicates something like a reward for faithful service, because their love for Christ itself points to a divine work in them. As Augustine put it long ago, "He would not have wrought in us something He could love, were it not that He loved ourselves before He wrought it."[13] Some contend that this passage suggests that God's love is not spontaneous and unmotivated; he loves those who deserve to be loved. But, in addition to the point made by Augustine, there is the further consideration that loves of more than one kind may develop together. C. S. Lewis points out, for example, that *erōs* often is found along with friendship or affection. Thus the fact that God loves because of what he is—loves with a spontaneous and unmotivated love—does not mean that he may not also respond to the love men show to his Son. The other passage mentioned earlier is from Paul. At the end of his first letter to the Corinthians he says, "If anyone does not love the Lord, let him be anathema" (I Cor. 16:22).[14] Loving the Lord is not a matter of peripheral importance; it is the central issue of life.

---

[11] See above, pp. 180f.

[12] Cf. Gustav Stählin: "The *hoti* in this saying of the Johannine Jesus is not to be misunderstood as though God's love for the disciples were dependent on their love and faith in Jesus, as a reward for this. Their love is a response to the love of Him who has come into the world and of Him that sent Him" (*TDNT*, IX, 190).

[13] *Lectures on the Gospel according to St. John*, CIII.5; *NPNF*, I, vii, 391.

[14] B. B. Warfield comments, "It is not of failure to love Jesus Christ supremely of which Paul is speaking; it is of failure to love Him at all" (*PTR*, XVI, 1918, 186).

Jesus also brings out this idea when he says, "He who loves father or mother more than me is not worthy of me; and he who loves son or daughter more than me is not worthy of me" (Matt. 10:37). We must remember that the place of the family in first-century Palestine was very important. Thus Jesus was making the greatest possible demand when he said the love that should be given to him should surpass the love for one's nearest and dearest on earth.

The verb is used to refer to Christians when the letter to Titus closes with "Greet those who love us in faith" (Titus 3:15). In any first-century letter we would expect a greeting at this point, but here it is not the normal secular greeting—its references to love and faith make it clearly Christian. Perhaps this is the place to notice that a number of letters have a reference to greeting with a kiss, using the cognate noun *philēma*.[15] This is usually a "holy kiss" (Rom. 16:16; I Cor. 16:20; II Cor. 13:12; I Thess. 5:26)[16] and once "a kiss of love" (*agapēs*; I Pet. 5:14). The verb is also used to refer to a most unholy and unloving kiss: that with which Judas betrayed his Lord (Matt. 26:48; Mark 14:44; Luke 22:47f.).[17] Because Judas had been separated from Jesus for such a short time it seems somewhat unlikely that this kiss was a normal greeting. Be that as it may, it certainly betokened friendship, and thus has always seemed to Christians a particularly heinous method of betrayal.[18]

Sometimes there are references to unworthy loves, such as those of people who love to stand praying in the synagogues or on the street corners where people will see them (Matt. 6:5). Of the same kind are those who love the best places at feasts

---

[15]This noun is used twice in Luke and once each in Romans, I Corinthians, II Corinthians, I Thessalonians, and I Peter. On every occasion the word refers to a greeting.

[16]See the note in my *The Epistles of Paul to the Thessalonians,* London, 1956, p. 109. For the use of the word group in this sense in Greek generally, see *TDNT,* IX, 118–24; in the Old Testament, pp. 125–27; and in the New Testament and the early church, pp. 138–45.

[17]In Matthew 26:49 and Mark 14:45 the compound *kataphileō* is used to refer to the actual deed. Some hold that this means "kiss tenderly" or the like. But this cannot be insisted upon.

[18]I. Howard Marshall sees the word order as significant: "The position of *philēmati* ... is emphatic and stresses the enormity of using a kiss in such a hypocritical manner" (*The Gospel of Luke,* Exeter, 1978, p. 836).

(Matt. 23:6) or greetings in the marketplaces (Luke 20:46). Worse still are those who love and who makes lies (Rev. 22:15). And there are those who love their own earthly lives too much. In John 12:25 the person who loves his life and will lose it is contrasted with the person who hates his life in this world and will keep it for life eternal.[19] A similar contrast is drawn between those who are of the world and those who are not (John 15:19). The world loves its own, but it hates those who are not worldly and whom Christ has chosen out of the world.

From all this it is clear that the *phileō* words are not as significant to the Christian idea of love as the *agapaō* words are, but they do underscore certain points. Although they do not establish the spontaneous, outgoing character of love as the Christian knows it, they fit in with that conception and help us see further aspects of it.[20]

COMPOUND WORDS

We can explore another aspect of our subject by examining compound words using "love." These are formed exclusively from *phileō*, because *agapaō* does not form compounds.[21] There are twenty-two such words in the New Testament; no less than sixteen of them occur only once, while three are found twice each, two occur three times, and one occurs six times. The most important word in this group is *philadelphia*, meaning "brotherly love," which is found six times.[22] We

---

[19]See above, p. 184.

[20]Cf. William Lillie: *philia* "differs from the love of natural relationships in being a matter of deliberate choice; we are born with our relations, we choose our friends. . . . What is evident in friendship is what may be called the mutuality of love; it takes two to make friends more truly than to make a quarrel, and a love that meets no response is a truncated love" (*SJT*, XII, 1959, 235).

[21]The only compound cited from *agapaō* appears to be *agapēnor*, which does not occur in the New Testament.

[22]The term is used in secular writings to refer to love for literal brothers and sisters. H. F. von Soden points out that there are "no examples of this more general use of *philadelphia* and *philadelphos* outside Christian writings" (*TDNT*, I, 146; we should, however, notice something of an exception among the Jews, though this was

have already noticed that this virtue is inculcated by exhortations like "Love one another."[23] Here we notice that the compound is used to emphasize the importance of the attitude. The compound may be linked with *agapaō*, as it is when Paul writes, "Now concerning brotherly love [*philadelphias*] you have no need of me to write to you, for you yourselves are taught by God to love [*agapan*] one another" (I Thess. 4:9). Paul uses another interesting combination when he urges the Romans to be "kindly affectioned [*philostorgoi*] toward one another with brotherly love [*philadelphia*]" (Rom. 12:10). His "kindly affectioned" goes back to *storgē*, which means "natural affection." The combination emphasizes the naturalness and importance of love within the brotherhood, a love that is to be deep and warm.

"Let brotherly love abide" is linked with another manifestation of love—namely, hospitality (*philoxenia*; Heb. 13:1, 2). The writer encourages his readers by telling them that some who have practiced this virtue have entertained angels without being aware of it (Heb. 13:2). Paul encourages the practice (Rom. 12:13; angels or no angels!), and we get a little glimpse of the way it worked in III John. John commends Gaius for entertaining the brothers even though they were strangers to him. He does well to send them on their way in a Christian manner. In fact, John thinks that it is the Christian's duty to receive other believers and in this way work for the truth with them (III John 5–8). Hospitality was evidently rated highly, as seems obvious by the number of exhortations to engage in it (I Tim. 3:2; Titus 1:8; I Pet. 4:9).

Brotherly love is to be practiced in addition to piety and in turn is to be supplemented with love—*agapē* (II Pet. 1:7). This is the consistent New Testament teaching—that going through the proper motions in the sanctuary is not enough in itself. There is no substitute for love, which is in the first instance love of the brothers and, in the second, love of mankind in general. We see this in the further exhortation to "purify your souls in obedience to the truth in sincere brotherly love" (I Pet. 1:22; the writer goes on, "Love [*agapēsate*] one another fervently out of a pure heart"). Again the point is that spiritual

---

confined to members of the race). We must not even assume that brotherly love was commonplace in religious groups.

[23]For a discussion of this concept, see above, pp. 203ff.

purity alone is not enough; brotherly love must also be practiced. J. N. D. Kelly comments,

> The writer's point is that, through submitting to the gospel
> and being baptized, his correspondents have entered a
> community in which 'love' is the rule of conduct.... In
> this relationship love becomes a caricature of itself if any
> tincture of hypocrisy is present; hence it should be 'sin-
> cere'.... The expression brings out the warm sense of
> being brothers which, as the NT shows (e.g., Acts xiv.2),
> bound Christians together in the apostolic age and excited
> the admiration or incredulity of pagans.[24]

When the writer returns to the theme a little later, with
the simple exhortation to be loving to the brothers (I Pet. 3:8),
he uses the adjectival form *philadelphos*.

"Love of mankind," *philanthrōpia*, is highly esteemed
by secular writers. It is the kind of virtue that we might have
expected would be referred to often in the New Testament.
But it is mentioned only rarely. It is used to refer to the attitude
of God, who is described as "our Savior" in a passage that
goes on to say that he saved us by his mercy and not on account
of works we have done in righteousness. The passage continues,
referring to "the washing of regeneration and renewal of the
Holy Spirit," to the gift poured out through Jesus Christ our
Savior, to justification by grace, to becoming heirs of life
eternal (Titus 3:4–7).[25] This is a thought that we have encoun-
tered often: it is God's love and not any human merit that
brings salvation. But apart from its occurrence in this important passage, the noun occurs only in Acts 28:2 in reference
to the kindness shown by the barbarians on the island of Melita
to the shipwrecked travelers. The corresponding adverb is
used to refer to the centurion Julius, who treated Paul and
his party "courteously" (Acts 27:3). Another such compound

---

[24]*A Commentary on the Epistles of Peter and of Jude*, London,
1969, p. 79. He goes on to note that the Jews knew of brotherly love,
and adds, "What is distinctive about the new Christian family is that
admission to it no longer depends on physical or racial kinship but on
acceptance of God's will and total commitment to Christ."

[25]U. Luck sees in this passage both a reference to God's love and
to the obligation of the recipients of this love to respond: "Inasmuch
as God has condescended to the world in His *philanthrōpia*, He is not
a remote or alien God, and life in this world under concrete obedience
to this God becomes a constant duty. God's saving work on man also
demands here man's right conduct in the world" (*TDNT*, IX, 111).

adverb is *philophronōs*, meaning "of loving mind"; it is used to refer to Poplius, who lodged Paul and his companions in the shipwreck "in a friendly manner" (Acts 28:7).

Such compounds are used to refer to familial love. For example, the older women are to teach the younger to be loving to their husbands (*philandros*) and to their children (*philoteknos*; Titus 2:4). This usage reinforces the consistent New Testament emphasis on the importance of family life (a point discussed earlier).

People are to be lovers of God (*philotheos*; II Tim. 3:4), and bishops are to be lovers of good (*philagathos*; Titus 1:8).[26] The verb *philotimeomai* is interesting. It means "to love honor, to have ambition" or the like. The New Testament writers use it to refer to the ambition to preach the gospel (Rom. 15:20), to please the Lord (II Cor. 5:9), and to be quiet (and unambitious?; I Thess. 4:11). Together these usages give insight into the way the Christians refused to accept the values of their day; they did not share the ambitions of the worldly. Yet even among those who accept the Christian way there can appear a Diotrephes who "loves being first" (*philoprōteuōn*; III John 9).[27]

Other compounds formed from the stem *phil-* refer to the love of evil things. Thus there are references to the love of money, *philargyria,* with its accompanying adjective *philargyros* (I Tim. 6:10; Luke 16:14; II Tim. 3:2); to loving oneself, *philautos* (II Tim. 3:2); to loving pleasure, *philēdonos* (II Tim. 3:4); and to loving strife—*philoneikos, philoneikia* (Luke 22:24; I Cor. 11:16). In addition, there are words that can have positive meanings but that are not used positively in the New Testament. For example, Paul refers to *philosophia,* which is often used to refer to a very important and highly esteemed academic discipline—but he links it with the "empty deceit" of those who try to deter Christians from the right way (Col. 2:8).[28] Similarly, there are references to philosophers,

---

[26]"According to the interpretation of the early Church it relates to the unwearying activity of love" (W. Grundmann, *TDNT,* I, 18).

[27]AG say that this verb is found "so far only in eccl. usage." But cognate words are found in secular writers, and we need not think that the vice is confined to Christians.

[28]O. Michel holds that we must assume that Paul is not using the term disparagingly, but that he is "adopting a designation which his opponents used with a claim to weighty authority and that he sets it aside with the polemical addition *kai kenēs apatēs*" (*TDNT,* IX, 187).

philosophoi (Acts 17:18), but these are the people who refused to take Paul seriously at Athens.

*   *   *   *   *

This word group makes an interesting study, but it adds little to what *agapaō* teaches us, and certainly it does not show to us the characteristic New Testament idea of love. Rather, it reminds us—in most of its occurrences—of the kind of love that runs through life, some of which is good and desirable and which Christians share with others. Yet sometimes the word is used in a warning about loves that should form no part of the life of God's servant.

Conclusion

*O*UR survey of the Bible's teaching about love has brought out one great overriding theme—namely, that the love of God is a love for the completely undeserving. Using a variety of words and images, the many authors of the Bible emphasize this truth. God does not love men because he finds them wonderfully attractive. His love is not limited to the beautiful, the good, the pious, the prayerful, or the kind. In fact, nothing in men can account for God's love; he loves because it is his nature to love. John expresses this overwhelming idea by saying simply, "God is love." Is there any better way of putting it?

That love means the cross, for God will do whatever is needed—even make a supreme sacrifice—to save the sinners he loves. The Bible does not tell us why the cross was necessary to save sinners; it simply tells us what the cross did. It speaks of justification, of redemption, of propitiation, of the making of a new covenant, and much more. It leaves us in no doubt but that this was costly—it cost the Son of God his life. But it is the way of love (in the sense in which the Bible uses the term) to sacrifice for others, to undergo the cross for the sake of beloved sinners. God's love is not simply a beautiful but detached emotion—it is a love that pays the price.

The cross is the measure of this love. Certainly there is no greater love than that which makes one lay down his life for others (John 15:13). It is easy to love when one can simply enjoy life with his beloved, making only minor sacrifices in the process. But it takes love of real quality to suffer deeply for someone who is not worthy.

That is the great truth on which the Bible insists. God's love is not merely a distant truth—it is the reality on the cross. It is a love that sacrifices, that brings salvation, that is constantly active on behalf of God's people.

It is thus surprising that this truth is overlooked in much

271

modern writing. I began this book by pointing to the curious fact that quite a number of outstanding scholars have written theologies of the Old Testament or of the New Testament without recognizing love as one of the significant themes by means of which the teaching of the Bible is to be interpreted. As I come to the end of this book, I understand this phenomenon no better than when I began. It still seems to me that the Bible's teaching about love is of central importance. I do not see how either the Old Testament or the New can be properly understood unless emphasis is given to the great truth that God loves sinful people.

Another surprising feature of recent writing is that many books about love written by Christian authors do not see love as the Bible does. George H. Tavard begins the preface to his book *A Way of Love* by saying, "Several periods in the history of Christian thought have been marked by an abundance of writings on the nature of love. We are in such an era. Psychological, psycho-analytical, sociological, philosophical, phenomenological, literary, theological, and biblical studies on love have been published during the past few decades."[1] In many of these recent studies love is seen as central to the Christian way, but it is love as the author conceives of it, not love as the Bible sees it. It is love that proceeds from the author's ideas, not from the cross, as the New Testament writers insist it should (e.g., Rom. 5:8; I John 4:10).

Ironically, Tavard himself might serve as a good example of such an author. He says much about *agapē*, including this: "Friendship constitutes the ultimate form of *agape*, the perfection of Christian love. In relation to God, *agape* means God-with-us, Emmanuel, the gift of God in his Son, born, crucified, and risen for us."[2] He says further, "Friendship, *agape* in the full sense of the term, unites human persons who identify with each other despite and within their otherness. But

---

[1] *A Way of Love,* New York, 1977, p. ix. He goes on to ask, "Do we intellectualize love because we do not experience it? Do we seek shelter from the deprivation of love among books by the mass media, which tend to reduce love to sex and sex to pornography?" These are good questions that must make us all thoughtful. He goes on to other questions like "Or is an authentic rediscovery of love taking place. . . ?" One would like to think it is, but in view of the persistent neglect of biblical emphases one cannot but wonder.

[2] *A Way of Love,* p. 54.

the widest otherness and the closest identity are experienced between a man and a woman. Thus the man–woman relationship forms the central model of the Christian *agape* as mutual self-gift."[3]

As far as I can see, he mentions the cross only once in this particular chapter—when he slips in the word "crucified" between "born" and "risen" in his description of God's friendship. It cannot be said that he takes the cross as his starting point. In fact, he does not even bring in the cross as a useful illustration of what love means even after he proceeds from his non-biblical starting point. He prefers to emphasize "the man–woman relationship."

Now I do not want it to be thought that I am unmindful of the virtues of Tavard's treatment of our subject. He has many penetrating and thoughtful things to say, and if we all took notice of what he has written and made a diligent attempt to put it into practice, there would be a good deal more love about. I gladly acknowledge my own indebtedness to him.

But that does not entitle me to say that what Tavard has written is biblical—it is not. It does not take the cross as central, and the Bible does. To choose to start anywhere else is to engage in a non-biblical treatment of the subject, whatever nods one may make in the direction of the Bible. Perhaps I should add that I am not singling out Tavard as a special offender—it just happens that I have been reading his book recently. But he is typical of modern authors: one could document the same attitude expressed by any one of a host of writers. Tavard does go awry in a particular way. For example, he identifies *agapē* with friendship without a word to indicate that friendship was highly esteemed in the ancient world and designated by *philia,* a word that the New Testament writers virtually never used (it occurs only once—in James 4:4). After this, it is curious that he comes close to identifying love with *erōs*, which most see as quite different from—even opposed to—*agapē*. These interpretations are peculiarly Tavard's—but his neglect of the cross he shares with many other authors. And my whole book is a protest against this—against the ignoring of the authentic Christian experience of love that is expressed in Galatians 2:20: "The Son of God loved me and gave himself up for me."

---

[3]*A Way of Love,* p. 59.

But this is not the way we use the word *love* today in our western community. We accept without question the fact that the term is often used to refer to sexual passion. When we speak of love we usually mean love between the sexes, something we see as an overmastering emotion that has nothing to do with the will. Nobody chooses to love like this—nobody says, "I will now love so-and-so." Rather, he "falls in love." Because this kind of love fascinates us, we excuse almost anything done in its name. Denis de Rougemont observes this: "To go by literature, adultery would seem to be the most notable occupation of both Europe and America. Few are the novels that fail to allude to it."[4] He is surely right. The modern novel rarely misses a chance to depict adultery.

Few of us realize that this idea of love is by no means obvious and by no means universally accepted. It is comparatively modern,[5] and it is certainly un-Christian. It seems to have begun in the Middle Ages, the age of chivalry. The typical knight spoke abjectly of himself as the humble and gentle vassal of his lady (whereas in fact he was the proud and violent vassal of his lord). Beneath his elaborate courtesy lay his desire (which he shared with the lady) to fulfill his passion in adultery rather than in marriage.[6] Ironically, the "courteous" knight married in a calculated, ruthless way, his goal being to enlarge his fortune or perhaps to cement an alliance between families. Little consideration was given to the feelings of the unfortunate bride. It was even doubted whether there was any possibility of love in marriage, so strong was the emphasis on the passion that leads to adultery.[7]

We have inherited this view of love, and it has led us astray. We do not seem to realize that this is far from being the only meaning that love can have. In other times than the me-

---

[4]*Love in the Western World,* Philadelphia, 1953, p. 4.

[5]Cf. W. Warde Fowler: "The modern idea of passion with marriage as its consummation . . . was unknown at Rome" (J. Hastings, ed., *Encyclopaedia of Religion and Ethics,* VIII, Edinburgh, 1915, 465).

[6]Cf. the passage from C. S. Lewis cited on p. 122, n.27 above, wherein the characteristics of "courtly love" are listed as "Humility, Courtesy, Adultery, and the Religion of Love."

[7]De Rougemont says, "It was even contended—for example, in the famous judgment delivered by a court of love in the house of the Countess of Champagne—that love and marriage were incompatible" (*Love in the Western World,* p. 25).

dieval and in other places than the West, very different ideas have been and are held. The ancients, for example, thought of the kind of love we champion as a sickness (cf. the way Menander refers to it). Among peoples like the Hebrews or the Greeks or the Romans, parents usually arranged marriages. Love was not so much an overmastering passion as it was a feeling that developed from responsibility and respect. Love certainly existed (cf. Gen. 24:67), but it was not the kind of love that we so often talk about today.

"The cultivation of passionate love began in Europe as a reaction to Christianity (and in particular to its doctrine of marriage) by people whose spirit, whether naturally or by inheritance, was still pagan."[8] De Rougemont makes this statement, using italics in order to emphasize it. It is important that we see that the Christian concept of love is not the passionate concentration on one person as a sexual object that so often masquerades as love today. De Rougemont may or may not be correct in his idea that it originated in an Eastern heresy[9]—but whatever the origin of this concept of love, we must see that, for Christians, love is not this sexually oriented passion. In its concentration on sexual fulfillment, this recent idea is much more limited than the wide-ranging, sacrificial love to which Christians aspire. If we look to modern novelists or modern western society to define love, we will not understand Christian love.

We should further notice that passionate love is not the wonderful thing modern writers (and lovers) so easily assume it is. To them it always seems an enrichment of life, the grand passion without which life is not worth living. But it is not. It is, in fact, an impoverishment, a love with severe limits because it shuts out everything and everyone but the beloved. As de Rougemont puts it,

> Passion is by no means the fuller life which it seems to be in the dreams of adolescence, but is on the contrary a kind

---

[8] *Love in the Western World,* p. 70.

[9] He says, "It was not Christianity that caused passion to be cultivated; it was a heresy of Eastern origin. This heresy began by spreading in precisely those regions which Christianity had not yet fully evangelized and where pagan cults still flourished in secret. Passionate love is not Christian love, nor even what has been called 'a Christian by-product.' It is rather a by-product of Manichaeism" (*Love in the Western World,* p. 300).

of naked and denuding intensity; verily, a bitter destitution, the *impoverishment* of a mind being emptied of all diversity, an obsession of the imagination by a single image.... There are no longer either neighbors or duties, or binding ties, or earth or sky: one is alone with all that one loves.[10]

Not only is the modern concept different from the biblical one—it is vastly inferior. It strips life of its greatest good and replaces it with what at best is selfish, tawdry, and defiling. I do not, of course, mean that there is no place for passion in the Christian life. On the contrary. Passion, though not the overmastering passion that shuts all else out, is an emotion important in a full, satisfying life; life is flat and dull without it. But I do mean that it is not passion that constitutes Christian love.[11] Passion was common in the orgiastic religions of the time when Christianity made its appearance, but the Christians rejected this approach. They had a distinctive idea of love, one that centered on the cross.

My first point, then, is that we know love in the New Testament sense only because we see it in the cross; my second point is that to see this love is to be affected by it. As the hymn writer puts it,

> When I survey the wondrous cross
> On which the Prince of glory died,
> My richest gain I count but loss,
> And pour contempt on all my pride.

It is impossible to retain one's pride and self-sufficiency and at the same time have a proper appreciation of the fact that one is a sinner, saved only because the Son of God died on Calvary. The modern attitude that seeks success at any price, that is concerned only with personal achievement, no matter how much suffering this involves for others, cannot be embraced by anyone who has felt the impact of the cross. It is a humbling experience to know that all one's hopes for time and for eternity rest on what Christ has done, because one can do nothing

---

[10] *Love in the Western World,* p. 120.

[11] Cf. Daniel Day Williams: "The Bible does not reject the language of human emotion or even of passion for the divine love, yet it never makes the ecstatic or emotional fulfilment of familial or sexual experience the key to the experience of God" (*The Spirit and the Forms of Love,* Welwyn, 1968, p. 20).

to achieve salvation. This is an emphatic rejection of the approach of many in our modern world. Where that world affirms pride and self-sufficiency, the cross speaks of love and self-sacrifice.

And love begets love. When God's love reaches us, it transforms us. Truly understanding what Christ did in dying for us and truly responding to that love means becoming a different person. Christians have used many ways to describe the change that takes place when anyone becomes a Christian. They refer to conversion, to being born again, to passing from death to life, to putting off the old man and putting on the new, to dying with Christ and rising with him, to coming to live in Christ, to presenting their bodies as a living sacrifice. Are not all these just so many ways of saying that the miracle is the replacement of self-centeredness by love? This is not something we can do ourselves, and for this reason Scripture relates love to the activity of God's Spirit. Love is a sheer miracle, not the crowning human achievement.

Christian love means love for fellow Christians. This is admitted on every side, and it is important. The early church stood out against the background of pagan society because of the quality of brotherly love that was so characteristic of its membership. Pagans might mock the phenomenon of Christian love, as did Lucian of Samosata, or they might take it seriously, as apparently did those of whom Tertullian wrote. But they could not deny the fact that to be a Christian was to love the brotherhood.

A modern Christian does well to ask, "Why is this not the verdict of non-Christians today?" There can be few places—at least in the western world (and none that I know of)—where outsiders spontaneously comment on the love Christians show to one another. On the contrary, they often refer to Christians as people far too frequently occupied with bickering and backbiting. They see us as prepared to squabble bitterly and indefinitely over theological minutiae. They marvel at the multiplicity of our divisions and our readiness to make more. I am aware that much of this is false and malicious, and that our divisions are sometimes a matter of conscience. I know that Christians sometimes must say, "Here I stand. I can do no other."

But I still feel uncomfortable when I look at the Bible and at the church of which I am a member. I ask, "Why do we not show the love of which the Bible speaks?" I ask, "Does the

Bible consider anything else in Christian life to be as important as love?'' I remember that Jesus spoke of love for God as ''the great and first commandment'' and of love for the neighbor as like it (Matt. 22:37–39). Granted that our critics are often bent on faulting us and that nothing we can do will please them in the end; yet I must still ask, ''Why is the impression we make so different from that which our predecessors made? Were not their critics equally unsympathetic?'' I can ask such questions, but I cannot answer them. I can only write my book and plead with my fellow Christians, as I plead with myself, that we show more love within the Christian community. There of all places there should be love.

And, of course, love should not stop there. When we understand love in the light of the cross, we understand that love is to be shown to the unlovely and the unworthy. No one who takes the cross seriously can think otherwise. The Christian who has been transformed by God's love revealed in the cross cannot be other than deeply concerned for sinners. That is what love means. And as he responds to God's love he becomes a loving person. It is love that brought him life and therefore it is love that he brings to life.

The Christian who has come to understand the meaning and the place of love cannot but speak the word of love to the modern world. It is a world that says much about love but that understands love in its own self-centered way. Like the men of Qumran, modern man loves those he conceives to be ''the sons of light'' (i.e., those of whom he approves) and hates ''the men of the pit'' (those of whom he disapproves). His love is selective, and it centers on himself. He cannot conceive of love in the Christian sense as anything other than impractical idealism—an idealism of which he does not approve.

If it were not so tragic it would be funny that modern man dismisses Christianity and the Christian way of love on the ground that it does not work. Will anyone in his right mind claim that any of the modern alternatives do work? Certainly the stress on the self-centered life does not lead to blissful happiness; only fierce competition results when self-absorbed people confront each other. People try to get the better of each other, and in this sad process laws are broken, rights are violated—and police forces grow larger. Crimes multiply, crimes of violence being the most ''popular,'' because violence is the simplest way for the physically strong to get their own way. The result is that everybody loses. We lose by the depredation we suffer, and we lose by the increased taxes we pay to support the protection we have come to need so much. The more self-centered our society becomes, the more crimes we commit, the more police we need, and the more jails we fill.[12] There is scarcely the need to elaborate the point because life in any modern city is a vivid illustration of the truth that selfishness leads ultimately to suffering—for everyone. Where is there a system that works better than the way of Christian love?

"Beloved, let us love one another, for love is of God."

---

[12]When I was in New York some time ago, a statistician released some figures showing that in that city murder is the most frequent cause of death for men in the 17–40 age group. This is one more sad reminder that self-assertion leads not to happiness but to loss of life on an alarmingly large scale.

General Index

Index of Authors

Scripture Index